This Is Not
The Story
You Think
It Is…

This Is Not The Story You Think It Is...

A Season of Unlikely Happiness

Laura Munson

AMY EINHORN BOOKS
Published by G. P. Putnam's Sons
a member of Penguin Group (USA) Inc.
New York

AMY EINHORN BOOKS
Published by G. P. Putnam's Sons
Publishers Since 1838
Published by the Penguin Group
Penguin Group (USA) Inc., 375 Hudson Street, New York, New York 10014, USA • Penguin Group (Canada), 90 Eglinton Avenue East, Suite 700, Toronto, Ontario M4P 2Y3, Canada (a division of Pearson Penguin Canada Inc.) • Penguin Books Ltd, 80 Strand, London WC2R 0RL, England • Penguin Ireland, 25 St Stephen's Green, Dublin 2, Ireland (a division of Penguin Books Ltd) • Penguin Group (Australia), 250 Camberwell Road, Camberwell, Victoria 3124, Australia (a division of Pearson Australia Group Pty Ltd) • Penguin Books India Pvt Ltd, 11 Community Centre, Panchsheel Park, New Delhi–110 017, India • Penguin Group (NZ), 67 Apollo Drive, Rosedale, North Shore 0632, New Zealand (a division of Pearson New Zealand Ltd) • Penguin Books (South Africa) (Pty) Ltd, 24 Sturdee Avenue, Rosebank, Johannesburg 2196, South Africa

Penguin Books Ltd, Registered Offices:
80 Strand, London WC2R 0RL, England

Published simultaneously in Canada

"Cabin Poem," from Jim Harrison's *The Shape of the Journey: New and Collected Poems* (1998), and "Older Love," from *Saving Daylight* (2006), are reprinted by permission of Copper Canyon Press, www.coppercanyonpress.org.

Library of Congress Cataloging-in-Publication Data

Munson, Laura.
This is not the story you think it is— : a season of unlikely happiness / Laura Munson.
p. cm.
ISBN 978-0-399-15665-6
1. Munson, Laura—Marriage. 2. Wives—Montana—Biography. 3. Man-woman relationships—Montana—Psychological aspects. 4. Happiness. I. Title.
HQ759.M937 2010 2010001614
158.2—dc22

Printed in the United States of America
1 3 5 7 9 10 8 6 4 2

BOOK DESIGN BY NICOLE LAROCHE

Some names and identifying characteristics have been changed to protect the privacy of the individuals involved.

Penguin is committed to publishing works of quality and integrity. In that spirit, we are proud to offer this book to our readers; however, the story, the experiences, and the words are the author's alone.

To my husband

The map's no good without the territory.
We always said we wanted adventure. . . .
I love you.

To my father,
John Chester Munson (1918–2004)

Here's your blue Duesenberg. Though I don't suppose you need a car wherever you are, namely in my heart. Thank you for believing in me.

I've decided to make up my mind
about nothing, to assume the water mask,
to finish my life disguised as a creek,
an eddy, joining at night the full,
sweet flow, to absorb the sky,
to swallow the heat and cold, the moon
and the stars, to swallow myself
in ceaseless flow.

—Jim Harrison, "Cabin Poem"

Contents

Are You There, Clarence? It's Me, George Bailey's Wife

5:00 a.m.

Summer. Montana.

At this moment in my life, I am strangely serene. In fact, I may have never felt more calm. Or more freed. Or more certain that these things owe themselves to a simple choice: to accept life as it is. Even and especially when it really fucking sucks. Even and especially if my husband left last night to go to the dump after announcing that he isn't sure he loves me anymore . . . and nine hours later, still hasn't come back.

You might think all this would find me in a place of intense pain. Panic, even. State of emergency. But I'm choosing something else. I am choosing not to suffer.

How is this possible? you might ask.

Let me introduce you to my bedside table (see page 338), which at present holds a perversely vertical half-cracked and sometimes devoured stack of books telling me all about it: inner peace, harmony, love, non-suffering, freedom . . . from the Buddha to Jesus to the Sufis to the Christian mystics to Dr. Seuss and beyond. (I've always been a seeker of wisdom. I'm not picky where it comes from.) And they all hint at, or even proclaim, this simple truth: the end of suffering happens with the end of wanting. The end of wanting.

I've read this hundreds of times, in different word arrangements, ever since I had my first metaphysical thought a long time ago. But up until just this blink of a moment (that's how it happens, finally—in a blink), I have bashed myself bloody. Because with all this arsenal of wisdom, I have never been able to understand how not to want.

How, for instance, am I not to want my husband to walk through the door and tell me some drop-dead beautiful story about how he sat all night at the dump and was spoken to by heavenly hosts and sung to by an angelic choir and experienced an epiphany that resulted in him realizing what I've just learned? That we both have been psychically touched by the same odd angel who has let us into the secrets of the universe:

Suffering sucks. Don't do it. Go home and love your wife. Go home and love yourself. Go home and base your happiness on one thing and one thing only: freedom. Choose freedom, not suffering. Create a life of freedom, not wanting. Have some really good coffee and listen to the red-winged blackbirds in the marsh. Ignore the mosquitoes.

But my husband doesn't come home. He doesn't call. He doesn't answer his cell phone. And I get to practice this ridiculous "bliss."

Probably the wisest words that were ever uttered to me came from a therapist. I was sitting in her office, crying my eyes out over my then unsuccessful writing career and my husband's challenges at work, and she said, "So let me get this straight. You base your personal happiness on things entirely outside of your control."

"Yeah. I guess. If you put it that way," I agreed. "I'm not writing novels not to see them published. Fourteen of them to be exact—spanning over half my life! I'm not raising kids—two of them—a girl, twelve, and a boy, eight—pouring my entire heart into every fiber of their beings not to make sure they're healthy and happy and have the right size shoes and find a life that they love. I'm not married—to the same man, whom I've adored since my senior year in college—to live in loneliness. And I can't control any of those results. But I want them to be good ones. I'd be lying if I told you I didn't believe those positive results would make me happy."

"That's insanity," she said. "Just so you know."

"Fine. It might be insanity. But it's human nature to want. I can't deny myself my human nature. It's impossible."

"Really," she said, and she did that lift-of-the-eyebrow thing she does.

I know to pay attention when she does that. That there's more coming and it's gonna be good.

"There's a big difference between wanting and creating," she said. "Do you want to stop feeling anxious and depressed and scared and angry?"

"Of course. That's why I'm here in this office. But I'm not allowed to want, remember?"

"Fair enough. Do you believe you can create a life in which you are happy?"

"Absolutely. But doesn't it take two to tango?"

"Does it?" she said, her eyebrow raising. Then she saw my pain and filled it in for me. I love her for this quality. "It's when you stop wanting things outside of your control that you'll be happy."

Easy for her to say. Sitting there on her mauve couch with her manicure and her neat scarf and her presumably more-miserable-than-she clientele.

How can a person not want? You are born—you want to live. You get married—you want to build a life with your spouse. You have kids—you want them to live even though it seems at first like they're doing their best to try to off themselves—and later, you want them to be happy, and you want them to live even longer—long enough to provide you grandchildren. And you want them to live, too. In fact, you worry about them not living before they're even born. Because what would that do to your child, outliving their child? You want everybody to live, and you want to live until you are one hundred, still driving, mind intact, cheekbones and legs still not too bad, and then you want to die in your sleep. You want to be Katharine Hepburn. And in the meantime, you want a calling. You want to work hard at that calling—you want talent and you want success. How is it possible to live in this human body in this human world and not want?

Easy, too, for my fabulously famous, spiritually evolved novelist friend to say when I asked him in a letter: *How do you spend your life writing without wanting to be published?*

He responded with a phone call; that's when I know it's important news and that I should widen my third eye. "The only difference between being published and not being published," he said, "is being published."

Fine, Mr. I-hang-out-with-modern-day-prophet-sorts-and-get-scads-of-adoring-fan-mail-and-speak-at-sold-out-venues. I'm not sitting on my ass all day in a dark room, year after year, page after page, spilling my guts, martyring myself, my abs, my glutes, to the gruesome art of channeling the human condition for a whole lot of nothin'! Not wanting a direct line from this dark office to the bedside tables of people everywhere. Well, excuse my lack of spiritual enlightenment, but to me that's one thing: a colossal cop-out.

Or so I thought, until just this moment in my life.

Back to the novelist friend.

I retorted with, "The thing is, I'm good! I've been working at this craft for years and years, and I can honestly say with confidence . . . that I'm good! And it's not just me. Editors at major publishing houses love my work. My agent's never seen such positive rejection letters. But I don't have a 'platform,' they call it. I'm a no-name from Montana."

"You just need to keep writing. Stop thinking about getting published. But be careful. There's a vast difference between being detached . . . and being un-attached. You wanna shoot for the latter."

"But," I whimpered, "I'm in a spiritual cul-de-sac. I don't know how not to want. I'm very, very attached. Not in the least Zen. More . . . I don't know . . . Episcopalian."

He laughed. And I could tell he was withholding valuable information. Information that is only earned, not inherited. The Big Journey was all mine—just like Dorothy. God, I hate that.

But back to this moment in my life.

At this moment in my life, I am not sure where my husband is. He left last night to bring the trash to the dump after announcing that he's not sure he loves me anymore, and hasn't come home. He isn't answering his cell phone. He isn't responding to texts.

But I don't buy it. The part about him not loving me. As much as it's devastating to hear, I believe there's more to the story. I believe he's in a state of personal crisis. I believe this is about him.

I'm going to give you a challenge here. I'm going to give both you and me a challenge here. Let's try in all this not to take sides. Because how does it feel to take sides? Do we get to be right? Self-righteous? I think there's more suffering in self-righteousness than most of us are willing to fathom.

I see it like this: we all have our seasons of personal woe. I've certainly had mine. I know how much he hates his job, how much he punishes himself for not making enough money and not knowing where to go next with his career; how stuck and desperate he feels, especially in our small mountain town where the high-paying jobs are NOT plentiful. I know that he's suffering intensely. I know because I've been there. I feel his pain and I've told him so.

But he's not hearing my voice. His own is too thunderous. He has to come to the end of it by himself. Just like Dorothy and me. And I know it's more helpful to practice empathy here. Not anger. Or fear. Even though his words were like sharp sleet.

It's like when teenagers scream "I hate you" and slam the door in their parents' face. Does that "I hate you" have credibility? Or does the parent know instinctually that something upsetting happened at school? That it's not about the parent at all? I'm not saying that my husband is acting like a teenager. (Or, God forbid, that I'm his parent!) I'm just saying that I think there's more to the story.

My husband is a great guy. Loyal. Supportive. Loving. A true family man. Staying out to all hours of the night and not calling isn't something he does. But he's been doing it a lot lately. I figure it's his version of slamming the door in my face. And that's when I know something really bad happened at work. He apologetically calls it "blowing off steam," which is fairly easy to do in a place where there are countless lakes and rivers all around, a national park nearby, not to mention ten bars in three blocks.

On those nights, he sleeps on the couch in his office, a short walk from downtown. How do I know this? It's a small town.

Everybody is under a microscope here. People like to report on each other like it's an assignment for social studies class.

Without any prompting they'll offer, "I saw your old man gettin' after it at the bar last night." ("It," in our town, is beer. Not necessarily pussy.) Or, "Saw your hubby brushing his teeth in the office bathroom this morning at the crack of dawn. He had sleep marks on his face in the pattern of his office couch." The coda to these field reports usually goes like this: "Is he doing okay?"

"Why don't you ask him that question?" is my usual response.

So you can detonate your suspicious fantasies of him off with some woman in her fabulous log home on the lake. Even though I've had those suspicions, too. Believe me. Even though there is absolutely no evidence of it. Or arrows pointing me to that conclusion.

Here's a good place to ask you a very important question. It's a tricky one, and you might resist it at first, but I'd like you to really open your heart and mind right now because I believe it will help us all. It's a question I've had to ask myself with the same openness, and I promise you, it's intensely powerful.

I'll pose it to myself, in fact, because I'm doing this work, too: Just how important is it for me to know right now in my life . . . that in no uncertain terms . . . my husband is or is not having an affair?

Hang on—don't go away. Stay with me here.

It's such a powerful question to ponder. How will the definitive truth help my commitment to not suffer? Never mind my marriage. To what extent is knowledge power right now?

Because what exactly am I supposed to do with that information?

If he is, in fact, having an affair, is it a deal breaker? Is it the automatic end of the marriage? Do I issue ultimatums and temporarily kick him out and turn the family on its ass? Is there any leveraging power there for me? Like—aha! Now I can FORCE you to go to therapy because . . . because . . . because—wait, why?

If I wanted to make him wrong, I wouldn't have to work very hard. Because isn't the declaration that his love for me is in question, by nature, an act of unfaithfulness in and of itself? A violation of our marriage vows? It does, however, beg the question:

What is the "worse" I signed up for in "for better, for worse"? Maybe it would be a good exercise for minister types to make us write down our criteria when it comes to "worse." But truth be told, I always knew that "worse" could be really, really bad.

The definitive truth I know for sure is this: my husband is in crisis, whether or not he's having an affair. Whether or not he loves me.

And I love him.

So let's do a one-eighty. What if, just for now, I looked at it like whatever it is that has him not coming home is a symptom of something deeper in his soul. Some level of personal pain that is not mine to bear. Would I be any better off accusing him of infidelity, demanding the truth, or hiring a private detective and obsessing over a potential affair when there's absolutely no evidence of one? Stealing his cell phone in a rare opportunity and scrolling through to see if there are suspicious texts or strange phone numbers? Do I think so little of my husband?

And I ask us this: Who would I be in that moment, sneaking around behind his back? What kind of integrity would I have? How would that play out in my own soul?

And let me ask us this: How would that cell phone feel in our hand? Is it on fire, burning a hole in our palm? Is that a level of suffering we're willing to accept in order to get to some sort of truth? How will that truth set us free? How used to suffering are we in this life of ours? Dare I suggest that suffering has become our normal?

I'm not doing it. I've been there before in other aspects of life—lying to myself that some levels of suffering are worth it. I'm not in that lie anymore.

So for now, I'll be calmed by what information has come my way, without my trying to control or meddle or suffer to get to it. The general consensus is: he goes to the bar, drinks with the guys, and sleeps on his office couch. Sometimes there's fishing involved. It's that erotic.

Even the kids have come to understand lately that when Daddy doesn't come home at his usual hour, and sometimes not at all . . . he's got this steam to blow. Not that it's right.

Historically, my husband and I pride ourselves on our parenting. On our healthy relationships with our children. But we're not selling them myths. And times are tough. So we've told them that mommies and daddies are human, too. We all make mistakes. Adults go through hard times and don't always act responsibly. But we're still a family. Even when we mess up. We love each other and we protect each other. And we forgive each other.

But it's hard not to take his absence like a slap in the face. I can see it in their eyes. I wonder if they can see it in mine.

One of my husband's and my favorite quotes emphasizes being guardians of each other's solitude:

> *The point of marriage is not to create a quick commonality by tearing down all boundaries; on the contrary, a good marriage is one in which each partner appoints the other to be the guardian of his solitude, and thus they show each other the greatest possible trust. A merging of two people is an impossibility, and where it seems to exist, it is a hemming-in, a mutual consent that robs one party or both parties of their fullest freedom and development. But once the realization is accepted that even between the closest people infinite distances exist, a marvelous living side-by-side can grow up for them, if they succeed in loving the expanse between them, which gives them the possibility of always seeing each other as a whole and before an immense sky.*
>
> —RILKE

Guardians of each other's solitude. Their fullest freedom. Loving the expanse. (Though I'm fairly certain that when Rilke wrote those sagacious words, he wasn't referring to the bar. Fishing, maybe.)

I want him to have time alone. I cherish my own. We've always given each other that room in Rilke's "greatest possible trust." Still, regardless of his personal crisis, regardless if he's telling himself he doesn't love me anymore, is he willing to ruin the years of trust we've built?

And what about respect? All I've asked for is a phone call so that I don't worry. How hard is that? The commitment to healing and even to couples therapy would be great, too. But we're not there. Rather, much, much further away than I thought.

I'm not going to try to justify his behavior, because I know it's not justifiable. I simply want to understand instead of freak out. It's not behavior I'm willing to put up with for too long. Whatever "too long" will come to mean. But in the meantime, am I to react to the part of our society that wants us to lie about our marriages being somehow perfect? Until they're not. Black and white. One false move and you're out. I'm sure that in reality, most of us married people have had a lot more than even three strikes. No. This is not a time to react. This is a time for deep rooting, like the writer Terry Tempest Williams calls for.

But my brain winds and wends. Back and forth. Up and down. It feels like the county fair has inhabited my mind—complete with sketchy rides, carnies, and sugar-amped kids crying over lost balloons. So loud and disorienting. I want it to pack up and move on to the next town. I want my mind to be an open grassy field again with crickets and dandelions. Besides, my husband isn't there to ring the bell with the mallet—to win us all a stuffed animal, which, in that one summer moment, is the most important thing in the world. I am most certainly at this county fair alone.

Fear lunges at my throat. It scares me to think what life might be like without him on my side. But I know at least this: fear is not my friend. Better to return to empathy right now, rather than fear.

Even so, I'm worried this morning. Though I try to let it wash over me in waves, I have to admit that I am very worried. Like Mary in *It's a Wonderful Life* when George yells at their kid playing Christmas carols, meets with the broken banister knob one too many times, and takes off thinking he'd be better dead than alive. Yet like Mary (and I ain't no Donna Reed), even though she does bust out a "George, why must you torture the children!" . . . in my heart of hearts, I know that nothing will be gained by really letting loose on him, or giving him ultimatums. But, oh, for a visit from Clarence the guardian angel. Like George Bailey, I know that so much of my husband's crisis is directly related to the stresses of money and unrealized dreams. And as much as I want to try to heal his pain, I know that I can't. It's not possible. This is his work. He's going to have to pop out of this equation on his own.

I understand that equation. The treacherous terrain of shame built on years of career failure. It took me the better part of two years with a really good therapist to trudge through it. How can I ask him to do it all on a summer's day?

Still, this morning, sitting here typing these words, fast and furious . . . in my worst moments, I'm weak. I go back to old ways. I get hooked by fear and I careen toward the center of suffering: What if it IS another woman???

Now, I know, dear reader, there's a strong possibility that you've got your hackles up. You want to tell me I'm being a fool to put up with this unacceptable behavior. You want me to fight.

Well, I do, too. I'm a good fighter. I'm famous for cutting to the chase and expediting genius makeups at Mach speed.

But I'm opting for a different strategy, and I'm going to believe it will work in a way that fighting, persuading, and demanding never have. Because whether or not he comes back to me, I will be ultimately empowered by my commitment not to suffer. It's a way of life. A way to life. And it's about many and no religions. Plug it in wherever it meets your life. We all want to be free, don't we?

And yes—this strategy is new to me, too. I'm sure it'll be shaky at times. But I'm going for it. And I'm going to write my way through it. Both for my process. And for yours. For anyone in any situation in which one is tempted to go into panic mode, or worse, victim mode, rather than taking responsibility for one's own well-being.

I look up at my Author's Statement taped above my desk, next to the photos of my son running midair on a beach, my daughter wearing a halo of daisies, my husband kissing me on our wedding day. I take my Author's Statement very seriously. It came to me one day, and I typed it up and printed it out and put it next to the picture of the mountain bluebird that comes back in the spring when there's still snow. My daughter calls him Hello, Friend. He is the very symbol of hope after a long Montana winter.

It says: "I write to shine a light on an otherwise dim or even pitch-black corner, to provide relief for myself and others."

That's what this book is all about. Maybe it will help people. Maybe even save marriages, and jobs, and children's hearts from breaking. I wish I had this book on my bedside table right now. If only just to know that I am not alone.

If my husband and I come out the other side, together, in love, still married, and unsuffering, then this summer will have been worth it. This book will be worth it.

And even if we don't, then I know I will be a better person for living this way.

So stay with me. Like a gentle friend. Maybe we will both learn something that will change our lives. I'm willing to try. On our behalf.

The Cloud of Unknowing

8:45 a.m. Same morning.

At this moment in my life, my children are stirring and I'm wondering how to handle this. How to tell them or not tell them about their daddy's suffering. If I should attempt to translate, in a language they can understand, how he sat me down yesterday and told me that he's absolutely miserable. Stuck. That his company is totally broke. That we're in insane debt. That our savings are dwindling. That we might lose the farmhouse that we custom built so that our children's bookshelves hold their exact collections of toy horses and trucks, plumb and true. The land that holds our dogs and horses, cat, beta fish, and even my daughter's beloved pet rat.

And especially I'm wondering how not to let on to the fact that he said, looking into my eyes for the first time in months, that after more than half our lives together, he needs to be alone before he puts a bullet in his head. That he's not sure he loves me anymore. Or ever did. That he's not sure that he knows how to love.

This last point gets me out of my head, and into his heart: he questions his capacity to love.

I, on the other hand, do not question his capacity to love. I've been a witness to and a recipient of his love for a long time. For him to be thinking this way, there must be a disconnect deep inside him. And I think of the times when I have been at my lowest. What is that like for me? Have I questioned my capacity to love? Maybe I have. But I find that I can access love for myself and the world around me almost immediately when I enter into the act of creating. Especially if I can create something beautiful.

Creating beauty is something I've valued all my life. My mother and grandmothers inspired it in me. They knew the names of things—fine things. And they taught them to me with seriousness in their brow. It wasn't an issue of snobbery. It was an issue of aesthetics and family pride. Tradition. The care of legacy, one generation to the next. Like china and crystal and sterling batons.

Only ours hasn't been a relay race. It's been rather a slow evolution of principle and will, from the *Mayflower*, through the Revolutionary War, Civil War, the homesteading days, and beyond. You should see the stack of Bibles I have on my shelf, going back to the 1600s. The handmade lace made by so many young women for so many trousseaus. The tea services and fussy silver vessels for things like toast and buns and gravy. As little as it has to do with my Montana life, that was the beauty in my childhood and I loved it. Still do.

Because for me, those things went beyond beauty. They stood for safety. When there were hybrid tea roses in a polished silver vase by my bed or the table was set with the best Limoges and Steuben and Irish linen, then I knew I could trust my little world to be in harmony, at least for that rose-scented sleep, that shiny meal with family gathered around.

I've repeated that beauty in my Montana home and gardens, to the degree that it's applicable, and so, yes, I'm sure I have let down many grandmother ghosts. But living in Montana for fifteen years has inspired me to see a new kind of beauty. I keep my eye out for it as I wander around in nature. A heart-shaped rock is as beautiful as a hand-painted porcelain heart-shaped figurine. A verdant patch of moss as pleasing to touch as a piece of silk chenille. Nature's beauty has worked in me. And the longer I live here, the more I feel connected to the Designer of that beauty. However you choose to refer to that Designer.

What a wonderful world we live in that a thing like beauty is subjective. Truly, in the eye of the beholder. There's fathomless hope in that fact. I don't care how a person sees beauty. I just care that beauty is beheld. Created. It's something I take seriously and have passed to my children. Because when we're creating beauty, we align ourselves with our Designer. When we're receiving beauty, we're receiving "the kingdom" in its best form. And in that divine-aligned act, we're creating and receiving ourselves, not separate as us and them, or me and you or it. Maybe that is what it is to be truly alive. To love. To be in our true nature. Maybe that is what's missing for my husband. And why he feels he cannot love me.

I want my children to be surrounded, then, by beauty today.

But here's the most painful part—the conundrum that shows me my husband's inner war and challenges my commitment to non-suffering to the core. His final words before he left for the dump were: "I just want a woman who doesn't have any baggage."

So . . . does he really question his capacity to love? Or just to love me? Trying to wrap my mind around his confusion puts my brain into contortions—and I want to abandon beauty and thoughts of his limping heart and go straight into bitterness.

Here's where I land and it's not graceful: my husband, the father of my children, thinks there's someone out there who is better for him than I am. Somebody who's gotten this far in life unscathed. That he then, in effect, believes in fairy tales. And fairy-tale princesses. And maybe even fairy-tale princes, too. (Even though he's terrified of horses.) But this sort of thinking cuts, and I put on the brakes. I even laugh, trying to imagine a human being without "baggage."

Why am I able to laugh—to hope for and even achieve any level of calm this morning? Any hope for a beautiful day with my children? Why am I not rifling through those books on my bedside table looking for underlined passages; a few inspired words of my own in the margins like prophetic life preservers, pre-flung to myself on some other morning in my life, early, with tea and pillows around me snug—husband asleep gently snoring next to me, before the world awakes?

Why? Because I know what they're all trying to say. Under their Bo tree, or at their Golgotha, or in their ashram in India, or their church basement addicts' meeting with the bad coffee. I know. Finally, I know. You get to the end of suffering. Or you don't. That's it. You choose.

And I can't say it enough: I am committed to the end of suffering. Being told I am very possibly unloved by my husband sealed the deal.

You don't need any more books. Well, maybe this one. (For $24.95, in hardback, preferably published along with my fourteen, at this moment in my life, unpublished novels, for a huge advance, and a swarm of press, and a world tour. Oh—and I almost forgot—a Pulitzer. Or not. I don't care anymore. I'm done with suffering. I am. Are you convinced? Am I convinced? We'll see, won't we?)

While we're being cynical, let me add here that, yes, I am well aware that there is far worse suffering than this. And yes, 'tis true that I grew up in tennis whites at a fancy-ass Chicago country club, went to a New England prep school, and was a debutante, for that matter. But I'm here to tell you that those things don't make it any easier to be happy. Not happy in the way I mean happy. Not free. In fact, those things can make it easier to pretend that you're happy. There's suffering in pretending. Suffering is a relative term, and is only as important as it ultimately pertains to you—that is, if we want to change the world. And I do. But before we can do that, we have to start with what we can control and be responsible for, and that's good ol' number one.

And you, too. You and me. We need each other, at least in these pages. We're in this together. What's the condition of the heart and mind of your husband/wife/partner/friend/child/sibling/parent/relative? Are you sure about that?

At this moment in my life, for the first time ever, I have fingernails and not "bloody stubs," as I've liked to endearingly call them. A four-decade habit broken subconsciously. I simply looked down the other day, and I had fingernails. At this moment in my life, right after I finish this chapter on the end of suffering, instead of biting them all off, I'm booking my first manicure.

I used to say that happiness was a myth, constructed by the folks at Disney. We went to Disney World. Signed up for the dinner with Sleeping Beauty, who looked like she'd dropped a couple of Vicodins. Not so happy.

And neither was I. I kinda wished Uncle Walt's vision didn't leave the Magic Kingdom dry. Not even a rum drink at the Pirates of the Caribbean. But that's just because I still believed that happiness was a cop-out. In other words, something to be gained from the outside in. And that even if it did at one time exist, in the end, Disney killed it.

I also believed that freedom was a cop-out. And if your husband chose the trash and the bar or his office couch or even a woman over you, and it didn't make you want to put a bullet in your own head, and maybe his, too . . . you were one thing:

a sucker. A sucker living a sucky life. Everything sucky sucky sucky. And that's just the way life is.

So go have a glass of wine and bitch to your baggageless, still-skinny-at-forty-one girlfriend about your husband. The same one who's probably lying next to him right now, in a cheap motel somewhere on the strip, being complimented on her still-great ass, still-great cheekbones, still-great legs.

Oh no! Victim mode! I'm derailed. I . . . I . . . can't stop myself!

That asshole!

Breathe. Make some tea.

I don't want to breathe. And I don't want tea.

I want coffee! Black and strong and . . . agitating.

I want I want I want! How am I ever going to live up to this strategy—this practice?

But I know . . . it's moment by moment. By moment.

9:30 a.m. Same morning.

My twelve-year-old daughter comes in crying because one of her best friends won't talk to her. It's been going on for weeks, she says, and finally she can't stand it anymore. It's eating her alive. She needs advice.

And I tell her all of this. The theory, that is. The stuff about suffering. Not that her father's capacity to love is in question.

And she gets it. She's suffering because she's chosen to base her personal happiness on things outside of her control. And as she sits there on the stairs shaking and crying, I can see that she really does get it. Suffering is no fun. She doesn't like it one bit. She'd rather be happy. She goes upstairs to wash her face.

I'm not going to write much about my children in this book for obvious reasons, but I'll write this here: What if someone told you *that* when you were twelve years old? What if you'd spent your whole life understanding that we have a choice? And that we can choose freedom simply by committing ourselves to ending suffering. It doesn't have to be so hard all the time.

To that end, I decide that after this morning of writing, I'm going to take the kids to buy plants to fill our terra-cotta pots on the patio. We'll get chartreuse and aubergine sweet potato vine and mix in tall prairie grasses and maybe some white clematis to climb out of the pots and up the sides of the house. We're going to create beauty despite him. But not to spite him.

All through breakfast, neither of them asks where their father is and I don't tell them. They assume he came home late last night and left early today for work. It calms me not to have to share my burden. That it's not theirs to bear. Yet. It calms me to think of creating beauty today with them. Especially given the situation. It calms me that I've just given my daughter the pearl of wisdom that I took forty-one years to find. And that today my children will learn about botany and creating and receiving beauty.

But guess what? I don't want to be calm. I want to ditch this philosophy, and I want to rage and suffer! I want to want.

I want my husband to come home. Say he's sorry. Tell me he loves me. And pour himself a cup of coffee.

Breathe, I tell myself. *Remember you don't question his capacity to love. You don't question his love for you. You don't see this as a state of emergency. You simply know your husband better than he currently knows himself. This is not about you. Not yet. You're going to ride this out. For now. Just for now. Breathe.*

At this moment in my life, I know I can at least do that. Just breathe.

But I can't "just breathe"! I'm choking! I'm weak and small and scared. Aren't I?

And then I remember an excerpt from a book that has seen me through hard times before.

It's called *The Cloud of Unknowing.*

In it, an anonymous fourteenth-century Christian mystic writer asks us to choose a word. One word. And to fasten it to our hearts. That word, working in us, will bring us through the hardest times. Or so the anonymous writer promises.

In my life, that word has been many things. God, love, hope, truth, joy, grace, beauty, wonder, surrender, freedom.

Right now it is more simple than any of those things. It is not a deity or a goal or a state of being. It's an action verb. It is simply: breathe.

From The Cloud of Unknowing

Take just a little word of one syllable rather than two . . . Such a one is the word God or the word love. Choose which you prefer . . . and fasten this word to your heart so that whatever happens it will never go away. This word is to be your shield and your spear, whether you are riding in peace or in war. With this word you are to beat upon the cloud and the darkness above and beneath you. With this word you are to strike down every kind of thought, driving it down into a pool of forgetting. If any thought should press upon you, asking what you would have, answer with no word but this one. If your thoughts should offer, out of their great learning to analyze your word for you and tell you its meanings, say to your thoughts that you want to keep it whole . . . It is not a matter of analyzing or elucidating . . . No one can truly think of God. It is therefore my wish to leave everything that I can think and choose for my love the thing that I cannot think. God can be loved but not thought. He can be taken and held by love, but not by thought.

I lie on my back on my office floor.

No one can truly think of God. He can be taken and held by love.

It's clear to me that a crisis like this requires us not even to think of God. Like the writer says, to go beyond thinking. Into a place of forgetting, even. Maybe even beyond creating, receiving, aligning. Maybe this sort of crisis requires the individual, my husband and me both, to unlayer down to our most true naked nature. Where there is just the beating of the heart. And the breath. Held by love.

I read it again.

And I do. I just . . . breathe.

Rilke's World at Play in Rumi's Field

An hour or two until we leave
for the nursery. Another mug of tea.

Even though I try, as a rule, not to dwell too long in the past, it seems important right now to look back in time. At our beginnings. In order for me to get a grasp on what is upon us.

This was read at our wedding:

> *Loving does not at first mean merging, surrendering, and uniting with another person (for what would a union be of two people who are unclarified, unfinished, and still incoherent—?), it is a high inducement for the individual to ripen, to become something in himself, to become world, to become world in himself for the sake of another person;*

> *it is a great demanding claim on him, something that chooses him and calls him to vast distances.*
>
> —RILKE, AGAIN

Even though we stood at the altar of the prominent suburban Chicago Episcopal church where I'd been baptized and confirmed, and had sung in the choir—me in my mother's wedding gown, and he in a black cutaway morning suit, four hundred–plus people surrounding us on the rainiest day I can remember (rain and weddings: good luck. Steak knives and weddings: bad luck. I think it should be the other way around) . . . and even though a thirteen-piece swing orchestra awaited us at the country club reception to follow—the country club where F. Scott Fitzgerald purportedly met the inspiration for his Daisy in *The Great Gatsby* . . . even though we stood there holding hands, gazing into each other's eyes over lavender roses, knowing we were making our parents exceedingly proud at that moment in our lives . . . we both knew damn well that who we really were to each other were partners in crime.

Okay, maybe just gentle rebels of institution, finally, after six years of courtship, taking on the Institution of Marriage. We dared it to take down our spirits. We loved our spirits best of all. With every vow that we took, that was our private subtext. We had a favorite quote: "Out beyond ideas of wrong-doing and right-doing there is a field. I will meet you there."—Rumi. Rumi was our inner MC, there at the altar, that rainy day. In Rumi's field, the rules of institutions were reduced to puddles reflecting summer clouds—puddles we'd splash through, running hand in hand.

"Why buy into the Institution of Marriage at all, then?" we asked ourselves. Our answer: At the end of the day, it was nice to come in out of the field, dry off, hang up your coat in a world that felt familiar. Safe. Traditional. We never said we were opposed to tradition. Not when it came to family.

We weren't afraid of marriage, even when confronted by the worst pessimists. For us, marriage was not uncharted territory. On our wedding day, we were going where many of our loved ones had gone before. We were the cabooses—each of us by at least seven years. Collectively, we'd been to a lot of weddings. In fact, rather than bridesmaids and groomsmen, we had our young nieces and nephews as our wedding party—twelve of them. We were entering into family hallowed territory. And we liked that. We loved that.

Our siblings were older—much older in some cases. This gap in generations owed itself to the fact that our parents were World War II people, born prior to, or smack dab in the midst of, the Great Depression. The cigarette and cocktail generation of uncomfortable footwear that wasn't so hell-bent on the 2.2--offspringed family. If they popped one out at the end a bit by mistake, it wouldn't be a big deal. The kid would figure it out.

Our brothers and sisters came of age in 1960s counterculture, and had put our parents through enough of a crash course in dope and miniskirts and LSD and Grateful Dead concerts and anti-patriotism . . . that by the time we came around, all we had to do to stay in their parental favor was keep our hair a decent length and try not to do anything too terribly publicly embarrassing.

As a result, we'd both gotten away with murder, as it were—he in his New York suburb, I in my Chicago one. We loved that about each other—saw it in each other's eyes the moment we met: The two of us liked to have fun. And get away with it.

But it was also kind of lonely back there in the 1970s, being the cabooses; for all intents and purposes, only children. Like we'd missed all the fun. So when my husband and I met, we recognized each other. We'd spent a lot of our childhoods lonely. Longing for our older sisters and brothers off at boarding school and college. Wanting companionship. Wanting our families assembled. No wonder we were both so keen on building our own family in the not too distant future.

In addition to having older parents and siblings, from well-appointed houses, we had fathers who commuted to work in wool overcoats and felt fedoras, who dined and napped at private men's city clubs; well-dressed mothers who were fine hostesses, and had taught us how to shake hands and use the correct forks. We'd been sent off to ruddy summer camps, and then to New England boarding schools, and then to a private liberal arts college in Ohio, where we met.

I was, at the time, heartbroken by the sudden end of a three-year relationship, and after sitting in the dark for a few weeks in my room, some friends convinced me to go to a frat party. I didn't really go to frat parties at that point in my college career. I'd just spent a year studying in Florence, Italy, and had experienced for the first time in my life what it felt like to be free-spirited and inspired. The whole college frat scene, simply put, paled in comparison with the Renaissance. But there he was. Looking like Michelangelo's *David*. So handsome and cocksure and able.

My husband has soft edges. Wavy hair. Round muscles. A huge smile. His sisters and his mother have this smile, which can sometimes make it weird for me because I'm used to seeing that smile and thinking, *Gosh, I want to kiss that.*

That's what I thought that night, standing at the top of a frat house staircase, looking down into a mosh pit of partying, and saying to my friend, "What's that guy's name?"

But I didn't listen to the answer. I descended the staircase, went up to him, and said, "Hi, I'm Laura."

"I know who you are," he said. "Everybody knows who you are."

"You like theater, then?" I said, pleasantly surprised. I'd been a drama/film major my first few years until I discovered writing.

"Not exactly," he hedged. "I just meant that . . . you're beautiful."

I blushed. Which was a lot for an obnoxiously PC feminist who'd deactivated from her sorority on principles of image discrimination.

And then his dog, Mickey Jagger—a mutt Lab cross in a red bandanna—bit me.

So, like a gentleman, he took me back to my house, butterfly-stitched up my thumb using camp counselor–esque techniques, kissed my finger, and left.

And the rest is history. More or less.

When people ask me why I love my husband, I don't gush. I'm a WASP. A smart one. A modern woman with very specific career aspirations. Women like me are not supposed to gush about why we love a man. We're supposed to act part lesbian, part cranky Yankee. What do we need men for?! So I give them my marriage elevator speech. It's short and it nails it. I say, "He's like a camp counselor." That's a lofty compliment. I had a crush on every one of my male camp counselors. I like to have fun. In relative safety, that is.

We said we were like two hot air balloons. We were going to float up above the institutions from which we hailed, and go somewhere far away and be fun and alive and free-spirited together. I called him my Radiant Stallion. He called me the Prettiest Girl at the Party.

To future financial world whizzes and ladies of the Junior League, I bragged about how he wanted to do cool guy stuff like fly helicopters. Scuba dive the Great Barrier Reef. Climb Everest.

He bragged about how I already knew that I wanted to be a writer; that I'd already started my first novel. He even said I had "great childbearing hips," at which some women would have taken offense. But I liked that he believed a woman could be a mother and a writer both. I knew I wanted to be both.

I also liked that he was a good driver. Competent and controlled. But that he liked speed. I'd always had a thing for speed. Horses. Cars. Boats. With so much pushing at me to fit into a fine small box—Tiffany blue, whether or not I belonged . . . speed felt like freedom. He felt like freedom.

Unlike me, he seemed unscathed by the pressures of society. He was the sort of man who didn't let things get under his skin. The sort who handled things. Calmly. Adeptly. But still with this element of danger that I liked. We'd crank Steely Dan and speed down the country roads around our college, blaring "Bodhisattva," not having the slightest idea what that word meant. I wasn't like "a regular chick," he said. I was more "like a guy." That struck me as a great compliment because it meant to me that not only did he see me as attractive and smart, but also as his friend. He prized friendship.

I'd never been in a relationship with someone like him. Being with him was easy. And it occurred to me that I'd spent a lot of time in my life being attracted to hard things. With this man, I felt like I could go anywhere. Be anything. And everything would be okay. He'd have my back. For a girl who knew she was about to part from her societal orientation, that seemed vastly important.

And let me be perfectly honest: it didn't hurt that the guy knew his way around a pair of khaki pants and a Brooks Brothers shirt. To me, that was code for: *We'll never go totally off the deep end, dear.* I never wanted to go off the deep end. I just wanted some reasonable adventure.

Ours began in a car. In fact, you could analyze our entire relationship by who he is in the driver seat and who I am in the passenger seat. Put it this way: with him, I've never had any reason to be a backseat driver. You can get a lot accomplished when you don't have to worry about who's doing the driving. (Calm down. I'm not saying that he's the driver in our relationship. Just in the car. It's a role. A skill. A vibe. It suits him. And it works for me. I've written novels sitting in the passenger seat.)

I've learned that in a courtship revving its way toward marriage, there's an agreement that the two parties come to mutually, either spoken or not. Ours went something like this:

We believed we were golden—that the world was full of shocking possibility with the occasion for joy and wonder in places we never dreamed existed. And we would find those things together.

Even though in our early years together we knew we were slightly reckless and wanted it that way, we also knew that whether or not we ended up together, we both had the full intention of one day being married people with children. In a house somewhere, not too different from the ones in which we'd grown up. Maybe more artsy and modern and informal, but still well-appointed. Beautiful like the beauty our mothers created, and new beauty, too—beauty we'd create all on our own in ways we'd come to learn all on our own. We welcomed that journey of self-discovery. We welcomed that unknown beauty. And we wanted children to pass on its legacy.

They'd know how to play the piano and the guitar, and they'd have strawberry stains on their hands much of the summer, and great tans. There would be meat braising in the oven, flowers on the windowsill, a dog carrying a tennis ball in its mouth, NPR on the kitchen radio.

We talked about these things in a way I'm not sure most twenty-year-olds do. Especially twenty-year-old rebels—who have every intention of leaving behind their comfort zones. Especially twenty-year-old privileged rebels who don't exactly have trust funds. Aha—the plot thickens.

We dreamed big in those early days. He'd be a wildlife photographer. Or fly bush planes in Alaska. Or lead helicopter skiing trips into the Rockies. Or run scuba expeditions in the Caribbean or off Australia. I'd write novels. We'd travel the world. And somehow, we'd be rich. Wouldn't we? Wouldn't the money just magically follow all that intentional living? In fact, didn't the world reward brave adventurers who left the comfort of money behind? Of course it did.

And one day, we'd settle down with all our money that had been sent to us in envelopes all around the world by the Bureau of Financing for Brave Ex-WASP Adventurers (mine would come from their special branch: Ambassadors of Elite Novelist Forces) . . . and we'd build a home somewhere as our base. And have kids. (See: money issues.)

We'd still travel the world—just with them in tow. It wouldn't hold us back. We wouldn't skip a beat. We saw what our siblings were capable of with their kids. From the height of our self-obsessed adolescences, we'd both gotten to watch our older rock-star-status siblings become mommies and daddies and housekeepers and businesspeople and learn how to carpool and ref soccer games and put on Thanksgiving dinners.

It looked wonderful. We wanted it. Just not immediately.

Anything was possible. We were powerful. Together, we were untouchable. My gut told me so, and his did, too. It wasn't much more than that, I don't think. We decided we could have it all. We'd live out the end of our adolescences in high form; and we'd do it together. And come out perfectly poised for the next phase. Together. And we could pull all of this off because we were not needy in our relationship. We were good at being alone . . . together. Rilke's guardians of each other's solitude. We had that in spades from the beginning. We always liked to play cards.

Reality, Cockroaches, Bums in the Basement, and Microbrew

Same day. Early evening.
A long day, this one.

Pots planted. Patio set up for summer. Teak table, chairs, umbrella, chaise longues . . . all positioned and ready. Kids playing soccer in the front yard, the fruit trees their goalposts.

I've stolen away to my office—the sanctum of my writing self. So many blank pages have been filled and edited here. It's like I've been writing all these years just to fill this exact blank page. My fiction writer wants to know: *Where will the plot go? How will it end?* But I can't do a thing to control the future of this story. All I can write is how it feels. What's going on in my mind. And the details, as they are given to me. In hopes that it will help you if you're in similar pain. I'm hoping for a little relief for both of us.

It's therapeutic, then, to think about the arc of my relationship with my husband. Who we were years ago. How we got here, to today. It helps me to stay on our team. Especially in light of it being early evening and still no call from him. I need to write about us for another chapter. To dwell in the sweet, charged, and turbulent terrain of the past. To write about us from that night we met as dreamers and partners in petty crime, to this Montana life.

I think back to when we moved to Boston. Of all the places to go in the world of adventure . . . Boston. Good-ol'-boy, whales-on-the-belt, cobblestony Beantown.

And why did we move there?

Because we forgot one small detail: we didn't have trust funds. And we didn't have an income.

And why else?

Because in Boston, we had beloved sisters and brothers-in-law and nieces and nephews and available laundry machines at our fingertips. The odd station wagon should we need it. Sunday dinners with the older generation of siblings we'd missed out on; had been lonely for. Sisters who'd served as second mothers—who remembered our first steps and first words, but who we'd never known as equals. We'd never known their secrets. Or helped them with their homework. Never read aloud to them. Or brushed their hair. I'm not sure how large that longing was for him as a little boy, but I know mine was immense. I wanted those missed moments—those dinners at the dining room table. Boston was like the last loop around the house before we launched our bon voyage.

And yet with all the pie in our sky of balloon aviation . . . we were still attached to the ropes of our fathers' financial assistance and our sisters' willingness to let us freeload. Just like most of the other recent college graduates that we knew. Only our friends from college were masterfully landing entry-level banking positions and paralegal jobs in preparation for law school.

Those sorts of jobs didn't bode well for our Big Dreamer Personalities.

So to support our mutually fanatical sushi habit and cover our other expenses (priorities in that order), we took night jobs at a popular Boston Garden post-game haunt called the Scotch 'n Sirloin—emphasis on the '*n*. The tips were big there, and so were the hair, the heels, and the clientele—many of them actual Boston Celtics.

For some reason, the owners thought the cocktail waitresses (women only) needed to be dressed like men, in tuxedos with red bow ties and cummerbunds, and the waiters (men only) as UPS drivers—brown on brown. It was all very steaky and lipsticky. My cocktail waitress training consisted of this: "You go up to the table and say, 'Good evening. What's yah cocktail?'"

"What if they're not drinkers?" I asked, all liberal-arts-collegiate.

"Maybe you can push them ovah the edge. There ain't no dough in fizzy watah."

We needed our days free. He had some college credits to finish up, and I had a book to write.

Outside of cocktail waitressing, I refused to start a secondary career, though the pressure was on. I knew I was a writer. Period.

Suffice it to say that when I was toying around with giving in to everybody's coaxing to get a career writing slogans for things like Keebler cookies, the former CEO of a major Chicago advertising agency sat me down in his garden studio and offered me some stern words.

Taking a drag on a Camel unfiltered, he said, "You're a writer of books. I can see the fire in your eyes when you talk about it." Then he pointed at me with his cigarette, slanted his eyes, and added a severe, "Don't let people tell you that writers need to be practical and take a job at an advertising agency! Write books! I wish I'd listened to my heart when I was your age."

And then he spoke some of the most important words of my life: "This is one of the hardest social demographics to leave on earth. Because this"—and he held out his arms to his artfully transformed garden shed and to his acres of rose gardens and to the rest of the North Shore of Chicago—"this is what much of the world wants." He leaned in, taking another drag so that he was shrouded in smoke. "If you can blaze your own trail and find success . . . then I'll know you're a genius."

I've referred to those words more times than I could count. He's dead now. He gave me wild geranium cuts from his Chicago garden that still come up every year in mine in Montana. And every time, they tell me that I am a writer of books. And that I was courageous to put that before social class. Even when I'm not so sure.

So, with big dreams and empty-ish pockets, we decided that until we could save up some money to travel the world, we'd be co-journeyers in a duplex in Allston, Massachusetts. We were happy in our little home, albeit a shoddy one. We wanted it shoddy. We were rebels, remember? If we couldn't be fabulous expatriates, for the time being at least we could be slumming it.

In short, we were pretentious idiots, but you probably already figured that out.

Our first living room art was a giant piece of driftwood we hauled back from a beach on Cape Cod. Our first dining table was a cardboard refrigerator box—an old quilt we found at a garage sale draped over it; we were proud of it. I somehow had my great-grandmother's sterling-silver candelabra, and that atop the quilt and cardboard brought me deep satirical pleasure. Especially when the wax dripped all over the place and the table smelled like it was going to self-combust. I felt unstable and dramatic, like Anne Sexton or Sylvia Plath or Anaïs Nin or Isadora Duncan or Sid Vicious or somebody.

Only I wasn't.

I was somebody who house-sat and nannied for extra money and showed up on time for work.

I wanted to be badder. I just wasn't brave enough—that's the truth. Leaving the comfort of my social class, writing my first novel, working night shifts as a cocktail waitress and riding the subway home late at night . . . took all the bravery I had. But never would I have admitted it. Never.

In the world I come from, something like not shaving your

legs is a high crime. A high crime I committed. And lived to pay for. So a cardboard dining table . . . Oh, never mind. Maybe you'll understand later, in the chapter where I describe my version of what it is to be a WASP. Or maybe you could just agree now to forgive me for being privileged and still having the audacity to claim there's ever been pain in my life. And you'll be kind. And I won't have to write the damn chapter about WASP society. I'm sensitive about this. There's nothing I loathe more on the page than poor-little-rich-girl syndrome. But I'm telling you—I grew up with some of the richest people in the world. And pain is pain is pain.

I used to say that I was thankful that I didn't have a trust fund. That there was no serious money in our family—tempting me and even dogging me into staying in that world. No inheritance being controlled by a fickle old dowager who needed a great-grandchild to be named after her, or else! Sure, for the most part, I enjoyed the privileges of my peers. But at the end of the day, my currency was limited.

I was rich in china, crystal, silver, mildewy chintz quilted sofas, and wobbly mahogany furniture. But not a lot of dough. Or in other words, I could probably get into any *Mayflower*-descendant-based private club in the country, but am not sure I can pay my current therapy bill. (I like to remind my mother that our thirteen *Mayflower* ancestors were rebels, leaving home for a new life.)

My husband calls it "all blue and no green."

The truth is, it's never been my goal to be rich. Not really rich like the families of my youth. I just needed to have enough in my bank account to pay the price for leaving the world to which my mother had committed her entire life—with the express intention of ensuring that her children swallowed it whole. Is there a dollar value on that one? Have you ever paid that price? Maybe now you understand. Good. Thank you. Now I don't have to write that chapter.

I still have dreams about our little Allston expatriate life. We were so eager and dramatic without much real-life drama. We liked to think that we could create it. Like we were preparing movie sets, we painted rooms uncommon mood-inducing colors. Romantic Comedy indigo in one room. Psychological Thriller puce in another. We almost got evicted for painting our kitchen brick red and covering over the old wood floors with black and white checked linoleum. Hey—we wanted it to look like a sushi bar—red and black. We liked red and black. Oh, the possibilities of the drama that could ensue between a couple in their own private sushi bar.

Perhaps we took the idea of slumming it a bit too far. In those early Boston days, we had to sleep with the lights on to keep the cockroaches off us. There was a guy living in the basement who screamed in the night and who pushed a shopping cart around Boston all day. He was somehow related to the landlord, who lived in the other half of the duplex. We called him Bum Brother. Every so often, he ended up in our apartment as if he had a key, as if he was starving for sushi. Luckily, my husband was, and still is, tall and muscular. The whole thing was, as my grandmother used to say, "sub-par." Very Bates Motel. A lot of screaming "Shut up, Muthah" at all hours in thick Boston accents.

We considered it like a renegade honeymoon before the real honeymoon, which we were beginning to think might actually be in the cards one day in the not so far away. When we'd have bridal showers and things would match and monogrammed towels would hang off shiny chrome towel racks, just so, as if they'd magically grown there, awaiting summer visitors with their own monogrammed towels back home hanging in their own version of just so.

Only weren't we rebelling against those monogrammed towels and all that they represented?

Needless to say, we were confused.

We were confused the way that anyone leaving his social origins is confused. Like the advertising CEO had forewarned. Not at all "genius." No, Boston was too slippery for us. Too many party invitations from people who were already enjoying success as businesspeople with sensible haircuts and designer shoes and housekeepers. As much as we loved our families and our friends, each in their own way had chosen the world we felt destined to leave. Making it even more confusing. We knew we had to cut ourselves off from the land of old comforts, nurturing as it was. That is, if our dreams were going to come true.

So we started to imagine life somewhere else.

But where would we go? We didn't want to go anywhere entirely off-the-grid, did we? Just someplace where the temptations of "home" were far away.

"What about Seattle?" I said one day, reading *Outside* magazine. A lot of people were talking about Seattle. And miraculously, no sooner did we start throwing around the name of that city than we landed a job managing an apartment building on the stunningly beautiful Queen Anne Hill in Seattle proper. He'd be inspired by the mountains and the water and figure out what he wanted to do with the next stage of his life. I'd have more time to write since our rent was taken care of in our managerial role.

Seattle felt like a world of possibility. Maybe now we'd get ahead. Maybe I'd meet writers and artists and musicians. My people. Maybe I'd get a novel published and we'd travel the world sooner than later. Maybe I'd even get back to Italy. I was pretty sure he was getting sick of hearing about my year in Italy.

We could pull off that sort of thing—having the best of both worlds. Right? The two us together, especially. We were golden, weren't we?

Such high opinions of ourselves.

Marriage. Children. We were talking about the possibilities more and more.

But first, we had to prove ourselves as successes in the world. Especially since we'd taken the road less traveled. We didn't know anybody who'd followed that road all the way out to Seattle. Not in 1989.

It was during the huge Northwest beer boom and, despite his degree in journalism, he took a job at a microbrewery. The adventures in the world of beer seemed imminently more interesting to him at twenty-three than working for a newspaper. It immediately made him one of the coolest cats in town.

I set up my writing studio in a room of our new apartment overlooking Lake Union and the Seattle city skyline. I decided to work at a funky café full of writerly types scribbling freehand over cups of what was probably the best coffee in the United States at that time. This was when there were only a few Starbucks—before they changed the logo, cropped off the mermaid's crotch, and taught middle America how to spend four dollars on a cup of coffee.

Over the next few years, we moved around north Seattle. I had three offices, under a four-foot eave, with a tiny broken window at the end, and a sawhorse for a desk. I loved that office. Apparently LSD was piped in through its walls, because I wrote a book in it about a woman who could see fairies. But that's how Seattle was for me. Wide open and pressure free. And my writing started to evolve from anger into playing. Eventually, it would find its way to gratitude, but that would take a few more years.

While I was busy writing, he was busy turning that brewery into the fastest-growing brewery in the Northwest. He became like a local celebrity. We never had a problem getting a table at even the busiest restaurants. No one would let us pay for a beer wherever we went. And the beer was good.

It was a twenty-something's dream.

I joined a writing group, got the green light that, in fact, I truly could write, started submitting my books, and met with the standard publishing world rejection. But not all form letters. I got what I called "good" rejection letters. A lot of them. Handwritten notes with generous words of encouragement, like "While you are a talented writer, I suspect that this is not the one." Or, "Write on!" My favorite one was and still is: "This could be good if you reduced it by three hundred pages." Which I did. It almost went all the way. But finally, the editorial board decided that the main character was not lovable enough. Of all the main characters I've created in all my books, that one in particular was the most autobiographical. Add being unlovable to your pile of rejection letters and try not to put your head in the oven.

Yes, slowly, all that rejection was taking shape in the form of shame. I stopped telling people I was a writer. I couldn't handle the standard question, "Where can I buy your books?" But still, I persevered. I was a writer of books, damn it! The CEO could see it in my eyes. I spent a lot of time looking in the mirror trying to see his fire. I would not sell out and pursue another more lucrative career. I'd take on more jobs, and I did. I nannied. I temped. I worked retail. Drove a delivery truck. (Not exactly what my father had in mind when he'd jokingly repeat an old 1940s radio sign-off, "Write when you find work.")

We adored Seattle. It was a love story to match our own. The salt air and ferryboats and the Dungeness crab and Copper River salmon and the dahlias and Skagit tulips and chanterelle mushrooms in Pike Place Market. Everything grew in Seattle—the doormats blossomed in springtime. Mountains all around—the Cascades, the Olympics, Mount Rainier peeking and ducking as you followed rainbows up and down the rain-fresh city hills. The sushi and the symphony and funky music and coffee shops. My skin and hair and body had never felt more stunning and alive. Apart from my year in Italy, *I* had never felt more alive.

The best part of it was that Seattle seemed to be snob-free. Artistically electrified. No one glazed over when I told them I was a writer, like they had in Boston. People took me seriously here. We all took each other seriously. It felt like a whole city of people inventing themselves. And the city reflected their efforts. Every corner pulsed with expression. Even the sewer plates were works of art. In the rain, for some reason, things are just a bit more dire. Like one good deluge might just melt it all away. I think we all felt a little bit like movie stars back then, for going full-throttle for our dreams. When we weren't busy lying in bed at three in the morning calling ourselves total ignoramuses.

It wasn't perfect. There was a time when my future husband and I needed to go off on our own—spread our wings, separate from each other. And we broke up. There was a lot of crying. I'd never seen him cry. I found out years later that he'd snuck into my apartment and stolen a sweater so he could "smell me."

We dated other people. But in time we missed each other. And we came back to each other, better than ever.

With the help of a great therapist . . . a few years later, we decided to get married. It was a very deliberate decision. We asked each other in a private ceremony by a river with candles and heart-shaped rocks we'd been collecting since our Boston days.

Friends questioned how we could be getting married after we'd broken up. And, God forbid, seen a THERAPIST. (A lot of those friends are divorced now. Almost all of them have been in therapy.)

I had one friend who actually came right out and said, "I think that anyone who moves west is just plain irresponsible. I mean, what are they running away from!?" (You should have seen her face when I told her a few years later we were moving to Montana.)

What I didn't say was, *Probably people like you.*

Instead, I forgave her for it. Because sometimes, when I was too tired to be rebellious and the fear of leaving so much privilege behind swept up my stomach in fits . . . when my parents confirmed their disappointment, despite their attempts at support and understanding, and their message was to wrap the whole thing up and come back home where I belonged . . . sometimes, I believed them.

I was a bad kid, after all. Rebels were bad. Ungrateful wretches. And working blue-collar jobs with a cum laude private college degree didn't add up to a whole lot of anything but stupidity. And yes, maybe even irresponsibility. Especially if you couldn't get a book published. Especially with "your UPBRINGING!"

Who cared that you wrote your ass off every waking moment that you weren't changing diapers or delivering flowers or making double mocha skinny half-cafs. YOU did not have SUCCESS.

AND you were SUPPOSED to have success. And you WOULD have success . . . if you'd . . . just . . . BEHAVED. And gotten a job at an ad agency writing ditties about Keebler elves.

So back to Rilke and Rumi. At the altar.

Despite our newly modified western selves, at my parents' prompting and after much consideration, we decided to have a formal society wedding in honor of who we'd both been for the majority of our lives. Our families. Our culture of origin. The friends and their families who had helped raise us. It was like our last good-bye. The final loop around the neighborhood.

Plus, it seemed unfair to expect the majority of our friends and family who lived back East to understand our renegade Seattle ways. We wanted to accommodate our loved ones. Our elders—so many of them. The generation below us—our many nieces and nephews. We didn't want them to be inconvenienced by our wayward western move. And it wasn't like the comforts of "home" didn't matter to us anymore. It wasn't like we weren't eternally grateful.

So, on our budget, we celebrated with our Seattle friends—a few kegs and a reggae band. And afterward, we went to Chicago. Met them in the middle. In my North Shore suburb where my parents put on the wedding that girls like me were supposed to have whether or not their "real lives" reflected it.

It was beautiful. Every detail "done to perfection," as my mother likes to say, but only if things meet her standards. And except for the pearl-white clamshells we gathered on the Hood

Canal and snuck into the flower arrangements to symbolize our lives out West, in her opinion . . . they did. It meant a lot to us.

We even ended up in the bridal section of *Town & Country* magazine, where we were supposed to, just as if we'd never left. We honeymooned in Paris—his parents' wedding gift to us. We wrote the thank-you notes for our gorgeous wedding gifts and beautiful bridal showers on our Crane stationery with our new monogram, which since I didn't change my name, inspired confusion among many. Confusion we liked. All six letters, like a new word.

And after it all, back we went, happily to Seattle. Launched for a good chunk of time.

We bought a home with the help of his father—a small but proper home. With a dining room. A dining room with a proper dining room table and chairs. A place for my grandmother's china cabinet.

And after remodeling the kitchen with friends in exchange for beer—which took a few months, as can be imagined—we unpacked all the wedding gifts. Everything was in its place for the next chapter of our lives. We even knew which room would be the nursery.

It was our first night. I'd made my Italian host Mama's special pasta pomodoro and was serving it into our brand-new pasta bowl, when my husband sprang open the newly hung kitchen door.

"Guess what?! I just got a job offer! A great job offer! At a new brewery. With an amazing boss who'd pay me well! Really well! With benefits! I'd be running it. And you wouldn't have to work. You could write full-time! And we could afford to buy a nice home with land. And we could have our children. And you could be a stay-at-home mother and write just like you've always dreamed."

My heart lifted, the pasta dangling midair. I pictured an old Northwest Craftsman, somewhere on Lake Washington or Bainbridge Island. Maybe on a beach where we could dig for clams and sail off to the San Juans with our future kids, gazing at orca whales and orange and purple starfish the size of steel drums. We'd become Seattle establishment all on our own volition and not because of who our parents or ancestors were. We'd be like those cool older couples wandering around town after the symphony. The woman in a long cape. The man in a pithy cap. The author and her magnificent husband with his chain of fabulous Northwest microbreweries. Our children could go to good schools and enjoy some of the privileges we had. Just in Seattle. Without the pressures we'd left behind.

"There's just one thing," he said.

I looked at him. I knew that look. My serving forks wilted.

"We'd have to move. In a month. To . . . Montana."

At that moment in my life I honestly wasn't entirely clear where Montana was. One of those huge rectangular states—like North Dakota. I barely even knew where Washington state was, much less Montana!

My heart sank. My beloved Seattle. My beloved friends. My

writing group. I knew myself here more than ever. I had contacted my true nature all on my own, surrounded by those whaleful waters. I didn't want to move from the city. I didn't want to have to find my true nature in strictly nature!

"We'd have to move where?" I said.

And then I remembered that just the week before I'd had the shitty idea of kneeling down by my bed like my grandmother did every night of her life, and asking the dear Lord—which was, at that time in my life, some approximation of Jesus and faceless, bodiless Love—to please give me the chance to write full-time. Crying like a baby, I blubbered, "I'm sick of working all these jobs and getting nowhere. I want time to write my books. I want to have babies. And have the money to stay at home with them. I want to be published."

"It's not like it would be totally rural. It's in a ski town," he said—an avid skier, to a girl from Illinois.

My heart sank deeper. Skiing wasn't my thing. I'd always said I'd never be one of those pot-smoking-hippie-trust-fund-wannabes who moved to a ski town. I loved the city. And I loved nature, too. I just didn't need nature in my backyard. I wanted cafés, movie houses, art galleries, independent bookstores in my backyard. Seattle was the perfect compromise. I had a house and a garden. That was as rural as I wanted to go.

But rebel adventurers don't say no to things like that. Not after they've begged God. Not if they're open to the journey. And that was what we'd meant when we'd called ourselves "two balloons."

"Okay," I said.

He even said it that night—raising his eyebrows, his voice going up an octave: "Two balloons."

What I didn't say was, *I thought we'd landed for a while.*

A month later, we were living in a large rectangular state with a total population that was just under a third of that of the city of Chicago: a place called Montana.

A place where I sit now, in the evening of the same day, a patio full of newly planted beautiful pots, my children in their rooms doing summer reading, wondering where my husband is. Fifteen years later. Almost to the day that we moved to this fair state.

Something tells me that dinner will be on the thin side tonight, the DVD player will be the babysitter, and I will be hidden away in my sanctum until the wee hours, writing my way through to the next day. When this marital mystery will hopefully be solved.

Montana

Wee hours, sure enough.

Still no word.

Put the kids to bed with a white lie. "Daddy's working late." Okay, not a white lie. A lie. There'll be plenty of time for truth. I just need to know what it is I'm dealing with first. In a family that prizes honesty, the lie feels like pollution in this star-swept night sky.

Montana. Big Sky. Big big sky. Something tells me this sky has forgiven many lies.

I first saw it, however, by day. Though, too, in a lie. Lying to myself all the way, across Washington and Idaho, that I was happy for the move. That I welcomed it as the answer to prayer. That I was up for this next chapter. Trying to hide my tears, stretched out in the backseat of our Volkswagen Vanagon, feigning sleep.

When we crested the hill that opened up to the glacial valley that would become our home—the swath of Flathead Lake, the mountains all around—two bald eagles flew right through the view from our windshield. I remember joking that it was like *The Firm*. Like his new boss was hovering in a nearby helicopter saying, *Release the eagles*. He knew I was not as keen on Montana as he wanted the wife of his new brewery director to be.

But from the beginning, Montana was everything we'd been promised. His job was great. He was well-respected. He made excellent money, especially for Montana. I had all the time and space I needed to write. Which was perfect since there were simply no distractions. Of the city sort. And I mean none. It was a real town, not a purpose-built resort town like Vail. Once a logging town, then a train town, it was a work-in-progress. And I immediately respected that about it. It wasn't putting on airs. In so many ways, it was exactly what I'd been looking for all my life.

Still, I was disoriented. I felt like I'd moved to another country if not another planet. No art galleries unless you grooved on cheesy horse art. No clothes shopping unless you liked nouns on your sweaters. You couldn't even get a *New York Times* back then. I made the mistake of asking once. The answer, after much commotion, was "Probably Seattle is your closest bet." In those days, fine dining came only in the way of variations on the steak and potatoes theme. And we didn't have the Internet yet, or cable. Thank God for the bookstore. I read a lot in that period of my Montana career—before nature became the biggest distraction I've ever known.

Within our first five years, the children came. A girl and a boy, in that order. We designed and built a farmhouse on twenty acres of prime land outside of town, with two ponds, State land surrounding . . . deer and wild turkey and hummingbirds and returning sandhill cranes and mergansers and goldeneyes and a loon that to this day flies over our house every summer morning at seven o'clock. Every so often a black bear wandering through. Coyote at night. Horses. Dogs. A cat that has lived many more lives than nine.

And by now, maybe we have, too.

We wanted adventure. Well, we got it. The Big Sky delivered. And after fifteen years, we're in love with its brand of adventure—miles of mountains and lakes and the stunning Glacier National Park just miles away. (Lest I be criticized for inspiring more people to move to our little gem of a valley, I'll warn the reader that we get less than seventy-five days of sunshine, annually. Great snow as a result. But it's ever so much sunnier in Colorado, for instance! Utah. Wyoming. But do come for a visit . . . We'll treat you like family. And now we even have a sushi bar! Some great boutiques and art galleries. Our own coffee roasting company . . .)

But the love affair took a while. We had skeptics. I was the worst.

Seattle was one thing. There were jobs there. There was always Microsoft, and by then the whole Starbucks thing had exploded; there was a Starbucks on every corner out there in Seattle if you needed a job.

"But Montana?" they questioned. I questioned.

Yes. Montana, I heard from somewhere deep within me.

By then, even I could admit I was afraid. But I claimed it the way I imagine the early pioneer women did, following their husbands' thirst for gold and land.

"I love it here. I can write. My kids run barefoot in the backyard. There's no social pressure," I'd say.

"What if something happens? Are there hospitals there?" I'd hear in return.

"Of course there're hospitals."

But we all knew not like the hospitals they'd go to in their lives—with the best doctors. Where the ultimately "responsible" people went.

"What if he loses his job? Then what? It's not like jobs grow on trees out there. How will you pay your mortgage? Aren't you being dumb to put all your eggs in one basket?"

"It'll all work out," I'd retort. But I wasn't so sure. "Maybe my books will start to sell. Our life here is good. We couldn't ask for any better. And I have time to write!"

The overture had begun to fall flat. By then I'd written many novels. I was becoming the girl who cried novel. I'm not sure any of them actually believed I was a writer at all. Hummingbirds make good witnesses, and the dogs at your feet, but not if you're trying to put anything on a résumé. Résumés require credits. And as fate would have it, essays, articles, and short stories in regional magazines and literary reviews don't count. You can't put good rejection letters on a résumé.

I tried to ignore them all and focus on my little family and my writing. Because other than publishing-world rejection, life was pretty good. I kept referring to that stage of our lives as Creation mode. We were building the foundations of our children's personalities. He was building a business. Me, books. I justified the lack of income from my pursuits by saying things like "Thank God I'm not getting published big-time right now. My kids need me. I could never justify leaving them for a book tour at this stage of their lives!" This was living time. Sowing. Not reaping. And, like I said, he was making good money, so it was doable to live on one income.

But then, after eight years, everything changed.

My husband had come to the end of his brewery days, and a new opportunity arose to start a corporate recruiting company with a few friends who'd been successful at it in a similar remote location. It seemed like a brilliant business model. Now, with the Internet, he didn't need to be in an urban locale. He could work hard, and then catch the last few runs of the day up on the ski hill. Play a round of golf in the summer and shoulder seasons. He could be his own boss. He could have it all, just like we'd always said: money and adventure and independence.

What they didn't factor into the business plan was what no one factored into anything: 9/11.

It hit his industry hard. And he worked like a dog for seven more years without the kind of financial success he deserved. And it took its toll.

My small writing successes covered about as much as my horse hobby required, which around here isn't much to begin with.

Things looked bleak. Our savings and investments were dwindling. And mildly put, neither of us felt golden anymore. One by one, we gave up or limited our creature comforts—the riding lessons, the housekeeper, the personal trainers, organic food, the gym membership, the dinners out. They were easy enough to let go. We prided ourselves on not needing those comforts in the first place. Still, we'd gotten accustomed to them.

But the house was different. We would not lose the house. He promised me we had enough savings to hold on to it at least for a few more years. But I saw doubt in his eyes every time he went to the loan officer.

There were the people who said it was time to pack it up, once and for all. To get serious and "come home" to the world for which we had been procured.

We didn't want sympathy. But we certainly didn't need judgment.

We were well aware of the fact that we'd brought this upon ourselves the moment we'd chosen to take such a one-in-a-million job in such a one-in-a-million place. I just don't think that we'd ever counted on falling in love with it so. The old adages were shrill in our ears. *You made your bed, now you have to lie in it. You get what you get and you don't throw a fit. You reap what you sow.*

There were people from the life we left who even seemed to be vindicated by our failure; saying, in so many words, they told me so. That really, I should have been more wise in my choice of husband. That I belonged with a guy who ran a hedge fund, and made sure we had the income to support a house in the suburbs and another one on a beach somewhere and the two country clubs that came part and parcel with the social rigors and regimes of those communities. That I owed my children the privileges I'd enjoyed—at least a private education, if not boarding school.

For the record: he could have been that man. He didn't want to be that man. I didn't want that man.

Still don't.

And the educations our children are getting are, we believe, rich. Because our kids are comfortable with who they are. And that goes a long way. From mountaintops to subway bellies to Harvard classrooms to canoes floating down small rivers.

Eleanor Roosevelt said, "No one can make you feel inferior without your consent." I have a good friend here in Montana who says we only get our feelings hurt when we actually believe that the mean thing somebody says about us is true. When we agree with them.

That was the problem. Deep down, we started to agree with them. Maybe all of this had been just a jaunt. And now it was time to suck it up and return. Maybe it was time to forget those sage words from the advertising CEO and make some real money to help keep our family afloat. But what? All I was qualified to do was mother and write.

Maybe I could get a job as a teacher at a private school—somewhere you didn't have to have a teaching degree. How would that be, standing up in front of all those privileged kids as an unsuccessful rebel, in the end, selling out to the institutions I had left? It makes my heart race just thinking about it.

The worst of it, though, was this: My husband was depressed and despondent. He stopped saying hello and good-bye when he walked through the door—which was more and more.

I missed our years of adventure. Of being those people running hand in hand in Rumi's field, splashing through puddles. And now that we had the home to return to—to dry off and hang our coats . . . where was he?

Out the door.

Now his eyes glazed over when I talked about my books. About my rejections, albeit still "good" ones. About my new ideas, regardless. That hurt most of all. He never was much of a fiction reader, but he always listened to my ideas and helped me troubleshoot my plots with enthusiasm. Was that all an act? Where was my partner? It all settled heavily on my shoulders. I'd always thought that no matter what, he'd believe in me. And that our love was larger than circumstance. Could career failure really take a person down? Him? Me?

Occasionally I'd offer little pleas, keeping them simple as I knew to, since he was prone now to defensive tirades. "Think of me—of our marriage—as a garden," I'd say. "You have to tend it once in a while."

It only made it worse.

He cleared it up for me one morning when he was walking through the door, once again good-bye-less. He said, "How do you expect me to tend you, or our marriage for that matter, when I can't even tend myself?"

It spoke volumes.

My response: survival mode.

I started to view my Montana world differently. Started to court the idea of packing it all up. This place of beauty we'd created. This farmhouse where we'd had fifteen years of Thanksgiving turkeys and Christmas geese and New Year's Eve prime ribs and Easter lambs. Wouldn't our ancestors, off of whose plates we'd eaten those feasts, encourage us to stay? Against the odds. To hold on to our land? Our house? They understood what it was to leave what they knew. To follow dreams. And to keep them even when they felt dashed. Wouldn't they tell us to fight to keep our home? Especially since it is a symbol of so much?

The wraparound porches where we've sat and marveled at countless thunder and lightning storms, hoping we'd dodge another bad fire season. The cottage garden up against the house full of delphinium and roses and herbs. Twenty acres of lush forest and meadow where I've ridden my horses and we've cross-country skied and sledded and skated as a family. Land we love like a relative. Land that has been our teacher, like the wise Indian chiefs whose spirits still roam these woods.

And the room I call my own—my coffee-brown writing studio with my desk full of good-luck charms and postcards from our travels in and out of Montana. My dream kitchen with the marble countertops honed and stained by years of lemon juice from homemade lemonade, the stainless-steel appliances that never quite come clean for all the eager fingers working their surfaces in pursuit of food "made with love," as my children like to say. And what about my dearest friend—my Italian stove, which has held countless meals, eliciting the words I love to hear, "Mom—it smells amazing in here!" The bead board ceiling and wainscoting, the dark-stained fir and larch floors—grooved by dog toenails. Six dogs over the years. Good dogs.

And the screened porch. The screened porch alone is a chapel in our home, with its bed for hot summer nights where we all lie together and listen to the peepers in the marsh and play cards by candlelight.

All of the potatoes we've niggled from the garden, and carrots that have wintered over, and forts in the woods—all the neighborhood gatherings—all of it gone to . . . folly?

No. We just couldn't make it so.

Fifteen years.

And so here I sit, at two a.m. Spent from regurgitating the soul span of our life together, seeing as clearly as I ever have the rise and fall of our "golden" years—still wondering where my husband is. If he has already moved away in his mind. And are we with him there, wherever he is?

You see, now, don't you, that I can't imagine NOT living with nature in my backyard? True nature—fertile, upheaving, and placid all in its singular morning breath, which I greet each day, first ablution, at my front door, regardless of frost or smoke or dark.

I can't imagine not having those children with the strawberry-stained fingers, running barefoot in the meadow, roasting marshmallows around the fire pit, playing with the neighborhood kids in the woods.

Even if we don't feel so golden right now, I know that our children do. They know that Montana makes them different. Different in a good way. And that they can go back and forth between the world their parents left and the one they call home. And feel the freedom of not having to be defined or confined by any of it.

Over the years we've had friends visit from the Midwest, the West Coast, and the East. They all arrive at our doorsteps, dumbfounded. Even the old skeptics. How did we have the guts, or even the audacity, to leave it all behind? they've wondered. But they get it upon arrival. "It's so beautiful here," they say, looking immediately ripped off by their existences in places with privileges that just hours ago seemed the crème of the crème. A country club swimming pool or a suburban nature trail looks a little silly next to what Montana delivers without even trying, like the most well-trained, effortless, gorgeous hostess. I think that those Montana-kissed visitors would especially feel sorry for us to have to leave.

But I wouldn't necessarily call it "guts." (Maybe "audacity.") Now that I look at it as I have in these chapters. It was more like . . . well, as much as I want to say *dumb luck*, I know not to call it that either. It was something in our spirits that we identified in each other the second we laid eyes on each other. I'm not sure we would have gotten here without each other. Not so intact. Not with so many dreams realized.

At least when it comes to the kids and the house and the land . . . I can honestly say that if I was somehow able to tell those twenty-year-olds, looking into each other's eyes on that first night when his dog bit me, standing around a keg at his fraternity, that we'd have all this . . . that we'd one day have so much to lose . . . neither of us would have been entirely surprised.

Because that's what we talked about that first conversation: family. Future. Our World War II parents, our older Grateful Dead–loving hippie siblings who suddenly had babies and jobs and houses and R.E.S.P.O.N.S.I.B.I.L.I.T.Y. We shared these notes of pride like alluring assets, like we were trying to impress each other by our prosperous families—who believed in family. Laying down our aces—our kings queens and jacks.

But we would never have admitted it back then. God, we'd never have dared to admit that to anyone, especially not out loud to each other. How horribly mundane. But it was there all along.

The first gift he ever gave me was a coffeemaker. A really nice one. The kind he'd be hoping to use to make his morning cappuccino, years from then. The one he used just two mornings ago.

At this moment in my life, I'm looking through my old books and journals, rereading the Rilke quotation that was read at our wedding, with my cocky bride's underlinings and asterisks around becoming a "world in [oneself] for the sake of another." I bought my first copy of *Letters to a Young Poet* while we were living in Boston. At the Harvard Coop. When I was working as a cocktail waitress and finishing my first novel. I have that Rilke book next to me now. My handwriting is loopy and my notes in the margins, pompous. Things like *Typical of a homogenous peer group* and *Yes—I already know this.*

Did I?

We had worlds to become, as Rilke reminded us on our wedding day, six years later from that first night we met, fifteen years from today. To refer to the quote, we were ripening individuals becoming something in ourselves, becoming a world in ourselves. That is no small task. And we are foolish if we think we can achieve it in a matter of years.

When I look back in my journals from my teens through my thirties, they are full of this point—over and over until finally I started to live past it: I felt like I was suffocating in those old institutions. Namely, the combination of WASP society, higher education, and the Protestant church. It didn't mean that I didn't love the people and places from those institutions, and that's what was so confusing to me. Why the CEO said it would be so hard, I suppose. I was interested in love. That was the Jesus message I'd gotten loud and clear. "Love the Lord your God with all your heart and with all your soul and with all your strength and with all your mind . . . Love your neighbor as yourself." That last part was tricky—it meant that we had to love ourselves, too.

How was I going to learn to do that? It didn't feel like the institutions, before whose altars I'd been taught to bow, were promoting that particular aspect of the love message. To me, it seemed more that they were promoting something that felt a whole lot like fear. That we were puny and fallen and needed to mind our p's and q's at every turn or things would go horribly wrong . . . but also that we were privileged and therefore should achieve great things; that is, if we did it their way. Makes me shiver in my boots just thinking of it. But somehow, it occurred to me early on that fear was the real enemy.

I remember the exact moment when that thought took hold. And I scour through my high school journals until I find it:

> *It's a brilliant autumn day today in Connecticut, everything scarlet and orange. I ditched field hockey practice and took a walk in the woods because we're reading Salinger's "Franny and Zooey" in English class and I couldn't figure out this one quote. It's the point of the whole book! And I knew I should get it, with all the thinking and praying I've done on just this subject. Here's the line: "Jesus knew—knew—that we're carrying the Kingdom of Heaven around with us, inside, where we're all too god damn stupid and sentimental and unimaginative to look. You have to be a son of God to know that kind of stuff." Suddenly,*

I stopped dead in my tracks. Thought, "That's because we're all too afraid to look there!"

Then I turned on my heels, ran back to my dorm with the phrase "Kingdom of Heaven" throbbing in my brain, and flung open my journal. I wrote, "It all comes down to this: love and fear. And love is greater than fear."

Now I run my fingers over my teenaged cursive. Leave it to Salinger—a Jewish/Catholic cum Buddhist/Hindu—to inspire my first real epiphany.

I remember how breathless I was with it. I wrote a whole paper about it that I'm sure amused my professor to no end. (Lots of exclamation points . . .) All about what phenomenal news that was! Because it meant that Jesus wasn't necessarily asking me to set my sights on the church or even him, but ultimately . . . on what we can know in ourselves of the Kingdom of Heaven—which is LOVE! I could do that! And Salinger was reiterating Jesus' point—that all I had to do was look . . . inside myself! I could be a container of love! And love was limitless!!! Which meant that . . . I, somehow, was TOO!!!

The man I met at that party in college seemed like he understood that limitlessness. Even more than I did, so busy in the brain. I wanted to be a force with him because of it. To have children and teach them this sort of freedom right from the start—just like Crosby, Stills, Nash, and Young had prescribed. I wanted them to know their true nature.

And I wanted to be a writer and to live hard and well and to soak it all in and write it all down and help people. Like Cynthia Ozick when she wrote, "I wanted to use what I was, to be what I was born to be—not to have a 'career,' but to be that straightforward obvious unmistakable animal, a writer."

And finally, after so many years, I've had the chance to laze around in Rilke's world . . . Rumi's field. I've had the time to write. To find the intersection of heart and mind and craft that is writing. To be that mother. That wife. Surrounded by open space and wildlife. The solitude and deadpan reaction of nature to my former years of restlessness. I arrived at that exotic place of my dreams and at that Kingdom of Heaven inside me. Quite by surprise. But not quite by accident. I've never believed that any of it was an accident.

Is it over now?

Please flip to the end and tell me that ours is a success story. We got what we wanted, right? We pulled it off. We just went through a rough patch or two.

And we didn't have to move back to the world we left, with our tails between our legs, or to uproot our family just for a job in an unknown city. Tell me that we found prosperity right here in the town we love. Against the odds. And that we didn't have to lose our land or our house to do it. And yet tell me that I'll be okay if we do.

Most of all, tell me that we're still idiotically in love.

Just two seconds ago, it seemed like we were.

Until the man who was my partner in everything that seemed to matter—two balloons—the man who became my husband, and the father of my children, announced that he wasn't sure he loved me anymore, deep in the mountains of northwest Montana.

But I don't believe him.

I just don't.

My Father's Blue Duesenberg

Noon the next day.

He called. Finally. He's been out at his buddy's lake house. There's no cell phone service there. That's why he didn't call. He needs some more time to think. A few days. No apology.

I know that thinking is the last thing he needs to do right now. He's been doing too much thinking lately. But I didn't say that.

I got off the phone quickly, so I didn't say anything I'd regret.

Then I spent the better part of an hour trying to find solace in the plates and sterling and demitasses from my grandmother's china cabinet. An old habit.

As a child, I loved watching her pull shiny things from this cabinet, naming them like prominent ancestors. Limoges, Herend, Steuben, Royal Crown Derby. She'd let me handle them. "Be careful." Serious business, her eyes warned as she passed them to my glad fingers. I'd caress them, memorizing them, knowing that one day I might be their lucky custodian.

She wasn't a materialist. That wasn't it. Nor were my mother and other grandmother, whose shiny things now share quarters in this cabinet. But the women in our family prized their fragile things. Like I said, they took care of them and passed them on, and they've lasted. They whisper, one generation to the next, that a family existed. In some level of comfort. Some level of safety. A long time ago. And when pulled from that china cabinet and arranged around a table, that family and all its toiled-after and inherited comfort exists now, if only in the new family, paying homage to tradition.

That's what these shiny things meant to me as a child. I needed the reminder, since a large part of my childhood was spent wondering when everybody would come home. When we'd be "the whole family," as I called it.

When I missed my siblings it was a common practice of mine to sneak around the house gathering up shiny things. Hand-painted china figurines, faceted crystal candlesticks, sterling urns like genie bottles. I'd hoard them into the dining room, where I'd lay belly down under the dining room table . . . playing with them, imagining all the "grown-ups" assembled around me, their fancy silk stockings and heels, their sharp-creased pant legs and buffed loafers telling me that yes, finally, "the whole family" was home. So it makes sense that I went to the dining room today, to the china cabinet, to hold those amulets of family. I pictured my grandmother dusting them off with her apron. "Be careful."

I long to talk to her right now. To ask her about husbands. The china cabinet is the closest I can get.

I loved her dearly. She lived with us for a chunk of time in my preteen years and I helped care for her—fed her and took her to the bathroom and snuck her, against my parents' words of caution, slowly on her walker across slippery marble surfaces, to the front hall where her old Steinway spinet stood, its ivory keys awaiting her liver-spotted fingers. It was my pleasure.

She was a simple woman, humble, and proudly old-fashioned—the daughter of a pig farmer. Which was why it was so remarkable that she'd once been on a path to becoming an opera singer. Instead, she was sexually harassed by her professor at Northwestern in the early 1900s, and went home to her college sweetheart, then had a son who was brain-damaged in childbirth, and then my father, whom she doted on desperately—her only other joy, singing solos in the local Presbyterian choir.

Given her world of lost dreams, she was not at all the sort to put her life's worth in a cabinet full of ephemera. But she was sentimental and tended to take things personally. So I'm not sure how she would feel about her wedding china now rubbing shoulders with the finery from all sides of the family—from a debutante's deep South, to the Yankees of the Northeast—all together in her china cabinet. Her inherited globe-trotting aunt's Imari demitasses was one thing, but the prize was her humble Illinois farm woman's Haviland china set, with the gold rubbed off the edges from so many Sunday suppers.

I wondered, this last hour or so as I ran my hands along delicate teacup handles and held thin china plates to the window light, if my mothers went to their breakable things when their hearts were verging on splintering into tiny shards across the house. I swear: I felt old pain in that cabinet.

And then I saw the six-inch scar in the wood dining room floor that my father, her son, made one Thanksgiving visit when he scooted his chair back a bit too hard. He was mortified. I was glad. He'd made a mark in my house that I'd have even when I didn't have him. I ran my finger over it today, missing him. Wanting to hear his voice.

But it's not possible. He's gone. If I called my childhood phone number, my new stepfather might pick up. A good man. And I'm happy for my mother. But it's still hard.

If you look at the dedication in the first pages of this book, you'll see (if, in fact, this book is ever published):

"To my father—Here's your blue Duesenberg. Though I don't suppose you need a car wherever you are, namely in my heart. Thank you for believing in me."

It's a version of the words that I've written in the first pages of every book I've ever written. In other words, this story cannot be told, or properly understood, without knowing some things about my father. Who died almost exactly four years prior to this moment in my life.

Now I stare at his WWII photo on the wall next to my desk, considering the thoughts that are swarming in my husband's head as sure as the mosquitoes around his fishing pole. What would my father have to say about all this drama on a fine summer day, my children playing at the neighbor's through the woods. I can hear them jumping on the trampoline, shouting, "Spray me!" A rooster is crowing midday. If I know this gang of neighborhood friends, it's probably a wet rooster by now.

This is precisely the kind of moment when I would call my father at work—a privilege not to be taken lightly.

His secretary would answer the phone and connect me directly, unlike my mother, who would want to talk.

He'd answer in his business voice, and I'd imitate it back to him, and he'd soften and say, "Weeeeeell, Laura. Hello." I'd hear his lips open into a smile over the phone line from downtown Chicago, Michigan Avenue, to wherever I happened to be: on a pay phone in boarding school, in a dorm room in college, at the post office in Italy, in a room in Montana, quiet except for a mad rooster in the woods.

"You decided to phone your old dad." Think Jimmy Stewart.

"Yep—" And then I'd have to stop myself because the tears would erupt even though I'd promised myself I wouldn't cry.

His voice would soften even more. "Uh-oh. What's wrong with my little girl?"

And then I'd just sob and gasp for a while and picture him in his business suit and want to smell his neck and go out to lunch at the University Club and take a nap in side-by-side red leather wingback chairs like we used to the summer I was an intern at the Art Institute.

"You know what I'm looking at?" he'd say every time.

"What?" wiping my nose; knowing what he was going to say, and maybe that's why I'd called him in the first place.

"The old piece of wood you gave me a long time ago. With the photograph of the antique car shellacked to it. Do you remember?"

And it would just make me cry harder because I could see his eyes twinkling in my mind. "Of course I remember. Your blue Duesenberg."

Then he'd kid me. "Well, I'm about ready for the real thing."

I'd break a smile through my tears and he'd chuckle. But we both knew that there was something to this old pact, which was: I get famous and buy him his most lusted-after car, a 1930 blue Duesenberg.

It was a deal we struck many years ago. Less about the car. More about him having utter faith in me having some level of brilliance that the world needed to know about.

My father always said I was going to be famous. He wanted me to be famous. He was fifty when I was born, having married my mother when he was forty. Late for his generation.

So from the start, we both knew our career together would be limited by time.

The fact that at my school the majority of us went off to New England prep schools at fifteen threatened our time together even more. That said, I figured (when I got old enough to figure—around ten years old) that we had about five good years together left. Fathers fell over in the backyard at sixty; I knew a few who had. The way my little mind wrapped itself around the subject, I figured we'd be lucky to even have those five years.

Plus, if you factored in my parents' social calendar, I missed him for both weekend nights, and wasted half the day on Sunday in church, where I at least got to harmonize with him on hymns and hold his big hand and play with his gold crest ring on his thick, dry finger. Push on his bulgy violet veins. Get glared at for fidgeting. His glares were never very scary.

I think our limited time together was the reason why I ran at him every weekday night and screamed, "Daddy's home!" jumping into his arms as he carried me up the stairs. Even though I felt so safe in his arms and so momentarily sure of this extravagance of father, I still sensed something sad about our future together. So I'd cling that much harder to him as he carried me up to the master bedroom and plopped me down on the ottoman, while he changed into his "work clothes."

They were as predictable as his other costumes: wingtips and Brooks Brothers suits and overcoats for Downtown and church; Gucci loafers and sport coats and flashy ties and pants for dinner and cocktail parties. And the rest of the time: khakis and white, unstarched button-downs—short-sleeved in summer; long in winter. Add to them: cream-colored wool socks, darned faithfully from extinction by my mother, and his trademark grass-stained dirty bucks that he'd nightly pull from his closet like old friends. He loved them so much that I once took a photograph of them, covered in grass clippings, waiting loyally like an old golden retriever on the garage doormat. I framed it and gave it to him for Christmas. He cried.

"Tell me about when you were little," I'd beg, letting the whirling red shoe buffer polish my hand in the dormer window.

And he'd launch into a story about his industrial town on the banks of the Mississippi River that he loved with all his heart—even more than his dirty bucks. But he always said, "You wouldn't like it there. It's not like the North Shore of Chicago."

But to me, Granite City, Illinois, sounded exotic because it wasn't the North Shore of Chicago. Exotic in its industrial, small-town American milieu, where people went to the picture show, got penny candy, rode homemade go-carts, and visited their fathers at the plant.

But mostly it seemed like a magical place because it had spawned my father.

The added fact that he was such a gentleman now, with all the right clothes—the kind of gentleman with a shoe buffer . . . on top of the fact that he talked with tears in his eyes about digging forts in vacant city lots and his beloved home on a street not good enough for even a name ("C" street, it was called then) . . . made me know that my father was a rare creature. Again: think Jimmy Stewart. Add in a little Andy Griffith and Dick Van Dyke (who, my dad liked to point out, was born in Danville, Illinois, like he was a long-lost brother).

I'll never forget the night when I ran at him and leaped into his arms and was guided back down to the kitchen floor. "You're too big for me to carry you." It was the beginning of the end of something I knew I'd never have again for the rest of my life.

Parental love is different from other love. It's the model for how we, eventually, have to love ourselves. It takes years of practice; years and years of a parent showing us how to love ourselves through their love cues. On a deeply subconscious level, I knew this. But by my estimation, my father and I didn't have years. He was fifty years older than I was. How could we possibly have years? A sense of doom gathered over my childhood that day.

My father's love for me was unique and went straight to my core. My mother's love was different. More about teaching: timelines and social skills and appropriate behavior. To me, his was the love to model. And yet he was the one most likely to leave me. Deep down, I felt I'd soon be on my own when it came to unconditional love. Either I'd have to learn how to love myself like that, and fast . . . or fake it till I'd make it. Which I did. For many years . . . in constant preparation for this abandonment, which is how I saw it. Why couldn't he have been in his twenties or thirties when I was born, like the other fathers?

Regardless of his good health, my fears were rooted in reality. He privately complained of heart pains and fibrillation, and refused to see a doctor about it. There were too many nights when he'd lie on the library rug holding his chest, while my mother and I would beg him to let us call the paramedics.

"Don't you dare! If you do that I *will* have a heart attack. Don't you dare. It's just an episode. It'll go away." And it always did. So I got used to sitting with him, not calling the paramedics, worrying that this time would be the time.

Bottom line: I grew up in the terror of being left by my father. The one who said I was special. So special that I deserved to be famous.

It didn't help that my sister and brother left for boarding school by the time I was seven, and the house cleared out to just my mother, father, and me—a father I was sure was about to drop dead at any minute. Oh, how I wish I could go back to that little girl and let her know she'd have him for thirty-one more years. I hate to think that perhaps I held out on loving myself the way my father loved me . . . to somehow keep him alive.

A daughter's love for her father can be intense. And mine obviously was. Not just because he loved me, mind you. But because I adored him. He was my hero and he knew it. He was a different kind of father. He wasn't in the financial world. Nor was he a lawyer or a doctor. He was in the train business. It seemed wildly romantic to me as a child. I *loved* that he was in the train business. That the bolsters and brake-beams his company manufactured were the guts of the freight trains I'd hear from my childhood nighttime bedroom, swishing along the Milwaukee railroad in the distance. That when I felt like I was the only one in the world awake, I knew there was a conductor out there blowing a coyote's whistle in the night, in part because of my father's company and his bolsters and brake-beams. That the train would be there even if he wasn't.

I loved the way he smelled when he'd come home from work,

like newspaper and Vitapointe hair cream—he called it "greasy-kid stuff." I loved the way he wiped down the soles of his shoes with a piece of paper towel first thing every night—so proper and thoughtful. I loved how he said hello to three people every day for years as he made his way through the Chicago Loop—a blind woman in a wheelchair at the train station, an Irish traffic cop on State Street, and a Korean grocery store owner in his building where he'd get his cup of coffee.

When my father did actually die, I went downtown to tell them that Mr. Munson was gone. They all just sort of slumped a bit—gave up their city-defensiveness for those three singular moments in downtown Chicago.

I loved watching my father's hands when he was buttoning his coat. He had thankful hands that moved slowly. He was thankful by nature. I loved that about him most of all.

He was, after all, a product of World War I and formed his character during the Depression. He didn't linger on the phone. "Your three minutes are up," he'd say, imitating the 1930s operators of his youth. He never left food on his plate—even ate the bone marrow and fat. He picked up trash on the sidewalk. When I'd hold his hand on a walk, usually there was a crumpled Coke can or a candy wrapper in the other.

Each evening after walking home from the train station, he did a lap around our formal redbrick Georgian home and came through the kitchen door with a grin saying, "Do you know how lucky we are?" and kissed my mother on the cheek.

My father was a car man. He loved a good American red convertible. He had one throughout his bachelorhood before falling prey to my mother's indelible graces. After that, his car life was pretty much reduced to station wagons. But he always talked about his dream car: a blue Duesenberg.

He liked to sit on the back patio after doing yard work and have a Coke. I'd sit with him, my little squirmy scraped-up knees bouncing around in our Brown Jordan outdoor furniture—the kind that leaves crisscrosses on the backs of your thighs. And he'd say, "Someday, Laura, when you're famous . . . I want you to buy me a 1930 blue Duesenberg. With white-walled tires."

And the feelings that would sweep over me went from flattery to pressure, because I hoped I'd be good enough at whatever I'd be when I grew up, to get my father just this Duesenberg.

For his birthday one year, I did my best. I cut out a picture of a blue Duesenberg in one of his antique car magazines, found an old chunk of wood in the garage, used a rusty hand saw to slice it down to size, and shellacked the photo to the wood block. On the back I wrote in crayon: "Here's your blue Duesenberg. For now. More coming soon."

When my father died, my mother went to clear out his office in downtown Chicago. He worked until the day he had his stroke, and died a month later at eighty-six. She sent me a few things from his office walls and desk, drawers and briefcase. Some short stories I'd written, which was a shocker. My father wasn't much of a reader. A Sunday church program with a copy of the sermon—my father was a sucker for a "good Presbyterian sermon." A few photos I'd taken of him—one on a horse in Wyoming, the last time he got on a horse. And the Duesenberg-bedecked slab of wood, which apparently he'd used as a paperweight for almost thirty years.

It's on my desk where I write. My father, after all, was the one who invented the idea inside me that I could one day be somebody who would make some sort of big difference. I aspire to that every day because of him.

It was a blessing. And it was a curse. Because how do you go at life being something small after that? How do you let down your father? How do you live, being the apple of your father's eye like that and only come up relatively broke, living in a farmhouse in Montana with a stack of unpublished novels in your closet, and a whole lot to say that doesn't seem to matter to the people who make writers "famous" and afford them the funds to buy their fathers their Duesenberg. Even when they're long dead.

When I decided to be a writer and move west with a man who didn't seem the least bit interested in hedge funds, it worried my father.

I liked that it worried my father.

I liked it because I knew that he secretly liked it. It came from the side of him that thought I was going to be famous. That wanted me to be famous. To step outside my comfort zone like his mother—which was exactly what he'd done, leaving his small industrial town for the lights of Harvard Business School, and eventually the North Shore of Chicago and all its shininess.

There was another reason he loved our little mountain town: the train came through it. The Empire Builder from Chicago to Seattle. He rode it many times as a young man—years before he was married; years before I was born. He'd get off to call on the foreman of the train yard and stay in the old Cadillac hotel; have a drink at the Hanging Tree Saloon where he'd hear renegades and wanderers talking about how one day ours might be a ski town. When I moved here, he wanted to know if, in fact, it had become just that.

I can't tell you how many times I've walked that patch of sidewalk where the Cadillac and Hanging Tree once stood and thought about his young man's shoes treading along that sidewalk. I've always considered it something between poetry and irony that the brewery my husband moved here to run is where the Cadillac once stood.

Sometimes when I miss my father, I go down to the depot and watch the freight cars change tracks. I think of him getting off the train with the Chicago still on him, looking around at the mountains and feeling the power and freedom of the wilderness—a place his daughter would one day know well.

He was a dreamer. I'm sure those miles of track conjured up some of his best dreams, especially when he hit the mountains. The mountains are good for dreams. Maybe he'd be a successful businessman one day. Maybe he'd move to an affluent town outside of the city, marry a beautiful wife, and have successful children. Maybe one of them would even be famous someday. I try not to think of that last part when I'm standing at the train depot, missing my father.

He'd watch Carol Burnett or Marie Osmond or Carly Simon and say, "You could do that, Laura." He'd watch Jane Pauley and later Katie Couric and say, "You could do that." He'd watch Julia Roberts and say, "You could do that."

When I told him in increments over the years that I'd decided I didn't want to be a television anchorwoman after all, or an actress, or a singer, he looked forlorn every time. His life was passing him by. And still no famous daughter and still no blue Duesenberg, which by then was a symbol of one thing: pride. My success would be his success.

Finally I announced, on Parents' Weekend my senior year in college, that I was going to be a writer. No, not for television. Or an advertising agency, or the movies. No, not a mystery writer or a romance writer. "No, Dad. I'm going to be a fiction writer. Literary fiction. I'm going to write about the stuff people do to each other. I think it will help people. I have a lot I want to say. And you know, the truth is, I've been writing since I was a little girl. My journals go back to fourth grade! I wrote a book of poetry when I was eleven! I've finally found what I want to be."

But he wasn't buying it.

My mother was indifferent. She wasn't the one who wanted me famous. When it came down to it, I think she just wanted a daughter she could relate to.

"What about being an actress?!" he balked. "Like Julia Roberts. You know you are every bit as good-look—"

"I don't want to spend the rest of my life worrying about the way I look. What kind of life is that? I don't want to go into a profession where the world drops you the second you hit middle age. Unless you're Meryl Streep."

"Well, you're every bit as good as Mer—"

"Dad. I want to be a writer. I want to do something that's not necessarily glamorous. That will call upon me to be my best self. That will make sure that I stay in a place of integrity." I remember saying all those things with impassioned tears in my eyes. You see, I'd recently been bitten hard by the writing bug. Out of nowhere.

I'd been minding my own business, taking a screenwriting course for my film degree. But when the teacher assigned a thirty-minute scene and I found myself fitfully, sleeplessly, rounding the corner to the end of a full-length screenplay . . . I realized that I'd been studying the wrong thing for three and a half years.

It helped that my film professor's reaction to my "masterpiece" was, "This isn't cinema! Take this to the FOOLS in the English department!" Though it didn't feel like "help" at the time—especially when I saw the D- he'd given it.

And standing at the desk of the dean of the English department, red-faced and desperate—holding a hefty stack of double-spaced typed words in my hand (little did I know that I'd spend the better part of the next twenty years in this state)—I realized my calling.

"Where the hell have you been?" he said, scanning the pages. And the next day, I was in the advanced writing class, writing my first short story. Which earned me an A+ and third prize in a statewide writing competition. I told this to my parents, that Parents' Weekend.

But they both stared blankly at me. It was off their radar—the writing life. They didn't know anyone who knew anyone who was a writer.

Maybe that's why I chose it.

I'm not sure if my father ever got over the writing thing. But he did memorize one literary factoid: "Agatha Christie had over twenty rejections before she got her first book published," he'd tell me over and over.

But as the years went on, I'd accrued many more than twenty rejections, and he stopped asking me for that blue Duesenberg. I'm sure it was because he didn't want to hurt my feelings.

Still, he had the paperweight on his desk until the day he died. And I know that that crummy slab of wood with that faded photograph was, to him, as good as the real thing.

My father was my advocate. My father knew the core of who I am. That I was born complex and passionate and a little sad. That I have a great penchant for adventure and a big laugh and a loud voice and that I like to talk. He used to boast that I'd had a boarding school professor who'd said, "Laura is an open book." A lot of people in WASP society would have added to that, "Maybe she could close it every so often." But not my father.

He never really read my books. He was a *Reader's Digest* sort of fellow. But he'd listen loyally as I told him about them on family vacations, where I'd read him excerpts, even though half the time he fell asleep. It didn't bother me. Do you know the value of someone who has so much faith in you that you don't even have to deliver? I hope so. I hope I'm not the only one so lucky.

It said it all when, in the ICU, where I lived off and on with him for the last weeks of his life, we were watching a Marx Brothers movie I'd rented—*A Night at the Opera*—and he laughed under his oxygen mask, "Oh, Laura, you could do that. You and I have always had the same sense of humor." Then he looked up at me, slid his mask off, and said, "You have always gotten me."

"You, too, Dad," I said, trying not to cry.

When he died a few weeks later, the grief was crippling. I knew the task at hand: that old fucker Self-Love. And after twenty years of harsh rejection, overwhelming financial burden, and an increasingly despondent husband . . . I wasn't sure I knew the least way through to anything remotely close to Self-Love. I'd, in effect, faked it till I breaked it.

We're lucky if we have one person in our life who truly gets us.

I've had two: my father. And my husband.

If only I could call my father right now and thank him for believing in me so, and ask him what a depressed forty-year-old man thinks about when his career is in the crapper and he's drowning in debt. When he thinks he doesn't love his wife anymore. When really . . . it's that he doesn't love himself.

I know what he'd tell me. He'd say, "You need your sleep. Go to bed. Tomorrow is a new day."

The Italy Cure

6:00 a.m. Next day.

Can't sleep. Back in my office. Steaming cup of tea. Need to write.

It's like when you want to confront someone and you're advised to write the "bad letter" first. Then throw it away and write a new one. This book is the "bad letter." Though I'm not sure it's so bad. I just need it to be honest if it's going to help me. You. I wish you could come over for tea this morning and sit on my screened porch. It's sunny there on summer mornings. We could talk about dreams coming true. We could talk about Italy.

It's fascinating to me how this pattern tends to repeat itself: just when you get strong, happy, and choose to powerfully fulfill yourself, that's when the shit hits the fan. (Be careful when you change the game. The world might not want to see you so happy.)

In short, my husband's disaffection, I believe, seems to have direct correlation with the fact that I've just come back from granting myself a twenty-one-year-old dream, which I paid for by my own means, extended to him, was refused but given his blessing to go for it. And I did. After twenty-one years of yearning for it, I went back to Italy—the place where I spent a year of my life awaking to my soul's journey.

I'd talked myself out of Italy daily, weekly, for years. Half my life. *Not now. Not with the kids being little. Money being tight. The dollar being so weak.* And yet returning to this place I love and these people who changed my life was one of my greatest yearnings.

We all have these purposefully unfulfilled dreams. Fill in here with yours: ________________________. Maybe you've wanted all your life to play the piano. And you have a piano. And it just stares at you from the living room, chanting, *You can't play me . . . you can't play me . . . your daughter can play me . . . but you can't . . . you've let down your dear grandmother.* It's a voice in your house that you've grown used to and that you loathe, yet for some reason, you tolerate it.

Italy, then, had become a symbol of arm's-length-kept happiness. A practice, if you will, of self-deprivation.

I didn't see it that way, of course. There are times when we'll do most everything we can think of to keep our carrots out in front of us and not in our bellies.

But with the help of a good therapist, I began to see how I'd chosen to suffer as a practice that had its payoff: I got to feel like shit. Moreover, I got to feel sorry for myself. And victimized by forces outside myself. In other words, I didn't have to take responsibility for my happiness. Happiness was an entity that would come in on the wind, when I so deserved it. Blown by the lungs of the publishing world. Certainly, nothing that I could beckon. Nothing I could choose. And certainly, given the state of affairs with my husband's business, I couldn't be so shamelessly selfish as to grant myself Italy. Maybe our annual trip someplace sunny for spring break. A cheap horse. That new pair of boots. But not the ultimate pleasure. Not Firenze and a local family that would take me in as one of their own and shower me with abiding love.

Even if I'd just lost my father and suffered the biggest rejection of my career—after four months editing down a book by a third for a big-time editor and having it turned down in the end because I was not famous. I was just a hillbilly from Montana who'd failed herself, her husband, her kids, and especially, her father. Who'd just died without his blue Duesenberg.

A trip to Italy, where I could recontact my soul? No. Better to fester in woe where I'd gotten used to the altitude, water, and air quality. But even I couldn't dwell there too long. I'm just not that good at being miserable.

After months of therapy—systematically going down the list of how I'd chosen to suffer over the years—one day I happened to bring up Italy. "I lived there twenty-one years ago. In Florence. My junior year in college. And I loved it so much. It was the first time I felt totally happy. Free to be myself. In my whole life. I haven't gone back since. And I miss it constantly." Suddenly I combusted into tears. "Sorry. I can't believe I'm crying. I sound like such a spoiled brat."

Therapists know to hurdle over comments like that and pay attention to sudden fits of crying. Her eyes bugged out and she said with ferocity, "Don't you ever, ever do that again."

"I know. I shouldn't bash myself, but—"

"No. I mean, don't ever, ever deprive yourself of Italy again. I'm dead serious."

As absurd and upper-middle-class and made-up as it sounds, she had the look of grave ground being trod. It was like I'd skipped a mammogram. Stolen from an old lady. Tripped a blind man. "Don't ever, ever do that again." What she meant was, *Don't ever spend half your life depriving yourself of something that you so purely and deeply love.* What kind of an imbecile would do that?

One that had gotten used to a certain daily dose of self-loathing. Suffering. Shame. (Agatha Christie's twenty rejection letters from my view: a fine friggin' stroll in the park.)

Suddenly, sitting in her office, in a blink, I could taste the end of suffering—so close. And I knew that the return to Italy would start the ball rolling.

Let's go back in time.

As you know by now, I haven't always been a Montanan. I didn't start out as a lover of nature and horses, mountains, rivers, lakes . . . open spaces. To recap: I started off preppy. Severely preppy. My boarding school senior yearbook prophesied that I'd be the floor manager at Laura Ashley in Greenwich, Connecticut, okay? But sometime in my late teens, I threw away the Lilly Pulitzer and took to vintage thrift shops, clunky hats, and chunky shoes. Cut my hair short. Became pale and a little gaunt. I wanted to see what else life could hold for me, outside the world of sororities and country clubs.

I had the sneaking suspicion that I was destined to be an artist of some sort, God forbid. And that didn't mean playing Marian in the local community theater rendition of *The Music Man.* I wanted what Joni Mitchell sang about. In other words, I wanted to "wreck my stockings in some jukebox dive." The only way out that presented itself to me was to study abroad. I took it hungrily.

With my mother's advice, I decided that Italy was the right match for me. Not prissy like Paris. Not rigid like Vienna. Not clean and bright like Salzburg. No, I wanted some grunge. So I went to Florence for the year. (Such grunge!)

My interests were less than academic or leather-driven or Italian Stallion. I wanted adventure. But not of the credit-card-emergency ilk, like so many of the other girls on my program. I wanted to do stuff like go to Turkey for a month with a backpack. Maybe buy some rugs and sleep on them in train stations. Go to Prague. See what was up with all the civil unrest in Yugoslavia. I just plain wanted out of the cookie-cutter preppy life that had inspired me to go to said small private liberal arts college to begin with. Pressure off! I wanted to be unsavory. Disgruntled. I wanted to grow hair under my armpits. And I definitely didn't want to hang out in the gorgeous trompe l'oeil hallways of our Italian school, smoking Marlboro Lights and drinking Diet Coke!

I'd chosen this program because of a woman I knew in college who'd come back from it just the way I pictured myself coming back from it. With kick-ass leather boots, a penchant for blood-red lipstick, and stories about smoking hash all night on church steps with gypsies. In other words, I was a pain in the ass; no better than the rest of them. But I thought I was superior and I thought that Italy had a cure for the rashy restlessness in my heart.

I'd also chosen this program because of a family. This woman had lived with a wonderful family, and she told stories of spending weekends with them in the Tuscan countryside. In a villa. Making pasta sauce with the grandmother, picking figs with the father, canning fig jam with the mother, and going to parties at other villas in the Tuscan countryside with the sister and brother, roasting pheasants on a fireside rotisserie.

She told me about their cousins, about the uncle, the famous artist, and about how they all spent weekends in the springtime together at their house on the island of Elba and how they invited their American students to come along. How they were such a healthy family. So nonjudgmental, so unencumbered and non-controlling and loving.

She painted a delectable picture of how these people pitched tents attached to carabiners on smooth rocks at the Mediterranean's water's edge and spent the day eating and sunning. She told me about their city apartment and how it was a good walk from the school, but if you walked there and back every day, you'd actually lose weight, even though you'd never eaten so much in your life; how along the way, there were countless cafés in which to duck out of the street and grab an espresso or a macchiato or a glass of red wine or grappa or prosecco.

"And the smells alone are reason to go to Florence," she said. "The streets are filled with one fabulous smell after the next, some rotten and wretched, the next sweet and flowery, then acrid and polluted, then musky and ancient."

I'd been reading Anaïs Nin's erotica at the time, and I liked to refer to myself as a "sensualist." (I know—ugh!) This Italy portrayal vastly appealed to me, and I applied, got in, got the family I wanted, and spent a year living with them, doing all the things I'd been told I'd do, dodging the American girls, shaking the confines of WASP society off my back—out of my soul. Feasting instead on the spirit of a place and a culture and a family that was the first free zone I'd ever really known.

I took every chance I could to wander the streets of Florence without my Baedeker as it were, just like the novelist character prescribed in *A Room with a View*, which had come out in film the year before. I strolled the city lanes purposefully getting lost, "O Mio Babbino Caro" blaring from my Walkman headphones, stopping to look up and around. I didn't want to miss one gargoyle, one little makeshift altar, one fresh fig. In between classes, I lay in the grass in Forte Belvedere, overlooking the city, reading Machiavelli and Dante. In fact, I befriended a priest who presided over Dante's church, and we'd go in at night and sit in the pews and talk about Gesù Cristo.

By day I'd scan the walls of my favorite haunts: the Uffizi, Orsanmichele, Santa Croce—imagining all the bones of Renaissance celebrities beneath my feet. At night, I'd climb over the railing of the Ponte Santa Trinita and sit on one of the stone outcroppings, staring down over the Arno and at the glowing Ponte Vecchio. I'd toast to my future with a *fiasco* of Chianti. I promised myself that I would never lead a mediocre life. I would carry the inspiration of the Renaissance with me for the rest of my days.

I indeed went to Turkey. Prague. Yugoslavia. Czechoslovakia. Greece. Too much to recount here. And my host family was a dream come true. (As you'll see in the next chapter.)

But as the year wound down, and I faced my reentry into the world I'd gladly left behind and learned I could live happily and freely without . . . I began to feel the old haunt. That I'd been lucky, that's all. That I didn't deserve my host family in the first place. That their love for me wasn't real but obligatory—they got paid, after all, by the school. That all those experiences were a dime a dozen. I wasn't any more special or brave just because I'd chosen to leave frat parties and BMWs behind. And high exposure to the fruits of the Renaissance certainly didn't assure you a decent entry-level job out of college, or even promise personal freedom from oppressive institutions. I'd always be a rebel. But I'd quite possibly never be free.

And here's why: because regardless of what my parents and siblings and grandparents ultimately thought about the choices I'd make in my life, I didn't know yet how to let myself off the hook for leaving it all behind. Even with the freedom of Italy embedded in my heart. That would take another two decades or so. I have always been my worst judge.

It would be Montana that'd eventually inspire my personal vindication. Where I'd finally believe that I wasn't bad or wrong for leaving. Or even good or right. That's the kind of freedom I'm talking about. Other than Italy, Montana is the only place where I've felt totally free to be my true self. I know. Yikes.

Still, for some reason not rooted in reality, it's easier to attach to beloved places of yore—and Italy remained the chief possessor and caretaker of my soul. Like it was still there, housed in a bell tower, waiting for me to come back to claim it. That's what I told myself, anyway. Unbelievable, the stories we tell ourselves and even live into. Maybe you have a few.

If you were to have met me, prior to just a small time ago, and we had the pleasure to chat for a bit, you would quite possibly know this: I lived in Italy. In Florence, Italy. For a year. A long time ago. I binged on it for a year, and purged it for twenty-one.

As with all "disorders," I've held Italy around me like a protective cape that doesn't really protect as much as it hides. A fantasy cape. A really great one. Prada. And it's in that cape that I write my novels every day. It's in that cape that I ride horses. And cook. And garden. The things that are mine and only mine. But in this cape there is wanting. It, in fact, is made of fine silk and cashmere-lined wanting.

My therapist and my writer friend are right: there is a vast difference between wanting and creating. Detaching and unattaching.

I found that out, because finally, this June, I went back to Italy.

It happened because, like with many things, I simply got sick of hearing about it. Or, in other words, I got over myself. Or in kinder words, I got out of the way of myself.

I ran into a friend in the grocery store and she was beaming and I told her so and she said, "That's because we just got back from three weeks in Italy." This from a woman who works two jobs, has an infant, doesn't speak a word of Italian, and doesn't have one contact over there in the Boot.

"I'd do anything to go back there. You know, I lived there for a year." Boo-hoo.

She stared at me and said, point-blank, "Go back! What's your problem?"

I pondered for a moment, scanning all my excuses. They all fell flat in light of her sparkling eyes. "I don't know what my problem is. Frankly."

I went home and, in just a blink (because remember—that's how it happens: in a blink), I called the airlines, learned I had enough miles to get all of us over there, contacted the family I had lived with, and found out they'd converted their villa in the country to a B&B and would give us a screaming discount. And after they enthusiastically offered us their car, meals with them every night for free, a cooking class, and transportation to and from the train station . . . and told me they loved me, had missed me, and couldn't understand why I hadn't come back for a visit in all these years . . . after that and twenty-one years of wanting Italy . . . I burst into tears, and booked it.

At first, I thought it would be a trip with my husband. He's been hearing about it for over half his life, too, after all. Plus, he's a Swiss man, with dual nationality, and it has always been our secret agenda that someday we'd take full advantage of that and live in Europe. I'd fantasized that this trip would open the door to that future possibility.

But he insisted that he had to work, that it would be a better mother/daughter trip with our twelve-year-old girl, that he'd be happy to stay home with our eight-year-old son, as long as I could arrange for playdates and summer camps to occupy his days.

I was disappointed until it dawned on me that without my husband, I wouldn't have to put up with any adult indifference to the Renaissance. Sure, a twelve-year-old might hem and haw a bit in line at the Uffizi, but that's expected. A forty-one-year-old adult male—hemming and hawing, sleeping in when there are markets to visit, cafés to stand in and drink espresso, Florentine food to gorge on, sculptures to cry over, paintings to stand before and say things like, "God—nothing's changed in hundreds of years." And "Look at her toenails in those sandals—it could be me"—any resistance to these toenails, these shots of coffee, these plates of pasta and stomach lining and rabbit and salt-brined fish . . . well, truth be told, it would break my heart.

So I said, "Fine. Great. Perfect. Thank you."

You might say, *I know where this is going. Sure you're happy. Sure you're calm. You just spent the month of June in Tuscany. With your darling daughter. Try a month in Afghanistan and see how you are then.*

But that's not where this is going at all. So pipe down. Get a glass of Chianti. Or better yet, a Barolo. Or a nice pomodoro-and-basil bruschetta, the crusty toasts scraped with garlic and drizzled with a really green olive oil. Sit with a plate of something nice and get comfortable. We have work to do. We need to find out where our husbands/wives/partners are. And I don't just mean geographically. Which means, of course, that we have to take a good hard look at ourselves, too. Damn it.

I'm going to make a giant stretch here, but it's worth the investigation. What if I had given myself Italy many years ago? What if I had given myself Italy every year for the month of June? No matter what my financial situation was. No matter what my language ability was. Or my children's ages. No matter how my Italian "family" took care of me or didn't take care of me. What if I'd saved my pennies and found a little villa to rent just south of Firenze and went there? Yearly. For twenty years. Who would I be? What would I want? What would I have created?

It's like you and that verbally abusive piano in your living room.

The answer may be moot. But the asking is worth it. Because I can tell you who I've been without Italy. And when I say Italy, you know I don't necessarily mean Italy. It could be anywhere, anything, that we've longed for, desperately, and not felt worthy of, for too long.

To really get to the bottom of this, let's stretch even further here and ask ourselves this: If we deprive ourselves of our greatest dreams, how are we setting ourselves up to be treated by our husbands? Our loved ones? Everyone around us? If we neglect our own souls, how are others to react to us? What are we creating? More neglect?

Think about it for a minute.

I'm going to pause here and return to my current life. In which I have a husband in crisis. I'm going to try my damnedest to take a walk in the woods with the dogs and not call his cell phone fourteen times. Even though he said there's no service at the lake—just to hear his voice on his message. I love his voice. The same voice that said, "I do." The same voice that said he doesn't anymore.

I'm going to wander the woods and try not to think.

I'm going to walk to the giant rock that has been my touchstone over the years. It's where I go to make little offerings of gratitude. Rather than begging for what I want in life, I simply bring little bits of nature to a fist-sized cave in its front face, and place them in it: red Oregon grape leaves in fall, deer vertebrae, twig crosses tied with dried meadow grass.

Only this time it won't be my usual *I surrender to the outcome of being published.* Or *I give thanks for my abundant life.* This time it will be a new one. Something truly impossible to imagine: *I surrender to the outcome of my husband's loving me again.*

Yet I doubt that I possess that grace. I imagine I'll just rest my forehead on its moss and lichen, eyeing at close range the years of little offerings—all that hope and thanks and surrender—and rock my forehead from side to side. Thinking: *Bring . . . him . . . home.*

Epiphany

The next day.

I sit here in my office—again in the early hours, kids still asleep, wondering what "a few days" means to my husband. It's been two. Does that mean he's going to drive up the driveway today after sitting on a lake, fishing and thinking for two days . . . and say something good? Or very bad? Or is "a few days" code for *I'm not coming home at all?*

Surrender to outcome, I think now, just as I thought yesterday, walking through the woods. But the forest was too loud. As if it wanted me to drop to my knees like the night in Seattle when I begged for the time and space to write and have children and do it all under one roof. It seems to me that the power of that Seattle prayer was not in its begging nature, but in the fact that I had dropped to my knees in surrender. I just didn't have it in me yesterday.

Instead, I turned and ran home—through the brindled summer forest, taking the deer trails and a few my husband had cut for nature walks—jumping out of them to the wild forest floor with wind-fallen snags like a giant's pick-up sticks, hurdling over them through to the clearing to my yard, my door, up my stairs, to my room . . . to my suitcase.

And I started to unpack from our Italy trip.

I held my shoes in my hand and looked longingly at their souls—scuffed leather that had just a week before touched the streets of Firenze, shined by the stone aisles of the Mercato Centrale, softened by the thin lanes of Tuscany. Just days ago, really, when my footsteps were still lithe and carefree and not fleet and spooked in the woods.

God, I'm tired. Is he punishing me for living my dream? I thought, as I unpacked. I'm getting sick of trying to gracefully navigate my way through playing Mommy to two kids again—two kids who are wondering what's up with Daddy—on top of keeping house and reconnecting with my son, who is feeling sort of left out with all this Italy talk . . . all on the fumes left over from the revved nights lying awake, panicked and jet-lagged.

At least I can tell the kids where he is. Where he says he is. I try not to look into the night sky and wonder if he's telling it lies, too.

Unpacking helped.

In therapy they talk a lot about "unpacking." It's usually no fun. Stuff like remembering the horseback riding instructor with the red afro who called you a rich bitch through a megaphone for reasons unknown, and the piano teacher with the twelve cats who you're pretty sure came on to you while you played "Lara's Theme" from *Doctor Zhivago*.

But what I unpacked yesterday, the kids still playing in the woods (thank God for the woods), was a suitcase full of treasures. Hand-marbleized paper from Il Papiro on the Arno. Swaths of silk from a tiny vine-covered factory whose fabrics adorn the Grimaldi Palace in Monaco and the Kremlin. Bottles of Tuscan olive oil, bags of dried cannellini beans, and a bundle of jewel-toned market scarves for Christmas presents.

I unwrapped a bottle of herbal tonic I bought at a seventeenth-century *farmacia. Digestivo,* it read. For stomach maladies. I opened it and swallowed a bit. But just a bit. I knew I'd need that tonic for later, however my marital adventure played out.

I sat on my bedroom floor with my treasures around me like a little girl after an Easter egg hunt, and thought of Italy. The spell, though he tried, was not broken. It was too powerful.

That was the nature of our trip—this Italy reunion with my daughter: powerful. And yet perfectly normal. Natural. Unstaggering. Grounded. Calming. Fueling. Steady. Flowing. Beautiful. Filling. Patient. Relaxing. Real. There.

The first thing I noticed in Italy were the trees. When you're twenty, you don't notice trees. You don't look down from the airplane and think, *Wow—I didn't realize that a Mediterranean climate would lend itself to conifers.* Perhaps this has something to do with where you've lived your last twenty years; for me it's been mostly in Montana, surrounded by trees, mostly conifers, so that's what I noticed from the sky. There were a lot of trees down there. And terra-cotta roofs. And clustered villages, with their central piazzas and churches and campaniles.

I noticed, too, and it looked strange to me as well, that there I was in this steel flying machine Leonardo da Vinci only dreamed of, throwing himself off the hills around Florence with a winged contraption attached to his back, and I was about to land down there where an airport exists just two inches, by my mile-high estimation, from that little cluster of a village where Leonardo probably scratched a diagram of his flying machine on a napkin at some café: Italy, I saw, was still old.

The next thing I noticed was that Italy works a lot more smoothly than it did twenty years ago. It's automated. There are ATMs everywhere—Bancomats, they're called. People have cell phones and laptops. They can override the general frustration of sharing medieval alleyways with Vespas by at least complaining about it to a friend, via satellite, with some cash in their pocket. This somehow makes it more bearable, this drawing a ticket and waiting in line, practicing your best charm, knowing that without it, you may have to stand in yet another line, and even then not get your lost luggage squared away. It's not that there are rules as much as there are variations on rules. And charm works. That's the next thing I noticed, and remembered, too: charm.

Gone are the *pappagalli*, pecking at you with their horny

overtures as you walk by. All those *Ciao, bella*s are over with. I asked a cabdriver. He told me in no uncertain terms that Italian women have changed. They put out. An entire subculture has evaporated into its bedsheets. It makes the walk from the train station to the cab line infinitely more pleasant. (Although, as a forty-one-year-old who misses her twenty-year-old body, I have to admit that there was a tiny place inside me that was looking forward to being objectified as an attractive woman publicly. Oh well.)

Instead of displaying all that displaced horniness, the Italians were, as my daughter put it, "like one big hug." I couldn't have said it better.

We arrived at Milano Malpensa, half asleep, our luggage lost, and went on to the foreboding Milano Centrale train station, holding paid-for tickets to an express train that, we were told, *non esiste*. All the people we met—from the guy selling panini on the train we finally took, to the cabdriver who brought us to our little hotel at midnight, to the old man who showed us the four keys we'd need in order to get into our room—all but two of them were one inch away from giving us their home phone numbers in case we needed assistance. The other two did. Italy is still old. And Italians are still like one big, prolonged hug. Un *abbraccio*. An embrace. Which insinuates that we hug back.

In just under a month in Italy, I accumlated a contact list a page long. I've never seen business cards passed out faster and with less privacy than I did this June in Italy. I have the e-mail address for a famous sculptor, a carriage driver, a taxi driver in

Milan (because he insisted that the best *gelateria* is not in Florence, but in his neighborhood in Milan, and he took us there for free to prove it) . . . e-mail addresses for a couple we met at a restaurant, well into the foreplay of a giant and bloody *bistecca fiorentina*, who wanted to know all about Miami and Las Vegas, an Italian count I met at a party at a winery who was fascinated by grizzly bears, an Israeli woman married to an Italian who liked my shoes, and many more.

And past charm, there is an undeniable pride. A pride that is somehow less broken than I remember it. The pride I saw this time was not just in the explosive think tank that was Italy five hundred years ago. It was something new. Just a little cavalier. Just a little nanny-nanny boo-boo. And they like to point it out: "So what if the dollar sucks right now? So what if the price of gas is stifling? So what if you hate your president? So what if you're embarrassed by the war he's gotten you into?" With all their embracing, they've got just the slightest glimmer in their eye that the mightiest power in the world is currently, and maybe forever, maimed. Second fiddle. And they like to bring it up, in passing, the way a widow shoulders a friend's head as she cries about her husband's infidelity.

So maybe I went to Italy maimed like the United States. Broken, even. Wanting to receive the embrace. The empathy. Wanting to hug back. To prove to myself that I could care for my soul again after the hardship following my father's death.

I went with my daughter because I needed her maybe to see

me that happy. And I needed for Italy to heal her, too. Though this is not her story, I can say here that my daughter is well aware of life's realities. She's seen the effects of career stress on her parents. She's seen how they've at times divorced themselves from their own souls. She's seen a mother's crippling grief—a mother mourning the loss of her father. She's dealt with preteen drama and knows her world is about to launch into all the challenges we've been preparing her for. She needed Italy as much as I did. I brought her there the way people take their elders to hot springs and medicine women. And Italy delivered.

First stop: *David*. Of course. Because even though I once spent three hours in this museum listening to an art historian lecturing about this sculpture's historical significance . . . let's be honest: David's hot. Despite my speech to my daughter about the relevant classical nature of the nude, I have a thing for David.

I had a postcard of David over my college bed. Not Paul McCartney or Jim Morrison. David. Over the same bed where I first saw my husband's ass. I told him he looked like Michelangelo's *David*. I asked him to stand in that exact pose and he did.

And twenty years later, there David was in all his glory. Naked and alabaster, holding court in his own mausoleum. I love watching people's expressions when they stand behind David. No matter who you are—regardless of gender, sexual orientation, race, culture, education—you can appreciate a great ass. Some people admit it with a smile. Others act as if they're reading an interesting newspaper article, one eyebrow raised. Still others get red in the face and dash off. Especially when they're twelve.

So my daughter did a quick drive-by, and moved on to another gallery. But I had to stand there behind him for a while. And other than for obvious reasons, it occurred to me why:

I hadn't seen David since I met my husband. Since I told him he reminded me of one of the most beloved sculptures in the world. I needed to revisit my twenty-year-old sense of male. And maybe even of my husband.

My reaction, however, was a letdown. Not a spot of erotica in it. David looked sort of fed up. Buried alive, even. Not unlike my husband in his current state.

Maybe David misses the rain and the exhaust, the pigeon shit from his old digs as guardian of the Medici Palace. Maybe he's uncomfortable now that they put him as king in his own "palace" (the Galleria dell'Accademia). Now that he has slaves flanking his court. Michelangelo's slaves.

I've always loved that Michelangelo believed his sculptures were already in the block of stone, in the same way the human soul is found within the physical body. Michelangelo kept his slave sculptures unfinished, to show how we enslave ourselves.

Maybe David looks different to me because I am aware that he is unburdened in a way I wasn't all those years ago. He gets to be finished and free from his original chunk of marble, save for his feet. So . . . maybe not so free. But that's the price of being an idol. I wonder what went through my husband's mind when I compared him to an idol. Did he feel like a king? Did he feel like a sculpture released from stone? Did he feel destined to fall?

At twenty, I spent a lot of time looking at the slaves. Especially Atlas, the weight of his "unfreed" head, heavy on his shoulders and hands. In that year in Florence, I'd stand before their burdened selves and think, *That's me. All the weight and pressure of what I am supposed to be on my shoulders.*

This time it was different. It was sad to see them. My empathy for them felt old and diminished. *You're still here? Unhatched?! My God, you know they've invented this thing called therapy. Most health insurance pays for it. It's really great. And God, your backs must be killing you. I have the number of a great chiropractor.*

Back in the Florentine din, I was happy to be barreling past real people, enslaved or free, but still alive. Weaving through tour groups to our next stop: the Uffizi museum.

You can reserve tickets now, making those two-hour lines of yesteryear five-minute VIP jaunts past nodding docents who somehow like you for your foresight.

I love those old familiar halls—originally the Medici palace's private galleries for Cosimo's stunning Renaissance collection. I can picture Catherine de' Medici's ancestors wandering through them at night like Isabella Gardner in her Boston-born Italian villa full of art and ghosts. These "home" museums hit me hard every time—not pantheons or altars with steps and pillars, but the odd corner. The not-exactly-accidental view of normal life going on below. The errant bird alit on a windowsill.

We went through slowly, stopping stunned, as was my usual reaction, in the Botticelli room. *The Birth of Venus* is faded and dull, and when I looked to see the last time it was restored, it was the year I lived in Florence—1986, which is why I remember it so vivid and pink. Now I trust Venus better; she's like me—a little faded maybe, the accumulation of twenty years dulling her a bit. And the nudes from the Renaissance make my figure look worth the half shell.

Now, I wonder what would happen if David and Venus were to look eye to eye. It might be a lot like what happened between my husband and me a few nights back when he told me he wasn't sure he loved me anymore. Tired . . . fallen . . . idols. A word to the wise: never ever think you're "golden." And never ever base a marriage on it.

It's better to think about Firenze. The feeling of walking those old streets again. To walk and sweat and not gain weight. To not feel bowel distress. To not feel that pain in my right gut that has me sure I'm dying of something foul and painful. To not care what's ahead of me, or need to know how to get out if need be. To not care what's in my purse—if I've remembered my emergency items like Halls, or homeopathic calming pills; to not court my obsession with lip balm. In the world of neurosis, I'd count myself at the low end of the scale. But that doesn't mean I've felt free.

In Firenze, I felt stunningly free.

I simply could not wait to return home and to share this state of mind with my depressed husband. To inspire his own healing. This better-than-ever person that is his wife.

I wanted a photograph of myself feeling that alive again. That calm and happy. I reached for my camera, but let it go. I didn't need to take that photo. I'm here with my daughter. We don't need to prove it to anyone. We'd already proved it to David, or better yet, the Slaves. To the faded Venus. The supine Donatello's *David*, on his stomach, being restored by women in lab coats at the Bargello who reminded me of department store Clinique clerks. The Perseus, the Sabine Woman in the Loggia, the Neptune white man of the fountain.

Hello, again, I shouted from my heart, not my lips. *We're all here again. You'd love Montana. So many trees.*

And with that declaration came one of the most profound moments of my life.

It was the morning of our last day.

I actually heard a voice. I know—oh God—not that. But seriously. I did. I heard a voice. It was my voice, ostensibly calling to me from said bell tower, and yet it felt as close as the pillow beneath my head.

It was an epiphany—a big one, if I may be so bold. A trajectory of the epiphany in boarding school when I finally understood what Salinger was talking about at the end of *Franny and*

Zooey. About where the Kingdom of Heaven lies. Back then I guess I hadn't lived long enough to want anything as badly as I have in the last twenty years. And I lost track of what I wrote in that English paper with all those exclamation points.

I was lying in bed that last day in Florence, looking at my daughter sleeping with her mouth open, listening to a dog bark on a balcony above the streets of Florence—the Vespas whizzing by, the polite exchanges of *Buongiorno,* the smell of coffee, and yes, exhaust, and something very old.

But I didn't feel the panic I'd thought I would, knowing I had to leave all of it behind. The desperate need to go out in that world beyond the thick wooden shutters and our own tiny balcony just one more time alone—to feel twenty and charged. The frenzy to contact my old footprints, in a state of ravenous adventure. I didn't need to be anywhere other than in my bed watching my daughter sleep.

In not quite a twenty-year-old's voice, but not quite a forty-year-old's, either, I heard, quiet and with morning breath, *It's all here. It always was.*

Forget Puccini. Forget Michelangelo. It begged me to forget, as the anonymous fourteenth-century author of *The Cloud of Unknowing* advised. A pool of forgetting. Forget age, class, career, marital status, and even motherhood.

It was a voice from my deepest place. From my truest nature. My most simple and honest self:

It's all here, it told me. *It's in you.*

It was a moment of enlightenment. The other-side-of-the-rainbow to what I'd considered the elegantly obnoxious comment delivered by my writer friend years before: "the only difference between being published and not being published, is being published."

It drove me crazy until that morning epiphany in Italy. When I awoke to the gift of understanding.

You see, I'd given myself something I wanted desperately—something I'd been wanting for as long as I'd wanted to be a published writer. The difference was that Italy was an outcome I could, short of travel disaster, control. I was responsible for this happiness. I was responsible for my own love force, where happiness hatches. And in that, there's no insanity. Just like the therapist said.

In that last morning, the dog barking, and my daughter asleep next to me, and the smell of coffee, I finally got it. It wasn't hyperactivated like a piece of blue sea glass being sucked from my palm, back into the sea—not desperate and fleeting and sad in its arrival for its certain departure. No.

It felt natural. Normal.

What a waste: all those years of wanting . . . of suffering from not having—for something that feels so natural. As natural and uncomplicated as waking up in your own bed in your own room in your own house, before the thoughts come in. All the trouble begins when we open our eyes and start thinking. Wanting things. Thinking about the shape of our day and the people in it. And if we've really got it bad, the trouble begins with our eyes still shut tight.

I decided in that moment to remember to let the waking hour stun me with its simplicity. To deliver me my true nature. And to receive its calm, empty self.

I finally got what my author friend had meant. He wasn't being smug in the least. Or even that spiritually enlightened. He was simply saying that our happiness—our ability to love, to be in a place of harmony with ourselves and beyond—is not outside ourselves. Our happiness is not outside ourselves. It's just as natural as waking up to a dog barking somewhere in the distance. Smelling coffee. And seeing your child asleep next to you. Even when you know that the day will be full of challenges. Even when you know you have to move on. That the bed in which you wake is quite different from the one you'll wake in the next day.

It's important to think of who you are in that meditative waking trance. Not where you are in the world. Because you may think that you have arrived there in that state. That you had to cross the ocean or pay your dues by years of hard work and even rejection in your field of work. But what if there really isn't anywhere to get? What if you're already there, no matter where you are or where you wake? Doesn't that feel easy on the brain? Maybe the bumper stickers don't lie. What if there is no there there? Maybe we don't have to cross oceans after all.

God, it's so *Wizard of Oz*. Sort of pisses me off.

My epiphany, boiled down then, to this:

Our happiness is not outside ourselves. It's all here. In us. It always was.

And that means, as I sit here in my office in Montana, my suitcase unpacked, my new fingernails tapping a staccato on my very old keyboard, a postcard of a Renaissance Jesus under it, and a few other prophets, too, as well as my Mecca: the Duomo in Firenze—my children still asleep in their beds, soon to wake to their own simple selves . . . my husband still gone, maybe, too, waking to a place of true nature . . . that it's all here. Here. At this moment in my life.

I knew it. I just had to go to Italy to find out for sure.

No Grace Period

The third day,
on the other side of "a few days."

Still no sign of husband. I've been jet-lagged and restless through the nights, tossing and turning and walking the pearly moon–lit rooms of our house. And like I heard the voice in Italy saying, "It's all here . . . it's in you," now I hear more words: "Trust me. And go back to sleep." And I do.

And in my waking hour of this third day without him, my eyes open and immediately start tracking back and forth like they're looking for something. I ward off the thoughts, blinking and staring hard at the mighty conifers outside my window, ash lavender in the dusty dawn. But there is a lumbering force behind me. Pushing at my mind. Trying to knead me into knowing that something dear to me is missing. That I should be afraid.

And that bastard knowledge is there. Consciousness, like an

ambulance chaser of dawn. And I know—I know that I am alone in my bed. Our bed. Our king-sized bed.

That's when I see my treasures laid out on my window seat where I've left them like talismans, and I smile because there is another thought there, but a kind one, an old one I know well—perhaps large enough to fill the space in the bed next to me. And it brings with it good news:

I must be okay.

Because I want to cook.

I want to cook something utterly consuming. Something I've always wanted to cook but haven't had the time or the know-how or, in Montana, the ingredients. I want to make cassoulet.

I've always wanted to make cassoulet. The proper way—how it's made in Toulouse, France. But it takes days. Which is what I have right now, I figure. I want a complicated, lengthy project that results in gluttony—all evidence savored, digested, and lost down the septic tank. It seems altogether apropos for the mood I'm in: jet-lagged. At war with my mind. Trying like hell to care for my soul.

So I throw on my bathrobe and whisk downstairs to scan the freezer for the variety of products I've been gathering from the local meat farm for just this occasion: pork loin, garlic sausages, lamb shoulder and bones, salt pork rind, and ham hocks. I take them out and lay them on the counter to defrost while I sort through the meat drawer to uncover the pancetta and prosciutto—my guilty pleasures.

Then I go to the garage freezer to dig out the duck our neighbor gave us as a Christmas gift last year. And the rendered goose fat in a mason jar in the pantry—from another friend's hunting expedition; another feast. It's one of the things I love about Montanans. We are proud of our gifts from nature—dried morel mushrooms, jars of native homemade preserves—huckleberry, serviceberry, thimbleberry. Smoked whitefish and trout. Turkey and elk jerky and sausage.

I'll bring it all out, whether or not he's there to appreciate it. I'll set our dining room table with my great-aunt's linens and my best sterling and china from the china cabinet. I'll go all-out like it's Christmas dinner. This will be a feast.

Besides, one thing I know he loves . . . is my cooking. Maybe it will summon him home.

And maybe it does.

The kids and I are in the kitchen making a glorious gamey mess. My wannabe-tough-guy son in a flowered apron. My daughter leafing through our jazz CDs. They know today could be the day Daddy is coming home from his camping trip, and they're excited to impress him with our creation.

We hear a truck in the driveway and the dogs don't bark, which means one thing: it's him.

The kids jump into action and run out the front door.

I want to take off my apron and wipe the grease from my fingers and somehow look cool and stunning. But I'm apron-bound—too far into my duck confit. The kitchen, at least, needs me. So I work and wait. And try not to think about George Bailey and whether or not, in all my husband's fishing and camping and thinking, he had a visit from his own Clarence, the guardian angel.

But I stay centered, eyeing the gorgeous Tuscan cannellini beans soaking in a glass bowl on the counter. I try to feed off of what I've just given myself after so many years. Remembering how I felt in Italy those last days—about my epiphany and the photographic proof I didn't need, and how I wanted to take this new me and practice. How, even given my husband's harsh words, I still want to practice all summer. On my family. Especially on my husband. Especially in light of his disaffection.

I have to believe this is just a temporary low moment in the long arc of our marriage. And I breathe in and throw back my shoulders like my father used to, just before he called on a customer in a train yard. I actually repeat the phrase he'd say to himself, "Shoulders back, Munson," and realize I've been hunched over like an old crone.

I tell myself that quite possibly he's going to come through the door with good news. And I'll get the chance to experience a marriage with him in which I'm being totally responsible for my own happiness. Regardless of the state of my writing career or who he's being. Or what changes may face us—a potential move from this life we adore, this home we've built, total mutual career reboot.

Standing at my kitchen counter, I'm centered and strong and brave. Radiant, even. Deeply alive.

And there he is. Dirty and scruffy and handsome.

I think of the moment I laid eyes on him. I still feel like he's my boyfriend, coming through the door with the fun and the cool. And his: "I know who you are. Everybody knows who you are." I want to fold into his arms, but know I am limited by his affections and it makes me mad.

Shoulders back, Munson, I think. I am no old crone.

"Daddy—you haven't seen our pictures from Italy!" my daughter says, her voice ringing like church bells in a small piazza campanile. "I put them on my laptop. I want to show you the slide show."

He sits down in his chair by the hearth like he's on old stomping ground. I love that he has a chair in this house. He smells like wood smoke. I'm glad. In case I wondered in a low moment if, in fact, he was truly camping. Which . . . well, I admit . . . I did.

He hasn't made any eye contact with me whatsoever.

Our son climbs into his lap. "Daddy, did you catch any fish?" he says like he's meeting his superhero. (And he is.)

"A few," he answers. "But no keepers," he says, sounding strained.

Our daughter puts the laptop on the ottoman and starts to describe our Italy photos. "And that's the kitchen of the family Mom lived with. They're so nice. That's the oven. It's wood-fired. And that's the mama. She taught us how to make tiramisù. And her tomato sauce. And that's the father. Doesn't he have the greatest eyes?! He's a blacksmith."

I dare to look at him. He's trying to appear interested. But I see pain in his eyes. My heart starts to sink, but I look at the copper pot on the stove, knowing there are duck legs slowly simmering in there, in five hours to become confit.

"I'm making cassoulet," I say, too desperately. It seems like all I've got, other than those photos, and they're not doing much to impress him.

My daughter's eyes are dancing along the laptop slideshow reporting the news of our happiness—". . . and that's a glass-blowing factory where we went in a water taxi from the Grand Canal, and they made me a glass horse right in front of me, and gave it to me for free! And Mom's Italian came back!"

An urge to crack a sick little joke hits before I have time to take it back, "Unfortunately, he didn't," I say.

My husband laughs and I laugh. We like to laugh at things just a little bit off. We've been laughing this way for twenty years. I try to make eye contact with him while we're smiling because I know he respects humor like this—more than cassoulet or Italy. But he goes distant again.

The phone rings and it's the neighbor kids and they want our kids to meet them at their fort. As they run out the door, I'm sorry to see them go. More afraid, actually. They're our buffer. But it's best that they aren't here for the conversation I know we need to have.

Our window is here, and we're well aware of it.

He looks at me as if he's never seen me before. As if he's trying to convert me into the woman he told himself would be back in his house, in his kitchen, making his life miserable. But I have to believe that I'm surprising him with my kitchen smells and veteran's apron and easy demeanor.

"We need to talk," I say to him.

He nods.

I am swarming with visceral panic. It's white and it's hot. But I take his hand, surprised by its firm grip, and we go out to the screened porch.

And we talk.

He cries. He says he's done a lot of thinking. He feels like he can't breathe. He needs to follow his gut. He knows what he needs to do. It's the hardest thing he's ever had to say. Something he never thought he'd say. But he doesn't want to be around me. He doesn't think he loves me anymore. He wants to be alone. He knows the kids will understand. They'll see how badly he needs to be happy. He'll get a place in town. He actually says, "You're not getting anywhere with your writing. You're bashing your head against a wall over and over, and I can't deal with it anymore. I never should have married a writer."

Is that what this is about? He's vilifying me for my lack of career success? What about my other successes? All he has to do is look around to see those in 3-D and Technicolor. All he has to do is look into his children's eyes. I have created so much that is a success. Plus, when's the last time he actually read anything I've written? Just because the publishing world doesn't deem my work worthy doesn't mean it's not.

I want to defend myself. Lament the state of the publishing

industry. Deliver him copies of all my "good" rejection letters. Remind him of how I've been on the mostly sane side of what most writers call home in Crazy Town. I'm not Bukowski or anything.

But as I've said many times:

"Sometimes taking care of yourself means letting yourself be misunderstood."

And through the old shame and new panic comes my Italy-self.

I stay calm. I think of Venus. Born from the depths of the ocean, being blown to shore by friendly wind. I think of my twenty-year-old self, so newly free; reborn. I think of my forty-one-year-old self having just met eye-to-eye with her again after all these years. *It's all here,* I repeat in my mind. *It's in you.* I will not retreat to the pit of suffering. Those ocean depths. He can't deal with my lack of career success? Or his own?

"I don't buy it," I say.

He looks at me, dumbfounded.

"I don't. I don't buy it." I tell him I think this is about him. He's come to the end of suffering. He's taking a stand. It's a good thing. Necessary and welcome. I understand what it is to suffer. I say, "But I'm not at all sure this is really about me. Either way," I add, "we have so much invested in this marriage, and there are little minds and hearts at stake."

I don't scream *I love you!* Or *Unchain my heart!* I stay cool. My proclamation of love wouldn't do anything but annoy him right now. Mine is not the love in question. Instead, I tell him he should go to a third world country with a backpack for a few months like he's always talked about. See if his parents will sponsor a trip to the Great Barrier Reef for his upcoming birthday. They're famous for sponsoring trips for their offspring. They believe in the healing powers of travel. They'd see it as an excellent investment in their son's well-being, and the consequent well-being of his marriage and their grandchildren's lives. Maybe a fishing trip to Alaska. His Italy.

"You need an adventure," I say like the twenty-year-old he once loved.

"Are you kidding? I can't ask my parents for money for a trip! They'd think I was being irresponsible."

I hold my tongue. But then I implore, "Use some of our savings, then. It's an investment in our future. It would be some of the most important money we've ever spent."

He says if he does that then he knows what'll happen. He'll come back knowing he has to leave. Or he'll not come back at all.

"Great," I tell him, trying not to be sarcastic. "If that's your truth." Which I doubt it is. But I don't say that. Instead I say, "But how will you know if you don't try? A trip for yourself will be a lot more imaginable for the kids than a bachelor pad in town—running into Daddy at the grocery store like all those other divorced daddies wandering around our little town with frozen pizza in their shopping basket. It's not age-appropriate to ask them to consider your happiness. It just isn't. They'll see it as one thing. Abandonment." I'm trying not to get mean. But it's hard. I picture the braided hills of Tuscany.

"There are so many shades of gray here," I tell him. "You're in fight-or-flight mode. You're seeing in black and white and you're talking crazy. There are so many choices here. And we have to make them together. Like a business."

"That's another reason why I can't take off. I can't abandon my business partner. I can't leave him high and dry with all we've put into this. I can't just take off on him."

I know his business is on its last legs. I know that he's months away from closing up shop. That he should have shut it down years ago. And it makes me mad that he's willing to give it mouth-to-mouth resuscitation and not our marriage. Not himself. "But you can just take off on me? Us? The kids? What we've built together?"

He's silent.

I hear the sound of gunning motors in the driveway.

"Who's here?"

A couple buddies. They're going dirt-biking.

He tells me he loves me as he rushes out to meet them. Those words utterly confuse me.

And then he doesn't call. And he doesn't come home that night. And I'm pretty sure this time he can't blame it on cell phone service.

In my worst moments, I think it would be easier if he somehow had an unfortunate accident on his dirt bike and died. Mourning seems infinitely more manageable than abandonment—for all of us he is about to leave behind in the name of "happiness."

The next day, I grill the sausages and assemble the cooked meats with the cooked beans to simmer. I decide we'll have the cassoulet for a noon Sunday supper—my Illinois grandmother's tradition. Why not? Why wait for my husband? We need diversion. Then I make some tea and sit alone on the screened porch, savoring the shameless musk of peasant food. And I think about the nature of happiness.

What is happiness? At this moment in my life, I honestly don't know if it's really anything more than one small step out of suffering. I can choose that small step—even though my mind is trying with all its bony might to tell me to freak the fuck out!

And lying there, I think of my old journals. And I think about freedom, not just happiness. Maybe this time in my marriage is really an opportunity to finally look at what it is to be free. Because at this moment in my life, I have never felt so oppressed, never mind those old institutions that messed with my mind as a kid. Freedom. Not just freedom from suffering or wanting. But freedom to accept my truest nature and dwell there, just like my old journals called out for. Maybe happiness is merely a byproduct of the greater state of being free. I think it's commonly referred to as "peace." That's what I want. I want peace.

I swaddle myself in blankets and pillows on the old mattress. And try to remember the last wise words I heard someone utter.

They come to me quickly. It was in a garden in Tuscany. A few weeks ago. From a man's lips. And that feels important. Like maybe it can attempt to undo what I've just heard from another man's lips.

It began with a nightingale.

Like I'm time-traveling, I let it all back in. I'm sitting quietly with the man who was my Italian father over twenty-one years ago, staring out over the hills around Florence with coffee—wishing my Italian was better. He refuses to learn a word of English, except for *hamburger*, which he says with disdain. I'm dying to try out my Italian. I want to say so much. How I've dreamed of him so many times, and we're sitting right here, but in the dream, we're speaking in English. And he understands me. He hears me and sees me and understands me, so alive in these hills where he's home.

Alas, we're in a reality where there is a major language barrier. I want to tell him that I have this sort of home in Montana. That he and his family inspired it with their long dinners discussing politics and world events; their generations of women in the kitchen cooking family love in family recipes—the *nonna*'s grandmotherly warning not to stir backward: "You don't want to undo the sauce!" Their pride in their country's history and hard work to preserve their land and homes is noble and contagious.

"I remember my first day here," I say in my best Italian. "I didn't speak a word of Italian, and you took me down there to the fig tree and you reached up and picked a fig, and then reached up to another tree and picked a walnut, cracked it in your palm, then put the walnut meat in the fig and popped it in my mouth."

I look at him and he has tears streaming down his face. He lets them fall, then he wipes them off with both thumbs. "It was September," he says. *Era settembre.* Like he measures his months by ripe fruit.

"I heard you are a famous writer," he says.

"No. No no no." I wag the whole of my forefinger like the Italians do, even though it feels beyond good to think there's a "father" of mine out there in the world who believes I have achieved some level of fame. I want to hug him for it. But I say, "Not famous. My short work gets published pretty often. But not my novels—not yet. It's very difficult. So much heart on the page . . . just sitting in stacks in my office."

He smiles. He thinks I'm being humble.

"I'm not famous." *Non sono famosa.* This is how this family is—they assume the best about you, never the worst. (Does that remind you of anybody? I have been blessed, then, in fathers.)

The look in his eyes explains, for a moment, his tears. Maybe part of what makes this the place he'll never move from and English a language he'll never learn and hamburgers something he'll never eat has to do with what happens the moment he pops a fig in an American girl's mouth at the age of nineteen. What happens in that moment, and what happens to her over the course of the rest of her life.

"I can see that you love your work. That's what's important," he says.

"It's true. That's why I keep doing it. I love it." I think of my husband. *What does he love?* I wonder. I used to think I knew.

"You must come back with your husband," my Italian father says, like he's reading my mind.

"Maybe it's better without him, this trip. This is very personal. I've waited a long time for this. He didn't want to come, anyway."

He smiles and lights a cigarette. He knows men.

I ask him what his secret is—being married this long—staying in love.

He stands up slowly and puts his hand at the small of my back guiding me, more like hooking me up to a pull he feels at all times, a pull toward his studio hidden away in the tangles of rosemary and shiny vines.

Quietly, he guides me under a low doorway, cupping my head like a cop with a criminal, and we're in a small shed full of tools. He is the fourth generation of blacksmiths in his family. I'm honored. I rarely let anyone into my office.

I'm also fascinated. "I just wrote a book where one of the characters is a blacksmith. Many many years ago, in the American West. Maybe you can help me with something I can't quite find the answer to."

He didn't expect this. He's seen brand after brand of American girl being curious about Italy, but not about metalworking. He cocks his head—a big gesture for him.

"In my book, the main character is losing his mind, going . . . *pazzo*, and in an effort to prove he's okay, he starts hammering his initial into the head of every one of his hand-forged nails. Is this even possible? I hope so, because it's a big part of my book, and something I love about it."

Then he goes to a shelf, and he pulls out a jar—a Mason jar, just like in my book, of hand-forged nails. I hold it while he fishes out a tool. He puts it in my hand, and I see that it is a stamp. With the letter R. His family initial.

"This is how you stay in love with your wife," he says, looking around his studio. "Just like your books."

Now I'm the one with the tears flashing on my cheeks. Because my husband doesn't have a specific life's passion that he can call work.

Then a bird sings, and he looks up.

I look up. People who notice birds are all listening in the same language, and it's always in the present tense. It makes sense that he's one of these bird people, too.

"A nightingale," he says. *Usignolo.* "Like Florence Nightingale. She was born here, you know. Hence her name. Her grave is in Santa Croce."

And I hold the nails in my hand and feel sure that someone popped a walnut-filled fig into her mouth when she was a young girl.

"What does your husband do for work?" he asks, tidying up some tools.

"He used to run a brewery. He loved that. But now he helps

people find jobs. He doesn't like his work. He's not happy. He can't hold anything in his hand," I say, gripping the nails, thinking of my closet full of books.

"Men need their work."

I want to say, *Well, I'm a woman and I need my work, too.* But this man is an old-fashioned Italian. And so I give an old-fashioned Italian response. Marriage is, after all, very, very old-fashioned.

I say, "But don't they need their women, too?"

He smiles. "Of course." *Certo.* And gives me a hug I know is intended for a wife who is showing the signs of marital stress.

"I'm sure you are a good wife," he says. Just as sure as he is that I'm a famous writer.

And from him, in that moment in my life, I am deeply touched. It's as if my own father has made a cameo appearance in my Italy gift to myself. Like he wants to get a word in edgewise. The men are saying something old-fashioned, but perhaps timeless: *Men need their work.* That doesn't mean women don't. But it's worth looking at, given my husband's expression when he gets home every night.

I think of how proud my Italian father is of his nails and hand-forged chandeliers and bed frames. My own father so proud of his company's patented train parts. How proud I am when I finish a book, even if no one ever reads it.

Pride.

When is the last time I saw my husband proud? Not since his brewery days. Eight years ago. That's what this is all about: pride.

At least I have manuscripts to hold in my hand at the end of the day. Whether or not they're published. What does he have?

God, I wish I could dish up some pride on a plate and feed it to him like the cassoulet I'll fill the better part of two days making.

But I can't.

This is what it is to surrender to outcome. He has to find his pride all on his own. It's the most helpless feeling, as I lie on the old mattress on the screened porch with my now cold tea. My back aching, my apron greasy and spent, my kitchen in a kind of post-op disarray.

But I remind myself what I can control: my work. My roles. My pride. I can still create beautiful things like cassoulet, regardless of his reaction.

And what now? Another day with my kids wondering where their father is. And what's the excuse today? I honestly don't have one to give. I wasn't granted one. How much truth can they handle? What do I tell them? Do I lie and say he came home late last night and left early for work this morning? I won't let him make a liar out of me. What now?

Like he's met with my mind, or at least his conscience, the phone rings. He's decided to put himself on the radar.

Turns out that he didn't die on his dirt bike. He apologizes. Says that he went out with his buddies late at night after dirt-biking. Slept in his office. Says he's coming home in a few hours.

"Can we count on you for lunch?" I ask. I have to, if at least for the kids' sake. "I'm serving the cassoulet."

"Yes," he says humbly. I can hear it in his voice: he's sick to death that he's putting us through this. But I can also hear that he doesn't think he has a choice.

So I leave it there. I don't chastise him for not calling. He might want me to. It might make what he's doing easier on him. But I know he knows his "sin." I refuse to be in the position of oppressor.

Instead, I get off the phone abruptly and put the cassoulet in the oven to cook, whether or not I can take him at his word. Even though it seems so suddenly important that he eat this culinary creation. That he receive my love if only in cassoulet. But I know this is ridiculous.

I hear the kids in the hallway. I have a few moments to catch my calm.

They run into the kitchen. "Is it ready?" they both chime, going over to the oven, still in their wrinkly pajamas. Summer hours.

"Almost!" I try to look cheery. "We're going to have it for lunch!"

"Wait till Daddy sees it," my son says, ogling the handsome copper pot through the oven window.

"But where's Dad? He'll miss it!" my daughter says, like she can take it if he does.

Luckily I have this to say:

"He says he'll be here for lunch." I avoid the part where she asked where he was. Maybe she can ask him that question herself.

God, what did Mary Bailey say to her kids? I try to remember an instructional scene from *It's a Wonderful Life*, but all I can think of is my father bawling his eyes out at the end, in the colored glow of our Christmas tree.

I take a deep breath and smile in a way I'm sure they don't consider real. "Daddy's going through a hard time right now. With work. A lot of people in our country are. A lot of people are . . . all over the world. We have to be patient with him. Remember how hard it was for me after my dad died? This is sort of the same thing for Daddy."

They both look worried.

"But no matter what . . . we love you and everything is going to be okay." As if Mary Bailey were pushing me from behind, I say, "Come on. Let's set the table like the Queen of England is coming for lunch. Even if it's just us."

And as much as I've learned to find beauty in the natural world, today I want the comforts of my youth. I want to fall back into the arms of my mother's and grandmothers' beauty. I want to be around their beautiful things arranged just so on the dining room table . . . that proclaimed and promised safety, comfort, home. That told me that soon the house would be full of parents, grandparents, older siblings home from boarding school or college, aunts and uncles and cousins . . . and that I was among them—old enough, responsible enough to handle their precious finery, even if it meant I had to wear scratchy clothes, hold my tongue, and keep my elbows off the table.

Old tears come to my eyes because I remember the hours I spent under our dining room table as a little girl waiting for "the whole family" to return. So much of my childhood was spent waiting for that to happen.

Which is why it's especially hard to set this table, given my current situation.

But we do it anyway. It becomes increasingly important to me, as if what I have to promise and proclaim to myself by just this table setting is that whether or not he leaves me, I'm going to be okay. Safe, comforted, home. Just like I promised my kids.

I drive this into my heart and mind with every laid piece of silver, every ironed-to-a-crease napkin, every spot-free crystal goblet. And we set this beautiful table . . . for four.

My Evil Twin Sister Sheila

Last day of June.

He came home for the cassoulet. Ate it in five minutes without speaking. Got up from the table, left his dishes, and went to the living room couch to watch baseball.

Usually on an occasion like that with a nice feast, we play a family game. Usually he brings his plate to the counter. Usually, he even does the dishes. Not that day. He was the lowest common denominator. On purpose.

As if to hearten him, as if to keep him home, the kids curled up with him on the couch, our son showing off his stat recall, our daughter pretending she liked baseball.

I sat at the dining room table amid my sparkling things and stared into them until the candles burned down, thinking about motive.

This is a dance he's doing. An aggressive one now. It's one thing to be in pain and go off like a dying dog for a while. I have room for that personal walkabout. But he's opting instead for something else, and I can see it plain as day. He's trying to get me mad. So he can play victim to an irate wife. He's trying to add to his "sins," which, like mine, are less dramatic than the average soap opera seeker would like. We're common garden-variety AM radio "sinners," I guess. If you want high drama, turn on the TV. But you don't want that from me, do you? You wouldn't be that sort of meanie, would you? You're my friend, right? Friends don't go sniffing around for sins, do they? They forgive and forget. Just like husbands. And wives. They know what's their business and what's not. Right?

Besides, I'm not dealing in "sin." Not in my marriage. And not in this book. My philosophy, my message is about trying to live responsibly and sanely with what is. Remember—we're not taking sides. We're not living in right and wrong. We're on higher ground.

Look outside your window. Take a breath. A deep one. We're in this together, remember? You and me. My husband and me. Moment by moment.

And in that spacious breath-ful place, I'm not in this dance he's doing. I may be in the larger dance of the marriage, but I can choose to sit this particular one out.

I can choose to stay over here and try to mind my own business; try to walk my line of non-suffering. Writing my way through what wants to become numbness or panic, whether or not this book ever finds its way to publication. At least I'll have it on my bedside table. I'm needing it more and more.

My husband comes into my office this morning. He wants to know if I'd be willing to take the kids to Wisconsin for the rest of the summer to visit our good friends at their summer cabin. It's the best solution he can think of that doesn't include our children thinking he's abandoning us.

I toy with it. Try it on for size. At least he's seeing that moving out will be interpreted as abandonment by the kids. (Forget about me for now.) At least he sees that this staying out and not calling and not coming home is the wrong message to send to our children.

And yet my leaving with our children reeks of something I can't quite locate.

"I've just had my dream trip. I'm home now. Here. Feeling strong and calm. Taking care of myself and our kids. I want to spend the summer in Montana. Riding my horse and gardening and writing. You're having the problems. You go." I can see that there might very well be some serious hardball in this before we're on the other side, if, in fact, we get there.

Still, I call my friend in Wisconsin. It feels important to have options. Lifelines. And I tell her what's up. She is the first person I've told, as if speaking it will make it official.

"Of course you can come. But I have to say—I think you're right in holding your ground. That's your home. Frankly, I'd kick his ass out of there."

"But that's not my strategy," I say. "I'm riding the storm. Trying to stay calm. I'm just confused about what kinds of demands I can make. Like . . . he's not coming home at night. And he's not calling."

I can feel her fuming on the other end. "I'll tell you what you can demand! You can demand that he grow the fuck up and take responsibility!"

"Yeah. But he can't right now. He can't see straight. He's got to care about himself before he can care for us. I told him to go scuba diving in Australia like he's always wanted."

"Well, what the hell's wrong with that gig? Why can't he do that?"

"He says it's too expensive. But if he really wanted to, he could find a way to make it work. I think he'd rather stay stuck, frankly. Hell—it took me twenty years to get back to Italy. I understand stuck."

"I'll tell you one thing—there aren't a lot of wives who'd give their husbands that much room."

"Yeah, well—I'm willing to, if it'll help him locate his heart again. I want his heart. I love him. And you know, I wasn't exactly a peach after my father died a few years back."

"What are you saying? That you deserve this? Listen, you were grieving the loss of your father. After a huge rejection from a huge publishing house that acted like they were going to take you all the way! Just cuz you weren't friggin' well-known! I haven't forgotten, missy! But hey—you were still reliable! You didn't stay out all night and not call!"

"Yeah. But I did stay up all night crying and drinking wine in my office, feeling like a total failure of a writer, watching old home movies of my father. God, I still miss him. I drank too much after he died. It couldn't have been fun to live with."

"So what? Everybody goes through their shit. Does that make you unlovable? And did you ever try to blame the whole thing on someone else? As I recall, you slapped yourself into therapy! It was a no-brainer. Men are wimps. I swear. He probably wants you to kick his ass out so he can call you the bitch and he can go be poor victim boy. I can promise you he didn't think he'd get a trip to Australia out of it. It's actually a brilliant strategy, my dear."

"That's what I'm hoping, even though I know I need to let go of what may come. It's a good way to live your life, no matter what. But I'm brand-spanking-new at it. And I'm not so good at it yet. And I'm still really friggin' jet-lagged for some reason. I just wanted a grace period, you know?"

"That would have been nice. Interesting what happens when you finally give yourself what you want. I'd say just mind your business. Guide by example. Don't ask him to do anything. Don't give him anything to push off of. He has to do this by himself. But of course, there's always a guest room for you here, and we can spend the summer together, cooking and reading books on the dock. Our kids would love to have your kids to play with. But I think you should stay. I've known you two for a long time. I believe in your marriage. I love you both very much."

"Thank you. That means everything to me. You're an amazing

friend." I pause because it's true. And I'm reminded that I'll need my friends during this period of my life. Instead of going into hermitage like I did after my father died and my novel deal got shut down. Hermitage can be dangerous.

Ultimately, though, I know I'm alone in this. That I have to be if I'm going to really get to the bottom of it; if I'm really committed to being free. Not dwelling in right and wrong. Good or bad. But really attempting to live in the moment of my true nature.

Still, a few choice friends are essential right now—sounding boards that I can trust not to judge me or act like they have all the answers or confront him. Especially friends who won't take sides and vilify him. Because, remember, I love this man. I'll need to choose those friends wisely. This is one of those friends. Too bad she lives more than a thousand miles away.

"But can I at least ask him to give it his best shot? Can I ask him to go to a therapist? I mean—I don't get it! He's willing to just throw it all away without any real work!"

"Not with the strategy you're using, I wouldn't. Just leave him alone for now. Ride it out, like you said. Frankly, it sounds like Hell, either way. But I've never heard you so calm. I'm blown away."

"Yeah. I'm even happy sometimes. I figured something out that I had to hear echoed back to me by my twenty-year-old self. In Italy. Happiness only comes from within."

She's a bit speechless. And then she says, "I'm really proud of you."

"Me too."

But not too proud to spend the entire day at a water park I've been avoiding for fifteen years, full of obese people eating junk food, because that's what my kids want to do—a shock to the senses after a month in Italy eating gelato and listening to nightingales. I actually witness a kid having a diarrhea explosion in the kiddie pool—luckily not the one my kids are in. And when I tell the lifeguard, he says, "The chlorine'll take care of it." And all the kids just keep on swimming in that water. There is simply no correlation between this water park, and Italy. And yet, *It's all here,* remember?

I have to do something special for myself after that, even though we're not exactly rolling in the dough. Like a true American I have to live outside my means and go get sushi. Like the old days when money wasn't a worry. Only back then, there wasn't much to spend it on. It's like a sick joke that now, thanks to the influence of the wealthy city transplants who've moved to our town . . . we finally have a thriving sushi bar. It's one in a small list of true city comforts in our mountain town. And tonight, it's exactly what the doctor ordered.

(Just maybe not the loan officer. And so what? Why not a splurge right now? Isn't this what splurges were made for? What did you buy the last time you felt like the world was crumbling around you? Okay. Maybe nothing. Maybe you're the type to make a list when you go to Costco and stick to it. You are my hero.)

Apparently my husband's seen the same doctor, because as I stand at the counter with the kids, waiting for takeout, I feel a gentle hand at the small of my back. I feel a tingle and turn. It's him. He's medicating his woe with sushi, too. I should have known.

"Daddy! Can we drive home with you? Please?" they beg, hungering for him.

It does not escape me that Daddy's home is still mine. Theirs. Ours. "It's okay with me," I say.

Both orders arrive at the same time, and he pulls out his wallet and says to the waitress, "I'll pay for both," which feels so good—so sickly good that he's at least willing to pay for my meal—that I lose my appetite.

I watch him take both bags, like he's holding a piece of me as he walks out the door with the kids, one on each side, tucked in close. I revel and reel in this feeling of unification. Of watching our kids woo their father home.

A wave of loneliness hits me. I need my trusted tribe outside that little party of three. A mother or a sibling. But they're all far away, and I haven't wanted to tell them any of this. They'll worry. And their worry will feel like a burden. I need someone I can sit with right here in my town who won't take it personally. Someone like my friend in Wisconsin who won't judge me or him and who'll hug me and listen if I feel like talking; leave me be if I don't.

And I think of just the right person. My friend, the horsewoman, who is currently boarding my horse. The two of them together would be the perfect medicine. I suddenly long more than anything to see my horse. To lean my eye into his, like a crystal ball. Feel his velvet muzzle in my hand.

As I drive to her house, I think of her life. She grew up in abject poverty. A latchkey kid from a family of eight that lived in a one-room house with no running water or electricity. Had holes in her shoes. Rode a horse to town when the truck was busted.

When I moved to Montana, it was people like her that I didn't dare tell where I'd come from. How could they possibly care about me or my feelings? Anything I'd say would be dismissed and judged because of it. So, like I'd edited myself in the social setting of my youth as the dreamy-eyed artist I wanted to be, this, too, would be my modus operandi in Montana.

But this woman showed me that truth is truth. Pain is pain. Empathy is empathy. The human heart does not discriminate. Only the mind.

I decide I'll remind her of what she taught me tonight. That my visit will be about gratitude and love. That I won't dump my problems on her even though she's one of the best listeners I know. I want to be free from my marital ordeal if only for a few hours.

She greets me on her front porch with a hug. She sees with her keen eye, however, that I am upset. "You look like you could use a ride in the woods," she says.

The sun still high in the sky, I call home to okay it with my husband. Because she's right. I need a ride in the woods right now more than I've ever needed a ride in the woods.

"Don't you want your dinner?" He sounds strangely incredulous. But I know it has less to do with my absence and more to do with spending money we shouldn't.

"Put mine in the fridge. I'll be home in a few hours. I need some fresh air." That's an exceedingly nice way to put it, in my opinion. Because I need a break. From all these feelings and thoughts. And I know the horses are the perfect way to bring me out of my angst.

As we saddle up our horses, hers an Arabian black, and mine a Morgan bay, wind chimes and guinea fowl tinkling and squawking in the background, I say, "I want to thank you for something you said. It was on a trail ride we took a few years back. Way up in the Salish Mountains, and it was autumn. The aspens were on fire. And we were talking about lovability and shame. Do you remember?"

She smiles. "I sure do. I'll never forget it." She likes to get right into deep conversation and sharing.

"You gave me a gift that day, and I bet you have no idea how huge it was for me." I mount my horse, glad for the feeling of his familiar body under me.

"A gift?"

"Yeah. You shared with me some really hard things that day. Do you mind me bringing them up?"

"Not at all."

"You shared that you grew up feeling ashamed of your house and your shoes and your clothes and the fact that you were poor." I check to make sure it's not heavy on her.

Her eyes are still bright and blinking, and she mounts her horse. "It was right after your father died. Do you remember the owl that flushed right in front of us? I just got goose bumps thinking about it." Goose bumps are her litmus test for truth.

Mine, tears. My eyes well up. I know she's saying it was a visit from my father. I could use one of those right about now. "It was a great horned owl. Right in the middle of the day."

"You don't see that very often," she adds.

I know to defer to native Montanans when they bust out a comment like that. But she's not the sort to try to lord it over you.

We head up the ridge, silent for a while, our horses a little frisky, leaving their herd so close to feeding time. What's not spoken between us on these trail rides together is usually what we remember. She's that kind of friend.

Finally I say, "And do you remember the shame that I shared with you?"

"Yes I do. It was one of the saddest things I've ever heard. You said that you'd always felt ashamed around people who'd struggled their whole lives financially because you'd grown up with all sorts of fancy things and fancy trips and fancy schools. And you didn't feel like you were allowed to complain or feel bad inside because of it."

I keep it to myself that I felt bad inside a lot, back in the days when I was supposedly so lucky. "I remember being scared you were going to turn around and gallop home without me. It was a big deal for me that you didn't judge me. That's what I want to thank you for."

"Why would I? You didn't judge me when I told you about my childhood. We were sharing. Honestly. Plus, you were giving me a gift by sharing your story. It was an opportunity for me not to be small-minded. And a chance to climb into someone else's world. Because when you're a kid—and even when you're an adult—you think that other people have it better than you. Especially rich people." She points at a white-tailed deer and smiles like she recognizes an old friend. "And just because you have fancy things doesn't mean your problems aren't real. Rich people can be poor in their own way."

This woman makes the world a better place. She lives on ground few people dare to even visit. She lives in love. She knows her true nature. She is as close to being free as I've seen in a human being. "Thank you for understanding," I say, watching as the deer realizes we're safe and goes back to foraging in the brush.

She leads us into a stand of ponderosa pines, bushwhacking off trail and up a sharp incline. She is fearless. I'm wondering if poverty does that to a person. I'm not sure fearlessness has anything to do with privilege.

Then she turns around and faces me and we stop. "It's hard when you feel different from the people and places around you. It's why I don't judge people. It's why I love horses. They're totally in the present. They've taught me so much about the freedom in that. And freedom from judgment especially is a good thing."

I want to share with her about my husband and the philosophy I'm trying to live out, but maybe it's better to think about judgment all on its own. Because it's judgment that trips me up in my low moments. "I try not to judge people, too," I say. "Even though I'm not always successful. But I try hard not to because I've always had a pretty loud, aggressive, mean judge in my head that likes to sit around all day banging her gavel in my face. So I'm sensitive to judges. I actually call her My Evil Twin Sister Sheila."

She laughs. "I used to have that judge. The horses helped me to let go of her. We're our own worst judges, I feel."

"I know. I've been thinking a lot about judges lately. And freedom. And true nature. Living in the moment. I love the natural world of Montana. It's like it requires us to be in the moment. It's so beautiful and dangerous and raw. Especially on a horse. With you." I move my horse up next to her as the woods open to a grassy field, an old dilapidated barn shining orange in the low sun. An old tangle of barbed wire and a rusted-out tractor, like people left in the night and nobody noticed. Just one of those moments.

She leans over on her Arabian's neck and strokes his mane. "Isn't it a beautiful thing that we came from such opposite worlds, and we are such dear friends? I don't judge you. You don't judge me. Because we meet here." She holds her hand to her heart. People who deal in the soul don't see fences.

"On the same trail." I'm crying now, playing with my horse's mane. "My father used to say, 'People are the same everywhere.'"

"Where you come from has nothing to do with how lovable you are, Laura."

Lovability. And its enemy, shame. I came here to be light and grateful, yet intuitively, my friend has brought me to the altar of my pain. To my knees. She has named my worst fear this summer: that my husband truly finds me no longer lovable.

I want to tell her about my husband. About how unlovable I feel. That he has deemed me so. Instead, for now I say, "I think that was the exact moment I felt at home in myself, that day on the trail. And like a true Montanan. Thank you." I reach out my hand to hers and hold it a bit long for simple thanks.

She grips it hard.

That grip brings me happiness. Not just a step out of suffering, but real happiness. When the lid to the heart opens wide and you fly a little.

Later, back at the barn, I thank her for the trail ride, and, she knows, for the happiness, too. And I stare into my horse's eye for a long time before I leave for home.

But it's a fleeting pleasure. Only lasts a few miles of country road. It's like my windshield is jeering at me—the standard Montana rock-pocked, spiderwebbed fractures, like the state of my marriage. And by the time I get to my driveway, I have to park at the mailboxes in the meadow for a while, trying to talk myself down off the cliff of massive suffering.

Because this part is driving me crazy: it's like watching someone drown when you know where the life preservers are. (I know, I know—*Codependent No More*. I've read the book.) But something deep inside me doesn't really buy that you can't significantly help someone by insisting that they go into some form of intensive, professional self-help.

Yet a deeper, wiser, horse-spun place inside me knows that people have to come to things on their own. If it's going to last. If it's going to be truly authentic and not just a compliant act; a lie. I don't want a yes-man. Obedient to me in all things—on the outside. Living the "I'm a good boy" myth. I don't want to be in a position where I'm the one deeming anybody good or bad. Bottom line: I know what happens to good boys. They go bad. I don't want a good boy, anyway. I want an equal partner. Who is dedicated to himself. And me.

For a minute I feel okay. I've talked sense into myself. I'm almost in my Italy state of mind.

But here's where I snag: it's not just him. It's our whole family that he's taking with him into that stormy sea.

My God. What's going to happen to us? (Panic.)

I sit in my truck, preparing to freak out. I start to picture myself alone, midwinter, my kids "at their dad's" like you hear uttered over and over again on the school playground.

That is not happening to me! That is not going to be my kids' childhoods! And what if I do end up alone? Who will I ever find in the middle of bumble-fuck Montana? I'm not young and hot anymore. Oh my God, I'm going to die alone! Lose the house. Live in some shitty little apartment in town. Be forced to sell my horse. Drive an old rusty Subaru. And he'll marry someone . . . rich. That he met at a party after a golf tournament. And the kids will like her better. Because she'll have stuff like TVs in the car, and doughnuts for breakfast. And she won't make them eat their carrots! Or feed the dog. And she'll have great hair. My daughter will want to braid her hair. My son will like her soft collagen-filled kisses.

The Beast—it starts to roar and rage and tear off its shackles inside me. An old beast I thought I'd slain. It terrifies me that I haven't.

And so, like a fool, I go to the place I did after my father died and I drink too much red wine after everyone's asleep, and bawl my eyes out in my office looking at old photos. And regret it the next morning.

Lying in bed, this is when The Beast surfaces—not only unaffected by hangovers, but seemingly aroused by them. My Evil Twin Sister Sheila that I told my horsewoman friend about last night on the trail. Only Sheila is an old "friend." Maybe the oldest "friend" I've got. Maybe you know her. (Please forgive me if your name is Sheila. I don't honestly know how her name came to be thus.)

Apparently the planets of Hell that live inside me were aligned just so the night before, and tah-dah—regardless of therapy, she's managed to ride in on her broomstick like Samantha's brunette doppelgänger, Serena on *Bewitched*. And this morning, Sheila is as loud as she was years ago.

You idiot! You can't afford to drink too much. You can't afford to be hungover! You can't afford any strikes against you. Let him be the fuckup. Not you! Now get your ass out of bed, go downstairs, and make bacon! I'd throw in some fresh biscuits if you know what's good for yourself.

Sheila knows one thing if she knows anything about me at all: I have abandonment issues. And I lie there wondering how much of my current predicament I've created to self-prophesy my worst fear. I hate that thought. It's like people who say they've given themselves cancer. Sheila's spent years telling me that if I got cancer, I'd deserve it.

Bacon and biscuits or not, he sleeps until eleven. I go up to our room finally to see if he's alive, and he belts out a huge brain-rattling, uvula tsunami of a snort. It wakes him. He says something pissy about me waking him up, and sits on the side of the bed.

I take a shower, and when I come out, I see him outside in the driveway putting his golf clubs lovingly and carefully into the back of his truck.

I resist the urge to run out and demand that he stay with us. *It's a weekend. We'll take a hike in Glacier National Park. We'll harvest the Swiss chard we planted on Mother's Day. Our purple potatoes. And we have beans!*

But I just slowly dry myself off, feel the brush as it drags down my scalp. Feel the silk from the loose pajama bottoms I put back on. Because hell, he's not going to be around. I can lounge with my kids and look like whatever I want to look like.

I hear his truck pull out of the driveway.

Downstairs, the kids are watching cartoons. They both

chime, "Dad's playing golf! He said to tell you," like they're truly happy for him. I'm proud that they don't have abandonment issues. Yet.

And after a day of sitting in a muggy screened porch huddling next to a citronella candle along with every mosquito ever created because the door to our screened porch has been broken for seven years—playing two games of Monopoly until my kids and I are not only stealing money from the bank, but throwing it at each other, he calls and says he's done with golf. He's going to the farmers' market. My territory.

I tell him we'd planned to go, too. We need tomato starts. My comment is as much about the future as it is about tomatoes. I saw him watering our plum tree the other day. He's got some future in him. Doesn't he?

"We could meet you there," I say. Five scared little words.

"Oh," he says. He doesn't sound like he wants to share the farmers' market. "Maybe I'll just go to the lake."

I want him to go to a lake . . . in Australia.

I want him to shake his head like a dog emerging from a lake and say, *Yeah. This was a stupid idea. I fucked up. I love you. This is precious, this life we have. And the Fourth of July is coming up. You love the Fourth of July. It was your father's favorite holiday, and it brings up all those memories. We'll go to the parade and we'll love each other and I'll look at you and love you like I've never looked at you and loved you before. We'll be okay. We'll grow old together and we'll travel the world like we said when we were twenty and we'll go to Italy and I'll sit with your Italian father and I'll learn about nails and family stamps. And work you can hold in your hand. And how husbands stay in love with their wives by caring for their own souls first.*

I want him to swipe tears out of his eyes with both of his thumbs.

The Supercool Wife

July.

There are no accidents. I have to believe this once and for all. Now is my chance.

It is no accident, then, that I have a friend whose husband has just opened up a helicopter school. Right down the street from our house, as the crow flies. As you may recall, my husband has been fantasizing about flying helicopters since I met him, twenty years ago.

I leak the info to him via e-mail, like a derelict buddy—like the girl who he met at the keg party twenty years ago.

"Dude—have you heard about the helicopter school that just opened? It's my friend's husband. They're doing a helicopter expo this weekend at the corner of the highway and Route 40. There'll be a four-seater there . . . plus the little Schweizers.

Remember that dream you had a long time ago—about leading helicopter skiing trips into the Rockies??? Well, here we are! I say GO FOR IT!"

And you wait for the e-mail back telling you that he thinks that might be his ticket. Flying helicopters. Professionally. Or even just as a hobby. You'll suggest he strap the drum set he bought and never set up to this imminent helicopter life. Land somewhere and beat the shit out of it.

Instead I get an e-mail from him saying he's moving out. His friend bought a house in town. He's going to live in it "until we sort things out." I sit, cluster-fucked in my office, staring at my computer screen, trying to process this.

I hear the epiphanous voice. Only now it says: *Trust me. Go slowly.*

I sit with another chosen friend on her front porch, a woman who has lost two husbands—one to a logging accident, the other to alcohol—and she tells me, "You can't panic. There's nothing there for you if you do."

"I know. But I'm also a powerful woman, right? I can steer, at least. I can send inspirational e-mails about helicopters and adventures and therapists . . . can't I? I can believe in miracles. I'm just not sure I can believe in my husband."

"Why don't you focus on steering you right now."

"What if it's another woman?" I whimper, knowing I'm going against my own philosophy.

"You can't go there," she says, stern. "There is absolutely no good in going there."

I try to let her words soothe the sore that keeps wanting to open. "I just wish he'd go to therapy."

"This is his work to do, Laura," she says almost sharply, like mind your own business. She's been in Al-Anon for years, and she knows all about what's her business and what's not. Which is why I've chosen to share with her what's going on with my husband. She has the skills to help me navigate this in a way even some of my closest loved ones do not.

Still, I can't resist e-mailing him a letter that tells him I love him and I believe in him and I believe he needs guidance and I know of a great therapist. I give him the name and phone number. It's a risk I'm willing to take. But it's his call to make—not mine. I risk it anyway and end the e-mail with: "Your soul is calling out for a major step toward self-care."

"Maybe so," he e-mails back. But nothing about the therapist.

I tell my therapist that he wants to get a place in town.

She rolls her eyes. She's seen nasty divorces, and apparently it all starts with a guy getting an apartment in town. "Can't you suggest that he go on a personal trip for a while instead?"

"I have. He says he can't afford to take the time off from work. He says it's too expensive. What else can I do? I feel so helpless just riding this out."

She reaches into a file and pulls out a sheet. "Make no demands. But do give him this. Take a minute to read it through right now."

It's from Divorce.com. It's a list of all the things a couple has to decide in setting up a responsible separation. Things like, Who can use which credit cards and If you've been at my house, you must write it down on a whiteboard, and that's only if I've given you the keys.

"We don't even own keys to our house!"

This list freaks me out. Are we really here? Isn't there a bunch of way worse stuff couples go through before they have to answer these questions? I've never even thrown a plate at him! Or packed a suitcase and left for the weekend in a huff. I've never even told him I hated him. I don't hate him. I love him. (I might have called him an asshole a few times, but doesn't everybody resort to that?)

"I believe there is so much more room for possibility," I tell her. "I feel that he hasn't even really tried to go to bat for our marriage. He's just put me into this shitty soup that constitutes his pain, and I don't belong there! I'm the fall guy. So he doesn't have to deal with his shit!"

"Give him the list. Just ask him to read it. That's all." I love this woman. She's got a plan. Her fingers so neatly folded in her lap.

"Truthfully, in the past few years I guess I've sort of suspected that things would have to get worse before they got better," I say. "But divorce was never on the map; not in my mind. And I don't think in his, either."

"Just show him that list of things he'll have to consider if he wants to separate in a responsible way. It's a strategy." She winks.

Aha. Strategy. She wants me to scare the living shit out of him. My Evil Twin Sister Sheila is turned on by strategy. I hear her groan in ecstasy and it makes me think twice. "But isn't that sort of playing a game? I don't like games."

"No. Not necessarily. It's just a strategy for how to handle what he's put on the table. He wants a separation. You believe he's a responsible man. Well, here's how to have a responsible separation. If that's what he wants. Show him the list. The strategy, in this case, is to have the truth come from a reputable divorce website, and not come from you." She raises her eyebrow.

"So he can't blame me. So he can't play victim. It's his idea to move out in the first place."

"That's right. If he wants to move out, this is what responsibility is going to look like. The strategy is not for everybody. But I believe it's a good one for you."

I fold the list and put it in my purse. "When do I give it to him?"

"You'll know."

The list feels like it's going to burn a hole through my purse and land on the floor, smoking. *What's this?* he'll say, burning his fingers. Cursing me for carrying around such dangerous cargo. I decide that it's not to be used lightly.

That night we sit together while the kids do their homework in the next room.

"Did you get my e-mail?" he says.

"Yeah. You mean the one about . . . the apartment in town?"

"Yeah."

"I think it's a dire mistake." I swallow and hold back the waterfall of words and emotions that want to come spilling out. But they come out anyway. "I know you say we can't afford it. But I really think you should take a trip. Find a cheap flight to Baja. Camp on the beach. Do some diving. Get inspired. Hell, drive down there if it's cheaper. Spend a few months there. Live off of ramen and fish you catch. That's ultimately so much less expensive than breaking two kids' hearts, and mine, too, just because you say you know what'll happen—you'll go and never come back. How can you be so sure? You might find your center again. You're derailed right now and you're blaming it on me. And I don't buy any of it. Go on a personal walkabout like the Aborigines."

He shakes his head.

Oh, the costs he's not considering. So I bring in my trump card. And it's not the list. It's way cooler for now. It's helicopters.

"Fine, then. Go and never come back," I say. "But in the meantime, go fly helicopters. It's one of your dreams! What are the chances of there being a helicopter school in this little town, much less in the entire state of Montana?! It's too perfect! Did you get my e-mail? They're doing an expo this weekend. You could get your license and then start a heli-skiing outfit. Something actually financially viable in a rural mountain town! It's got your name written all over it! You'd be getting paid for doing something you love! And maybe, since they're friends, they'd let you have a scholarship of some sort. Or barter for firewood or something. Maybe they need a good salesman and you can work for lessons and flight time. You could be a tremendous asset to them at this stage of the game!"

For a moment his eyes angle far to one side like he's seeing it all before him, his very own heli-skiing business in the Rocky Mountains. It looks like there's a molecule of hope that he's going to climb out of his world of hurt. Finally make one of his old dreams come true.

I try to keep my cool. But God, do I want to beg. Opportunities like this just don't come along in our little town. I think about the house. The kids. I swallow and say, "I could sell my horse. To free up a little cash. It's not much. But it could help with groceries. I could give up novel-writing for a few years and do only magazine freelance."

"It's not like we're that destitute," he says, like I've insulted him. Then he looks at me with something not at all like gratitude in his eyes. "No. I know what I need to do. My buddy has a house in town, and he'd let me stay in it for free. This is the way my life's always been. I go along and everything's fine . . . and then it starts to get all fucked up . . . and then I just need to go somewhere alone and bleed. Sting and burn."

I'm speechless. It's like he's been planning this all along. I wouldn't have minded a memo, before I took my marriage vows. I want to say, *So just how long does this stinging and burning . . . this bleeding—last?*

I think about the sting and burn from the LIST and eye my purse. This is not the time. I sit there shaking my head. Breathing.

Wishing I was in Italy eating figs with my Italian father on the terrace. Twenty-some-odd years ago. Or even a few weeks ago.

Sheila speaks in my defense for a change: Jesus, I never thought this guy would become so personally irresponsible. A house in town owned by his buddy!? Give me a break! He's got a dartboard or two, some really old scuba equipment, and some shitty couches where the mice in the basement live . . . that his parents bought him in Seattle, when you guys broke up. But then you had to go and get back together with him.

Yeah, Sheila. That's because I loved him. No one understands the mysteries of what happens in a relationship. It's no one's business anyway, so shut up! You have boundary issues.

Well, I'll remind you that you insisted that he go to a shrink if you were going to get back together. And he did. And he was better than ever! You need to haul this guy's ass to a good shrink!

Sheila—you need to read *Codependent No More*.

Still, as if he's heard her (chances are he's got his own Evil Twin Bum Brother Bob hanging out in his brain, egging him on that suffering doesn't suck) that night, sitting in our kitchen, he says, "Please don't make me go to some shrink."

And I see my opportunity. I see the difference between myself now and myself seventeen years ago when I was the person who made ultimatums and begged and cried. Notice the temporary results from that behavior. Notice the years of resentment that can build up. "Hey—I'm not going to make you do anything. It's physically impossible. Therapy has worked wonders for me. I know of a good therapist if you want his name. He's worked with a few guys in town you know. You could ask them what they think." But I leave it there like a little ticking stopwatch.

And interestingly, he says, "That might be a good idea."

We also agree that we need to sit down, somewhere without the kids, and have a good long "conversation."

I can tell he's planning in that conversation to troubleshoot his bachelor pad in town.

I, instead, have a bit more up my sleeve. And it's very, very hot.

He sleeps on the couch that night. I sleep in our bed. I wake a few times and read through the list. I never thought that my last hope would come from a website called Divorce.com.

I know this man. When he wants something bad enough, he gets it somehow. Here he is, staring one of his biggest dreams in the face, and he's dashing it before he's even explored it. I'm positive that he could make his helicopter dream a reality.

It's like he's given up. Like he wants to sting and burn. Like he never really had those dreams to begin with. Like they were lies. Or even worse, that he's scared of them. And now that one is staring him in the face, he's overwhelmed by it. Like he doesn't really want to be a success.

Who is this man? I don't recognize him. Where's the man in Boston who wanted to spread his wings with the woman he loved and see where they'd take him?

In the wee dark hours, now is the time for my disaffection.

I tightrope dangerously close to choosing sides. And at this moment in my life, I'd choose mine, of course. I've been the one in hot pursuit of my dreams. I may not have gotten my books published, but I've finished many. And I've honed my craft so that it's sharp and ready for action. I have that to put under my pillow every night of my life. I am proud of myself. Even when no one else is. I have my proof. At the end of the day.

What does he have to show for himself?

Did I marry a weak man? A loser? A person destined for stinging and burning? Who questions even his own capacity to love?

My father's one question to him when we announced our engagement was: "Can you hold down a job?" It was funny to us then, so brimming with belief in our futures.

I can honestly say that all my dreams have been real destinations. Weren't his?

I feel duped. I thought we were equals. Grounded in our love and dreams. But were we, instead, like the wax bride and groom standing atop the small frosting-coated circle of wedding cake, supported by pedestals, destined to one day fall? And not necessarily together? Aloft in myth and not grounded in reality. And then as the years stacked up, were we the shadow of James Joyce's prophecy when he wrote in *Ulysses*: "They discovered to their vast discomfiture that their idol had feet of clay, after placing him upon a pedestal"?

I'm thinking about discomfiture. Were we to each other then, merely idols? Only to find years later that we were like the statue that the Babylonian king Nebuchadnezzar saw in his dream:

though its head was made of gold, its feet were made "part of iron, part of clay."

I think of the time I asked my husband to pose like *David*. Maybe the moment I did that, I set us up for a fall. A big one.

God. I feel like puking.

It's not lost on me tonight, lying alone in the dark, that Nebuchadnezzar's statue, with its golden head, was shattered and destroyed by being struck on the feet—its weakest point. Maybe our hidden weakness was simply that we believed we were golden. Different. Special. What idiots. Or as my grandmother would say, "What lost lambs."

In our defense, we didn't have a bride and groom on top of our wedding cake. We didn't have those Doric columns holding us up. We didn't believe that it was the Institution of Marriage and society's backing of it that would be our support. We, as individuals and together, were going to be our support.

But were we up there anyway, in that sticky little circle? Did we think our dreams wouldn't come true without it?

What a sham. No wonder most married people get hitched when they're in their twenties. Now I understand why so many older couples get married barefoot on a beach. No cake at all. Lots of dancing and rum.

The most poisonous ingredient in our wedding cake, then, was this: liquid gold. That the strength of our union was not just our love, or our commitment to our individuality . . . or even a sideways belief in the myths of marriage . . . but a much more dangerous myth. The myth that being golden came with promises. The biggest one: we would be successful in our careers. And that success would have us and hold us till death did we part. That's the cyanide pill that too damn many married people carry around in their pocket, perchance WWIII breaks out. And by the time you hit your forties . . . usually, in one way or another, it has.

I see it clearly, lying here in my bed: my husband popped that pill when his job started failing; popped it and jumped. Did I stay up there until my father died and my own career seemed impossible? And then jump? Thinking I'd find him?

I didn't find him, though.

I guess I had to find myself. That's what I had to celebrate in Italy.

And where is he now? Where are we? Where am I? Am I back up on top, and he below, face-first in frosting, so he can play victim to me? How much of our marriage is based on who the fallen one is? I hate to think.

I'm sick with all this rise and fall. I want an equal partner. I want to love and be loved for better and worse and everything in between.

"How did we get here? I'm ashamed of us. It's not who we were supposed to be." I catch myself saying it out loud to myself, like the moon shadows on the lawn can tell me. Is it my fault? Have I not tended the garden that is him? Is this really about dashed dreams? Career failure? Or is it possible to really fall out of a love like ours? Is our love so susceptible?

I guess I'm a fool. Because I always thought that love, our love at least, was bigger than money or work or pride. From that first moment we looked into each other's eyes, I always felt like we were different. Maybe I was wrong.

My mind chugs along like the freight trains in the distance of my childhood bedroom.

Is this payback for not being a success in the way he thought I'd be? Is his love for me, after all, conditional? That thought flattens me farther into the bedsheets.

Are my faults responsible for his disaffection? Are they so unforgivable? Is the answer to that question important if I've taken ownership of my shortcomings? How badly does he need to make me wrong? I don't walk around making him wrong, even when he does his best to hurt me.

Isn't the fact that I'm my own worst judge good for something? That I know that I was supposed to have so much to be proud of at this point in my life. And instead, have lived so long suffocating in shame?

I pull up the covers high around my neck and take three deep breaths. Picture my horsewoman friend sitting on her Arabian horse, living in the moment as he has taught her to do. The judge exiled. The shame disemboweled.

But it's too much; the shame is thick tonight. Viscous like infection. Shame that my husband doesn't want to be with me. Shame that my books aren't published. Shame that, for all our dreaming, we've landed here in a place of relative despair.

Success. Shame. What is it to be a successful adult? A successful married person? How has shame played a role in our marriage? Is it possible that even though we left our social class behind, we still let it somehow define us? Because here we are, both of us feeling like failures, defining our sense of success by the very principles that we rebelled against. Shouldn't success be about love? Who we love and how we love and who loves us? Shouldn't this be the time when we wrap ourselves in each other's arms and be a force in the storm?

This is the sort of thinking haunting rooms all over the world right now. Men and women everywhere.

And I can see why I've tried to leave it behind. It's voracious. Rips and gnaws and devours. Like there's a cruel marionetter in a room somewhere, laughing his ass off, leaning back in his chair, stuffed and burping, his work done, his dastardly fingers folded neatly on his belly. If I don't go to sleep and stop this madness immediately, he and Sheila are going to have masochistic, exhibitionist, crazy sex tonight right here amid the moon shadows, and force me to watch from my window seat.

Trust me. Go back to sleep.

The God of the Fourth of July

Fourth of July weekend.

The Fourth of July is a big holiday in our family. Parades, fried chicken, corn on the cob, home fireworks, and then the big fireworks show across the road in a field. Our kids bring sleeping bags and lie on top of the truck while we tailgate on the back and oooh and aah. We've done it this way for years.

It's also my hardest holiday without my father, who used to drive his E Type Jaguar convertible in the parade back home in Chicago. He finally got himself his own dream car. He'd wave, tip his hat, and shift gears—all in a graceful hand ballet. The crowd loved him, begging him to "light it up." This silver-haired gentleman in his hot rod.

To my father, the Fourth of July was about more than patriotism, even though he'd sing along weepy-eyed to the choir from the local naval base, and had marching-band music in his car cassette player the day he had his stroke. It was about small towns and family picnics and bedazzlement. It was the holiday when our affluent town came together, public and private sectors, and it brought out something in him that I knew came straight from his childhood. He recognized himself on that day.And I recognized that part of him, too. It was a day to be simple. Humble. Grateful. And proud, too. Main Street USA proud.

But throw that Jaguar into the mix, and the Fourth of July became something even more poignant to him: it became about what could happen in the United States of America to a little boy from Granite City, Illinois.

Anyone who knew him absolutely loved that he got to be that little boy, all grown up, in that beauty of a car.

I got to ride with him in the parade once. It's the memory I think of whenever I'm trying to go to a happy place.

But still, on the actual Fourth of July, it's the memory that has me all day blinking back tears.

My husband knows darn well that I still need a fair amount of hand-holding on the Fourth of July. We've agreed to keep it light through the holiday and be a family. But we've also agreed to have a conversation that afternoon of the third just to touch base with the new news of him moving out. At four o'clock. I've made arrangements for the kids to be at friends' houses.

I've been to therapy and I have my spiel down. It's airy and spacious. Mature and self-responsible. I'm going to talk about how all relationships need breaks. This is a good and healthy thing. I believe in his gut's call to carve some time for himself—a personal walkabout. I've come to the end of our relationship being as it's been, too. I want to create something that works for us and our family. We've committed to being a family, and we need to create something that works.

Him moving into town doesn't work for me. Moving into town is so fraught. So dangerous to our children and the messages they'll get. His line "They'll want me to be happy" to me is a massive and lethal rationalization. Of course he's told himself that. How else could he possibly justify such an absurd slap in their faces? His happiness over theirs. Expecting them to want that.

Sure, they might pretend they understand for approval's sake, but he'll be carving a wound in them that will grow and fester and infect their lives. Our daughter, just coming into adolescence. Our son, too small to understand why Daddy is choosing something else besides him.

I'll suggest one more time that he go somewhere out of town by himself for a while. Or better yet, to get to the bottom of his pain in-house. Build a room of his own over the garage. A Man Cave. Set up his drums. Get therapy. Take solo, planned, weekend trips. But with an itinerary they can anticipate and trust he'll abide by. Limit his time with family, but be clear about when that is. And what that looks like to us. I'm all ready. It's everything I can do to stay calm. To keep my Italy mind.

An hour late, at five o'clock, he calls and says he can't make our appointment. He's going to a party up at the private golf club—to "network with a potential employer. It's my truth," he says.

I taught him that line and I'm regretting it. It was meant for emoting. Not justifying irresponsibility.

I ask him if he's planning on coming home tonight.

He says, "Probably not."

I ask him if he's planning on coming to the Fourth of July parade tomorrow.

He says, "No."

I ask him if he's planning on joining us for the rest of the Fourth—the BBQ, the fireworks.

"Sure," he says, like he'd never in his right mind miss that. Of course he'll be there.

I ask him what time he can commit to.

He says, "Two o'clock."

I tell him he's going to have to explain that to the kids himself.

I pass the phone to our daughter. I can see her face sucking up this news, pretending to watch the TV with half an eye. TV is something she can count on.

I hear his voice distantly telling her, and then our son, that he needs to do this for work.

Both kids say it's okay. They "understand," they say.

And then they proceed to scream at each other, torture each other, physically attack each other the whole night—through badminton games and backgammon, even a TV movie. They want their daddy.

The next day, at noon, he calls my cell phone. "Happy Fourth!" he says like everything's peachy. "What are you guys doing?"

"We just got to the parade."

"I thought we were meeting around noon at home," he says.

Home, he says. *Home.*

"No. We said two o'clock."

"Oh. Well, I think I'll go to the lake and hang out. Why don't you meet me there with the kids and we can swim and then go buy fireworks."

"I'll call you on our way back from the parade. Three-ish. The traffic is crazy."

"Okay—three-ish. Maybe I'll just go and buy some fireworks on my own, and meet you at home," he says.

Home. I flash to the other day when he was watering a plum tree he'd threatened to pull out and replace. We planted that plum tree on my thirty-fifth birthday. Home.

"The kids would love to buy fireworks with you. Why don't I just call you on your cell when we're close to town, and you can meet us at the fireworks stand."

"Okay."

Lately, he rarely answers his cell phone so I push it and say, "Keep your phone near you around three, okay?"

"Okay," he says, a little peeved. He doesn't like to be pegged. I don't like to peg, necessarily. But currently he needs some pegging. And it's the Fourth of July!

The kids stand at the sidewalk's edge scrambling for candy and waving flags, while I stand in the back with the taller people. Families. Couples. It's everything I can do not to feel lonely and really sorry for myself. All the traditions I'm missing back in my

Chicago suburb where I know so many people. Where I'd never be alone on the Fourth of July.

Proudly, I control the tears so that they pool just at the edge of my eyes and lacquer my eyelashes to my sunglasses. But they do not spill. As far as anyone knows, I am a happy mother at a parade with her children, her husband just up the street standing in line for hot dogs and Cokes.

"What time are we going to see Dad?" my son asks later, a bag full of candy in his hand. His red, white, and blue Cubs shirt drenched by the fire trucks.

"I told him I'd call him at three. We're going to meet him in town and buy fireworks with him."

He's very mathematical. "That's in ten minutes. It takes forty minutes to get back home. So we'll see him in fifty minutes. That's just under an hour. And then we can buy fireworks with him! He knows just which ones to get. Yippee!"

I call him at three. He doesn't answer. I try him five minutes later. Ten. Fifteen. He's blowing us off.

Honestly, I can't believe he'd miss a major holiday. And it means one thing: he's much further gone than I'd imagined.

It may sound strange, but if you've loved someone for a long time, maybe you'll understand this: I feel sad for him. His world of hurt is a wildly painful place if it's got him so by the throat that he's imprisoned there on a big family holiday.

It reminds me of that Robin Williams movie when he goes searching for his dead wife in the depths of Hell. It's not lost on me that the scenes of Heaven in that movie were filmed ten miles away from where I drive now: Glacier National Park. It gives me a little boost. I'm not in Hell. I'm here, in the mountains of Montana—a mother, with her amazing children, on the Fourth of July.

And there's a fireworks stand. I say, "Well, should we get some anyway? I'll bet the man behind the counter can tell us just which ones are the best."

"No. I want to wait for Dad," my son says, sad. "Call him again."

I do. He doesn't answer.

We go home, thinking maybe he'll be there, waiting for us.

He's not. We call him again. He doesn't answer.

We spend the next few hours playing a dice game called Farkle on the screened porch. My daughter tries him ten times on her cell phone. He doesn't answer.

My son says, "Dad's missing Fourth of July."

"How do you feel about that?" I say, my months of therapy kicking in.

"I feel like that sucks," he says. He's eight. Out of the mouths of babes.

"C'mon. Let's go buy fireworks," I say. "What are your favorites?"

His eyes light up but not totally. "The ones with the parachute guys."

At four o'clock, on our way out the door, my husband calls. "I thought you said you were going to call," he says, strangely sharp.

"I did call. Over and over. You didn't answer."

"Well, I hope you remembered that I'm helping my friend deliver his ice sculpture to the big party in town at four-fifteen."

God, do I want to rip him a new one. But I say calmly, "That's fine. We're running out to get fireworks. We've got food. We'll plan to eat around six-thirty."

"Well, don't wait for me."

My heart flat-out bounces into the dusty corner of our breezeway where I stand with the kids listening to the echo of those words; looking at me with those big orphan eyes I've seen in puzzles and on greeting cards. Not on my handsome, full-cheeked, sunny children!

"What?!" I say with venom.

"I'll call you right back," he says and hangs up.

He doesn't call back.

After we buy fireworks, we stop by a friend's who gives my kids Jell-O pie and takes me for a walk down to the river. Her husband asked for a divorce a few years back. Then he had a change of heart. Now he's here, blowing off expensive fireworks before it's dark.

"Do you think it's a woman?" she says.

"I doubt it. He's too fucked in the head right now to have another woman involved."

"There's some sort of tug that's making him act like this."

"It's money. He's lost his pride because he feels like a failure in his career." I'm not crying for some reason. I feel strong standing there in the mud, swatting mosquitoes.

We leave an hour later because we're sure he's back home. Ice sculpture delivered. Extra guilt fireworks in hand. We can at least redeem the last part of the holiday—the best part, as far as the kids are concerned—the fireworks.

But he's not there. There're no messages on my cell phone. On our home phone. On my daughter's cell phone.

We eat dinner and play more Farkle until it gets dark.

Then I pretend that I know what I'm doing and set off fireworks for the first time in my life. Big fireworks with skulls and devils and whores on their packages. With names like Dragon Farts and Sexual Sister and The Baditude Death Stalker.

It's hard not to flash on this, my father's beloved holiday: riding in his red convertible in the parade, waving flags, Dixieland jazz and Bloody Marys at a party afterward full of family friends in fashionable red, white, and blue starched clothes, tanned; pool-hopping until dark—a huge symphony playing John Philip Sousa under the stars and lightning bugs . . . lying on old plaid football blankets. And then the fireworks . . . my father tearing up as the military band sings, "O beautiful for spacious skies . . ." Holding his hand and tearing up, too. Feeling so safe and patriotic.

Now I'm under those spacious skies, so far away from Chicago, in Montana, lighting a fuse attached to something called Ass Kickin' Bone Crusher . . . running, ducking, alone. Feeling incredibly sorry for myself and hating that, too. That I've succumbed to self-pity.

But the kids are huddled in sleeping bags on the front lawn, cheering. And I admit, it feels sort of good. I get to be the hero with the pyromania problem for once. Yeah—it feels good. At least, with every light of those fuses, and every upward flare and every boom and every cascade, I forget about what's happening. I oooh. I aah.

But then it's quiet again. And I sigh and hear, *Go slowly. Trust.* Maybe the God of Fourth of July and my Italy voice are one and the same. And I breathe in everything I've ever believed and known and sought about God, and receive a level of peace that is nothing like explosive.

Then I think I hear him coming up the driveway and suddenly, I don't want him here. I want to be the hero. I want to drive them to the field across the road for the big display. Send them crawling up to the truck roof with blankets. I want to create this night for them. And I want the credit.

But I don't have to worry. False alarm.

We have our patriotic moment in the field. My children atop my truck. Me leaning against it . . . trying to muster that peace again, but without much success, especially with the heart-lurching boom of the fireworks. Mostly, I'm trying not to notice the other, grander fireworks display down the valley—where the big party is every year, where he dropped off the ice sculpture. And where he most assuredly is standing, ooohing and aahing—and I just wonder how he can possibly live with himself knowing his kids are without him at this moment in his life. In their lives. In mine.

When we get home, we crawl into bed together—in my

son's queen-sized bed. "Well, Dad missed the Fourth of July," he says, sad.

That's not all he'll be missing, I'm thinking.

Maybe he's out there somewhere thinking, *They're happy for me because I'm choosing my happiness. My truth. This is a good example to set.*

Yeah, right.

I stay with them until they're asleep. Then I lock the doors. I never lock the doors when he's home. We live in the country. But it feels safer that way, and I'm the parent here. They're under my charge. But then I realize we don't have keys. I don't want him to think I've locked him out. That's not what I'm doing with this strategy. So I have to choose: our safety, or his feelings.

There are endless possibilities in this for resentment to erupt.

I figure if he wants in badly enough, he'll find a way. I leave a few of the downstairs windows open, just in case he actually chooses *our* feelings.

Trust me. Go to sleep.

I do.

When I wake up, I hear snoring and I go to my son's bed and my husband is asleep in there with the kids.

He sleeps until eleven. Again. But we're not taking sides, remember? We're really trying not to take sides, you and me. We're really getting hooked though. Triggered. But we're trying our damnedest not to suffer. Not after yesterday.

I go downstairs and make breakfast. Coffee for one, no two,

no one. Fresh biscuits and bacon and blackberries. For three, no four, no three. Well, four maybe.

He comes down, walks right by me, and joins my daughter on the couch.

"You suck," my son says to him.

"I know. I'm sorry. There's no excuse," he tells them, staring at the Disney movie they're watching. All about a son leaving his father because his father lied to him . . . and his father waking the fuck up and going out in the jungle to find him. *The Wild*, it's called. I look at it and will it to wake my husband the fuck up.

"Tell us about the party," my daughter says, not wanting her father's feet to be made of clay.

He tells them all about it. "It was like the fair was in town. A Ferris wheel and a merry-go-round, and a roller coaster—all those rides you see at the fair. And that famous pop band was there. That one you have on your iPod. And they had piles and piles of the biggest, freshest shrimp you ever saw. And there were all sorts of Hollywood types there. And a retired NFL quarterback, boogying on the dance floor. And the fireworks went on and on—like it was the Olympics or something."

"Better than the ones across the street?" my son asks, sounding gypped.

"Oh, way better. They have a two-million-dollar budget. Two million dollars. And there was a huge air-conditioned tent. With real French doors. Like those there on our screened porch."

Our screened porch. The one he says he's leaving.

"Wow—" They both gaze at him in awe. Like he's just lit off the Olympic fireworks display himself.

"And right after they finished serving dinner, they served breakfast, with bacon and eggs and lox and bagels. Everything." He all but says, *You should have been there,* and I am fuming and I'm not going to hide it. What he did was wrong. How he's behaving now is despicable, I don't care how depressed he is.

I arrive with breakfast for our kids.

"Would you like some coffee?" I say to him, acidly. "Biscuits?" The consonants spark off my tongue, in holiday fashion.

"Nah. I'll get something myself." He doesn't look at me. He knows not to look at me. Otherwise he'd have to see the plain truth. And whether he can't see it, won't see it, or isn't capable of seeing it, I remove myself. I remove my anger. It will only get in the way of how that truth will fester in his heart today, watching Wimbledon on the couch, trying to divert and fascinate our children with his tennis trivia.

"Will you take us to buy fireworks?" they beg him.

"Sure," he says.

I let my anger grind away with the garbage disposal; drain down with the water. Anger is suffering. Especially when it's the kind of anger in defense of my children. But I try like hell to let it go and breathe. My throat is like a clogged drain. I cough instead.

We run into each other at the kitchen sink.

I remember how sad I felt for him yesterday in his personal Hell, and take a little joy in his badly sunburned back. "What do you want to do today?" I say, trying to remain calm. There's no sense in addressing anything difficult right now, with the events of yesterday under all our belts and a whole weekend ahead of us.

"Well." He looks at his feet, clay as they are. "We should probably have that conversation."

"I think that after yesterday, it's very, very important to give the kids a family day. A family weekend. And we can talk on Monday."

He agrees.

And then it gets even weirder.

The three of them are out on the screened porch playing, yes, Farkle, and I come in; lie down on the chaise. I lie there and notice how he's not looking at me. I'm in a pair of linen summer pants and a blousy sheer tunic I bought in Belize. I feel pretty. I've done my hair. I'm wearing jewelry. But he doesn't even acknowledge me.

It hurts. I feel like a fool, and gently I say to them all, "I'm going up to my room to rest for a while. Come get me when you guys go to buy fireworks."

The kids agree.

I go up to my bed and I read this. What I've written here, up to this page, where I am now. I read it and edit it like a novel I've written. But what's the use? What are the chances that I'd ever be brave enough to try to get it published? To think anybody would ever be interested in our story. Or my mind. Or my way of dealing with this crisis. Which clearly isn't working. For either of us, because right now, I feel like I'm going to puke. Right now I am suffering.

I remember my Author's Statement. Is writing my way through this time in my life offering me relief? Or is it making it more painful? I know that pain is a good guide. But I'm sick of it. I want a friendly Sherpa with saffron and magenta scarves who offers me tea, peace flags trailing from his pockets.

I opt instead for a look through my slide show of Italy. Instantly, I'm smiling and humming "O Mio Babbino Caro."

Then there is a sound at the bedroom door. A squeak and a closing and a lock. We lock the door when we're having sex. Only then.

It's strange because I've taken off my clothes. It's muggy and I need to be nude. I usually prefer light clothes, even if it's muggy. But I'm lying there nude.

And he comes in, gets into bed, and he starts kissing me.

"What are you doing?" I say.

"I'm kissing you."

It feels so good to be wanted, but I've got the slide show playing on my thigh and I'm in a weird position in the pillows and he's kissing me. And I'm wondering if I've fallen asleep and am in a dream.

For a moment I can joke because for a moment I feel like everything's going to be okay. "I thought you were leaving me. This is so mixed-message-y."

But I kiss him back and we have sex. Decent sex. Not great. I wonder if this is what good-bye sex is like. Guys can't quite say hello. But they can say good-bye. I hate generalizations about men and women. But this one fits.

Enter: The God of the Fourth of July:

Under the guise of buying fireworks, we go to the stand that just so happens to be at the same intersection of highway where my friend and her husband are holding their helicopter expo.

I hug her and she says they're crazy-busy and totally booked, but somehow, before I can even begin to hope, she has him up flying, her husband saying he'd love to hire a guy like my husband, who's local and a great people person.

I tell him he has no idea how much this could change everything. I try to give him every desperate-wife message I can muster, all in my eyes and in the way I hug him tightly, and I tell him that my husband is miserable. Talking about the worst. I stop there, hoping he gets it.

He says he was miserable, too. Until he started flying helicopters. His face is a ray of light. His smile so toothy. He says, "It's a dream to have your hobby be your job! This isn't work. I spend my day flying people to frozen lakes where no one can get to in winter, seeing moose and bear . . . and then fly home for dinner with my family. You can have all the boats, motorcycles, ski jumps in the world. But this is it for me. I've finally found it."

That's the man I married, I think but don't say. Instead I ask, not kidding in the least, "Can you please hire my husband?" I'm meddling and I'm well aware of it.

He nods. "I'd love to."

"Is flight school insanely expensive?" I ask.

He breaks down the cost and it looks bleak. It's one of those times when I'm just so desperately upset that my writing career isn't successful. Wouldn't it be ridiculously ironic if this book actually does get published and it's my husband's breakdown that actually affords his wildest dreams to come true? I can't even imagine that, at this moment in my life. But it would be worth it if only to help this man that I love. Maybe I'll add to my Author's Statement: "and to provide relief for my husband."

Until then, I figure maybe we could take out another loan.

All I can think about is my children's futures, parents divorced, the easy woman fix he might seek, might have already sought, and having nights alone without them—some other woman who doesn't deserve them, him, putting them to bed, climbing into bed with him, and my heart starts pounding like fireworks are going off. The panic place. *Please,* I want to beg him, *make my husband better! Give him a job! Something he can hold in his hand.*

What are the new words from my Italy voice? I can't remember. *Trust. Me. Trust me. Go back to sleep. Go slowly.*

"Wait till you see the look on his face when he gets back," he says.

I know that it's vital that when my husband gets back with this look on his face, he talk to this man without me around. So I skip out of there with the excuse of grocery shopping, and I stalk corn and potatoes and hamburger meat, jamming my cart down the aisles so people get out of my way like I'm in New York City, whispering to the God of the Fourth of July, "Please. I beg you. Let this be it. Let this be what cures him. Flight. Helicopters. Let him find a way to stay with us. To find a room of his own in the sky. And come back to us happy at the end of the day." His children can understand being left for flight. For a job that brings their father happiness and money . . . and most important, brings him home.

But I realize I am begging; the worst kind of wanting. I think of my therapist's words about creating. I am creating this moment by laying the foundation, and getting out of his way! Still, I want to know:

Who are you? Is yours the voice I heard in Italy? Are you the one telling me to go slowly. To trust and go back to sleep? Is it you I'm "trusting"? Are you God? Are you me? Does it matter if I hear you loud and clear?

I think of my friend's words: "Wait till you see his face when he gets back."

I picture that look on his face all through the grocery store, in the checkout line, on the drive back to the helicopter expo.

And I do see it on his face, the two men standing cross-armed next to each other, looking at the sky. He looks exactly like the guy who sped down those country roads with me in Ohio all those years ago. I'm ecstatic.

We go through another day. Another day where he wants to kiss me. Another night when we're sleeping in the same bed. Through the night. (Have I mentioned that often he sleeps on the couch when he's having a bad night of snoring? Maybe Bette Davis should be my therapist—a woman who said, "The key to a happy marriage is separate bedrooms." I wish we had a Bette Davis house.) He even climbs the ski mountain on his humble mountain bike like old times—before he bought his gross, gassy, loud dirt bike. Maybe I should have known he was in trouble the minute he rode that thing up our driveway a few years ago. The Montana version of a red sports car. Strangely, it coincided with his first bad year at his new job.

Then this morning, I e-mail him. "When can we have our conversation?" I write.

Tonight, he writes back.

In fact, he's driving up the driveway right now. I look like shit because I've been making cookies with our kids and playing lacrosse in the yard. I'm running upstairs to take a shower and what the hell should I wear for this conversation, anyway?

I wish you were here to tell me that my strategy will work. And that I can be this strong.

But I know I must detach from outcome. Go slowly. Trust.

The Conversation

Time stops.

It's helpful to point out here that I've spent the last year and a half, at the noon hour of Wednesday, in therapy. Therapy is not wasted on a forty-one year-old. It's the perfect time to go. Just when you're really sick of all your shit. Just when you don't want to cry another tear over your dead father or your career or anything else for that matter.

So I was the perfect person I needed in there with me for that conversation. I knew just how to talk myself down from his barbs, his defenses, his anger. I reminded myself when to breathe, when to stop-plug the tears, when to detect fear and, most important, bullshit. I had a mantra: *Don't go into persuader mode. Stay in inquiry mode. You are on a fact-finding mission. Also, Try not to cry.*

We went to my husband's office in town. The kids were at

home with a baby-sitter. I wore a dress he screwed me in one time. We sat at opposite ends of the couch. I leaned one elbow on the top of the couch. Casual. Open. Not gonna cry.

Here were some of his real goodies:

"I just don't know if I have anything left for you. I don't care about your writing. I don't care about your childhood wounds. I don't care about spiritual things, like you do."

Don't speak: It would be great if he could take the energy he's putting into telling himself what he hates, and put it into figuring out how he can take responsibility for his own happiness without taking down everything that we've built for the last twenty years. Including our children's happy childhoods.

"I just don't have it in me to work at this anymore," he says.

Do not speak: Work? What "work"? When did he do "work"? Is showing up for dinner and occasionally cooking and occasionally doing laundry and the dishes "work"? Hunting for the Christmas tree? Thanksgiving dinner around the table with our wedding china, crystal, and my great-aunt's silver . . . "work"? Building a house that our children play hide-and-seek in, where our animals all have safe soft beds and cool clean water . . . where the hearth is warm all winter and the kitchen alive with smells and good food . . . is that called "work"?

I try to put on the brakes, but I can't seem to stop my mind.

And me? Am I "work"? Is listening to my new idea for a novel "work"? Is walking through my four gardens, domed in honeysuckle and purple clematis and peach roses, "work"?

Does he not understand that what he's talking about is all work. And with little hope for payoff. And much promise of heartbreak.

Then he adds, "We're totally different people. You don't even like skiing. We all want to go skiing every weekend, and you never want to go."

Ouuuuuch! The Ski Button!!! Major button.

Do NOT speak. . . .

But Shit O. Dear. Here it comes.

Don't let it get hold of you. This is spiritual warfare. There are demons and gremlins and devils and Valdemorts and Darth Vaders swarming around us.

Don't cry: I'm sorry. When was the last time you asked me to go skiing? Years ago. I used to try to go with you, but you treated me like shit because I wasn't good enough. You hurt my feelings over and over. And still I rally and I go. And you ignore me the whole time. I don't remember where it was in the marital contract that said I had to ski. I ski plenty. You're an expert skier. You don't even like skiing with people unless they're expert skiers.

And yeah, there are other things to do on a winter snowy day than ski. Like the other things I make happen all winter long like sledding parties and cross-country skiing and dogsledding and horseback riding and snowshoeing—all those things that you never want to do.

But I am letting all this acid wash over me. Lazing my elbow on the couch in my pretty dress; open, not crying.

But The Ski Button is fierce.

Breathe! What about you?! You used to be an instigator. You used to come up with all sorts of fun when we lived in Seattle. You used to climb mountains. What happened to that guy? This is as much of a horse town as it is a ski town. I ask you over and over if you'd like to join me and you say no. Horses are too "unpredictable." At least I make an effort to ski.

"Totally different people"??? My ASS! I think we're so much alike, you can't see yourself anymore. And since when did our entire relationship come down to skiing? Haven't we always been about spirit? It seems to me that it's the same sort of spirit that loves to ski that loves to ride horses, and it seems to me that you are telling yourself a whole pile of bullshit to play victim to me rather than take responsibility for your own happiness and abide by your commitment to your family . . . and most of all LOVE ME! We are the same in spirit. Let's meet there!!!

Which brings me to the next thing I'm not going to say.

Not gonna say this: Speaking of spirit . . . who convinced you to dive the Blue Hole—one of your life's goals? Who made that happen, back in the days when we had dough? Who booked all that snorkeling and all that pristine beach time in places you loved so much you didn't want to leave? Me. Because I know you. It's not about skiing. It's about what's lost in your own heart. And damn it—I love you, by the way.

None of this do I say.

"If you make me go to a therapist, I'll put a bullet in my head," he says, as if he's got that gun in his hand.

But I don't say anything at all. I don't say: *Then why did you say you would before? Just to get me off your back? Therapy would do you wonders! It teaches you how to get out of victim mode. It's so freeing. You learn how to take ownership. You learn how to be responsible instead of running away from your problems. What are you doing to take responsibility? Giving up? Leaving? How far are you willing to run before you start caring for your soul? Can't you see how exhausting it is to run?*

"I know what I need to do. I'm moving out." And then he repeats his favorite line like the worst kind of sick-souled person. "Our kids will understand. They'll want me to be happy."

Here's where I speak. I pull out all the stops.

"That's great. If you want to create two codependents. Two kids who will grow into overly responsible control freaks who end up in fucked-up relationships and eventually, if they're smart, in therapy. Or people-pleasing enablers with abandonment issues, who also end up in fucked-up relationships, and in therapy. That's great if you want them to prize your happiness more than their own. Or just fake it to please you. That's great if you want to send them the message that your happiness is more important than theirs. That's great if you've done everything you can to try to make the family work, to keep it together, to make good on what you committed to when you decided to get married and start a family with me."

I feel myself hauling ass down Persuader Lane. I'm red in the face. I can feel it in my neck. And I switch quickly to inquiry mode. I've practiced this line with my therapist in an emergency phone session two hours prior and I love it. It's true. It's clear. It's straight. It's simple.

"What can we do to give you the distance you need, without damaging our family?" *What can we do* (aligning myself with him) *to give you the distance you need* (acknowledging his need and not getting in his way) *without damaging our family?* (I.e., *If you fuck with our children's happy childhoods, I'll take you down, boy.* But I don't say that.)

"I can move into town."

"What would that look like?" Inquiry mode.

I resist the urge to clasp my purse, because in it is my trump card. I can feel it pulsing, hot, in the Italian leather that just weeks ago hung innocently in a Florentine market—a symbol of my gift to myself. In its little parcel of power, there is the printed-out list. The one given to me by my therapist. A list of all the questions we will have to answer if he moves out. That is, if he indeed wants a responsible separation.

"Well," he continues, "nothing would change, really. I'd come home every night, have dinner with the family, hang out, tuck them in, and go to my place."

What? That's not a responsible separation. That's the most fucked-up thing I've ever heard! I have to hold back laughter here. I have to hold back standing up, slapping him across the face, and laughing so hard at him that I fall over backward, onto the couch, onto my purse with the hot little branding iron inside. I am aware of my sinewy, still-leaning elbow; my open body language. I check to make sure that my dress hasn't hiked up to reveal my ass-girdle, which I threw on at the last second to accentuate what he's saying he wants to leave behind.

I swallow and say, "I'm having a hard time seeing how that would give you the distance you need. I'm having a hard time seeing what that choice will do to our kids."

Then I eye my purse. It's time.

"Here's something my therapist gave me. She deals with the fallout of irresponsible separations all the time." I hand it to him.

"What's this?" he hisses, halfway committing it to his fingers. He takes a quick look. "Oh great. Money. Like you know anything about our finances. I think we both remember what a mess you made of our bills back when you paid them. What do you know about the stacks of shit over there on my desk that I have to deal with every day?"

He points to his desk. "And just how many more millions of dollars do you plan on spending on therapy, anyway?"

"Insurance pays for it, and you know it," I say calmly. How dare he! He's like a boy trying to pick a fight so he can give someone a bloody nose.

"Yeah, well, we still have to pay for some of it."

I don't say: *Well, if you're so stressed out about money, why don't you share our financial situation with me? Why won't you agree to see a financial advisor like I've asked over and over? To help us create a budget? How much do you thrive on living in a world of hurt?*

I know that his relationship with money is based in shame

and guilt. Mine is, too. We've both worked so hard at our careers with so little financial reward. We've both had to lean on our families for financial help and we're both ashamed. So I practice a little empathy and breathe. But it's mean, what he said. Really mean. Deep inside, I know that it's common to get mean when we're functioning on victimhood, rather than self-responsibility. But still. Jeez.

I breathe and swallow. "I would like you to read that list. It gives the questions we'll have to find answers for if you move out."

"Jesus—this is absurd," he says, reading the list. "You don't think it would be more damaging to have some idiotic white-board where I leave messages for the kids on the front door? We don't even have keys to the house!"

I get up and get some water. *Breathe . . . trust . . . let go of outcome.*

"Fuck this! This is ridiculous!" he spouts. "Oh, I get it. I get it. You're using the kids as leverage. You're threatening me with this list. You're going to make me answer all these fucking questions, aren't you?"

"I never said anything about making you do anything. I'm only sharing with you what a psychologist, who deals with the fallout of irresponsible separations every day, shared with me when I asked her what a responsible separation looks like."

He points at the list. "Oh great. Who's allowed to have sex with who?! Is that what this is about? You think I'm interested in another woman?"

I don't say: *A woman without baggage? An expert skier, maybe?*

I do say, "Are you being straight with me? Is there another woman?"

"Absolutely not."

I look into his eyes. I see ire. But I think I see honesty, too.

"Just where exactly is this house you want to move to in town? That's one of the questions on the list. Do our kids go in and out of this house?"

Now he hedges. "Well, it's not really bought yet. My buddy from New York is thinking about buying it."

"So you'd rent it."

"No. We can't afford it."

This is insanity. I want to go back to Italy. I want to pick figs and climb olive trees and stare at David's ass. This is insane and this is sad.

I say, "I want to know what we can commit to now. I'm not talking about next month. I'm talking about right now. You could get hit by a truck tomorrow. What can we do right now to give you the distance you need, without—"

"Would you stop asking that annoying question?! That's all you're doing. Asking questions! What can *you* commit to?"

Fascinating. If I was a therapist. If this wasn't my life.

"What can I commit to?" I say. "Well, I can commit to giving you the distance you need, but only without doing damage to our children. I can commit to supporting you in your path toward happiness. I can commit to holding down our home while you take a personal retreat—a walkabout. If Australia's too expensive, then get in your truck like you talked about, and grab your fishing pole and your bike and go on a road trip. I can commit to helping you create a space in the studio over the garage that would be your home office—your room of one's own where you could go to get some distance. I can commit to encouraging you to take helicopter lessons at our friend's flight school."

"So you're not going to let me have the place in town."

Good God. He's making this easy. "I never said anything about letting or not letting you do anything. I'm just not seeing how that arrangement will give you the distance you need. You're typically asleep by tuck-in time. So to ask yourself to drive into town, to sleep, and then wake up to go to work, in a place that doesn't yet exist for you, right now . . . that doesn't make sense to me. What can we create together in the life that we've worked so hard to set up, within our family and on our property, which won't threaten the kids? That won't feel like abandonment?"

Now he's silent.

I'm, of course, playing dumb. But straight. Of course this is an absurd arrangement. *And what's in it for me? I'm supposed to cook and clean and do everything, and then he waltzes in and out? What's in that for me?* I don't say that. Not yet. That's for when we're laughing about this in ten years, on a beach somewhere in the Caribbean.

"I just need some space."

"I got it. You need some space. You're also a father. And a

husband. And you've created a whole life which requires you in it." Part of me wants to say, *Grow the fuck up. These are problems of privilege. You're lucky you even have a family to play around with. A house to want to leave. A wife not to love. Skiing, my ass. Fuck off. This is a time to practice gratitude. Not to stay out all night, partying your ass off like a twenty-year-old. Grow up!* But instead I say, "Take a vacation. Go somewhere. Take care of yourself."

"I'm not going anywhere. I can't. I've got too much to deal with." He slumps a little like a kid who's gotten a hug in the midst of a tantrum. "I'm afraid I'm going to have a breakdown. I'm losing my mind."

"Honey. You're already there. This is a breakdown. Breakdowns happen. It's what you do with them that counts. I know from personal experience. Be careful. Go slowly. This is crucial time. And no one wants to have to answer that list of questions. And especially, no one wants to have to live them."

I think I'm a friggin' rock. I want to be married to me.

"What can you commit to?" I ask him, suddenly unafraid.

He looks out the window at the ski mountain, like he needs it for strength. His lips are a tight, thin line. "I can commit to our kids. I can commit to looking into the garage studio space. I can commit to looking into helicopter school. I can commit to . . . I guess I can commit to . . . calling up that therapist . . . and I can commit to a future with you. But not with any confidence . . . whatsoever."

That's when I start crying.

....

But by the time we're home, my eyes are dry. I heard the word "commit" six times, after all.

The next week we spend like a happy family. I see the strategy of the list working. He's looking around, seeing what he's capable of drastically fucking up. He sees that he's playing games with the dearest of his responsibilities. Which is, if you ask me, the very definition of neurosis.

My gut says to make more of those spacious, open-minded, modern statements. To get out of his way so he's stuck with his own grizzle to chew upon.

So I start talking in first person singular: "I'm taking the kids hiking up the ski mountain . . . I'm taking the kids boating with friends . . . I'm taking the kids to the lake . . . I'm taking the kids out for an early dinner." Thank God it's summer and the options are glorious.

And interestingly enough, I don't hear another word about that friend's house in town. But I'm not banking on anything. I'm in the moment where I need to be. Taking care of what I can. Leaving the rest alone. For now, at least. And that's all there really is. Now.

Sheila is still loud though, and I fight to believe him that there is no other woman. Sheila is too hungry in this area. She wants me to go off his team. Take sides. She wants me to suffer. She is my other woman, and I want her dead and buried.

The biggest fight, though, is the part where I keep myself

happy. Where I don't take him personally. Where I don't spend extra time making myself look beautiful; making myself irresistible. I don't want to live like that. I've always just been myself. I've worked hard at being real. Not wearing a lot of makeup, or caring about hair removal, or perfect abs. But it's not that easy. It's not that easy not to dance a little. Isn't that what this is? Aren't we playing at life? Aren't we playing with lives?

This week we'll see what happens. We've committed to another conversation. Tomorrow is his birthday. I feel like his gift should be a profound one. But I have no idea what to give him. I've given him so much. And based on how he's acting, I'm not certain he's ever received any of it.

Except for two things. Our children. I saw his fatherhood in his eyes when he stared out his office window to the ski mountain and listed his six "commits." His fatherhood is the ballast to the rest of his sinking ship. That's the man I know still exists in him. It's not leverage. It's not threat. It's all that matters in the whole world to him. Right now. And for now, I'll call that good. How can he love me if he currently loathes himself? The fact that he still loves his children shows me that maybe he's really not that far gone. Maybe the Fourth of July was rock bottom. Maybe he's going to fight his way out of Hell.

But I do figure out a good gift. A paycheck for a magazine article I wrote arrives just in time, and I give him a three-hundred-dollar gift certificate toward helicopter lessons. And a remote control helicopter. And a card with a guy on the cover flying a helicopter, happy. In it I write, "Go find a home in the sky." And I dare to write, "Two Balloons."

Our kids take a picture of us that night, on the beach at the lake where we've set up a little birthday celebration in his honor. He and I are smiling real smiles. Because we are looking at our children.

But how quickly the heart lifts and falls.

"I'm going out," he says, after we've gotten the kids to bed. "There's a guy in town who's got an interesting business opportunity."

I want to say that I trust him. But I have to say that I don't completely. The suffering that comes with doubt is the fiercest to slay.

I follow him to the door. I can't help myself. Calmly I say, "Please come home at a decent hour."

"The family is the prize," a friend told me to remember.

"I will," he says, peeved. "Thanks for the gift certificate."

He does come back. I hear him shuffling around at two a.m. Then I hear beer-thickened blasts of snoring throughout the night from the screened porch. Apparently the guy with the job opportunity likes to party.

I have to believe that our little family will survive. I have to believe in those two parents smiling on the beach.

This night adds another piece to my strategy. You can live in the moment and you can create and you can do it being unattached to outcome . . . because you can love something outside of yourself. And if you can love something outside of yourself, it means that love arrow started somewhere. And if you're paying attention, you can follow it all the way home.

Maybe he can find love for himself through his love for our children. And maybe, then, he can find love for me. I am going to live as though that has already happened.

Unlikely Happiness

Mid-July.

Everything this summer—the music at the dentist, the cartoons my kids watch, the radio talk shows—it's all speaking to me. I never realized how most everything is about fear of lost love, actual lost love, or residual pain from . . . yep—lost love.

To keep my head screwed on straight, over and over I ask myself: Who can I be in this? How can I stay away from anger? Victimization. Woe. I'm through with woe. But I'm not through with my husband. And I don't believe he's through with me.

Yet this is where I stumble: the wanting. The attachment to outcome. I want to be old with him. I want to travel the world with him like we talked about in our twenties. We have fun together. I know he agrees. He told me that once. "You're fun," he said. For some reason, it stuck in my mind as a high compliment.

It feels important to tap into childlike things that go easy on my heart—that give and don't take. So I open up *A Wrinkle in Time*, by Madeleine L'Engle—a book I loved dearly as a girl. I'd forgotten that in this story, the father is gone. The kids go to find him in the Fifth Dimension where he is prisoner to evil. And he's pretty far gone. The only thing he'll fight for is his children. Not himself. So his kids go to him. And he breaks through his personal Hell for them. Sweet Jesus.

Everything is speaking to me. Belting out the message that I am not alone. I feel like I am in another dimension, where my senses are sharper—the messages more clear.

Later, I'm in from watering the garden. My son is watching *The Incredibles*. "Remember," the little witchy fashion designer says, "you are Elastigirl! Remind him that he is Mr. Incredible. Now go find him and bring him back!" Something to that effect.

Sweet.

Jesus.

And *Mary Poppins*. The kids and I watch it one afternoon in a rainstorm, and after all these years of loving those books and that movie . . . I realize it's about a husband's crisis of identity from his loss of work, and how he regains his sense of self and joy through the love of his children and wife. S.J.

My grandmother used to say, "There are more eyes watching over you than you'll ever know."

I found that in Italy. They were everywhere, and they weren't just eyes. People appeared, led us to the right trains, the right streets, the right lines. People advocated for us. Spoke the Italian we couldn't.

Now I'm finding those watchful eyes here. If only in a hawk feather on a forest path. Aspen shadows dappling the ground outside my office window. The way my retrievers stay at my heels on the trail—not their usual behavior. How my body feels so thirsty in a mountain lake, so sated drying off in the sun. So snug on the back of my horse. I'm noticing the way the world seems to be moving slowly around me, buoying me. It's all here.

Maybe the voice I heard in Italy was the collective voice of my grandmothers and their mothers telling me what they know now—trying to save me from what they didn't know on earth. I'll listen carefully this year when I'm cleaning up after Thanksgiving dinner.

There are more eyes watching over you than you'll ever know.

As much as I feel the comfort of my legacy of women, I still haven't told my family of origin about my marital ordeal. Not only do I not want their worry, I don't want to have to hear their solutions. They will be very attached to fixing this situation. I guess that's what happens when you're the caboose by so many years. When you grew up not hearing their secrets, or soothing their woes, or being their equal. They think they own you in a way I can't be owned anymore, even though I spent many years trying, in an effort to feel loved. I need equals right now. Nothing fraught.

And my mother is so happy with her new husband after grieving the loss of my father. . . . They're traveling the world like honeymooners, I don't want to disturb it. She deserves this newfound happiness. I can feel her love in the china cabinet, as it were, and that's fine with me. No, what I need right now are easy people.

Angels. I mean it. Not tacky ones or New Agey ones or bossy ones. But real live angels are showing up all around me like my grandparents and my father are piping them through some mystical realm, right into my life. I feel them when I'm sitting with my kids at movies or in restaurants or at the beach or on our porch playing games. Even the way the grocery store checkout woman winked at me the other day felt like she was in on it. It's like they're saying, *Follow your instincts. You are going to be okay, no matter what.*

They arrived last night. Spontaneously. Two old friends—recent divorcées, on a road trip to Seattle. Happened to stop in Missoula on a whim. Wanted to know if I was around. It couldn't have been better timing.

I scurried around the house picking up, and in a few hours, there I was, on my porch, with two old friends. Two women I met traveling in Greece when I was trying to live Joni Mitchell's song "Carey." Women I've lain next to, sunning topless on a black sand beach. Women whose souls have always lain the same way with me ever since.

And it was like a gift from my grandmothers and theirs before. Like the voices in the china cabinet had come together on my behalf and brought me the comfort of women.

Because my husband was, again . . . not coming home until later.

He texted our daughter this news on her cell phone. There's

a networking opportunity at the private club up on the ski mountain. Might be a potential employer.

I was pissed. You don't text your daughter information that is meant for your wife. Even though your wife doesn't really text. You call her. She's good on the phone. But you might not call her if you thought you'd have to hear her potentially negative reaction to your decision to, once again, not participate in family life. Although, funny thing: this summer, with all your irresponsible behavior . . . she's been actually. . . . really fucking cool. Maybe you'll stay out all night again without calling to see if that rattles her. So you can say, *See—she's a bitch with baggage. I'm outta here.*

I am so not his bitch.

And I spill my story to these women, late-night, the kids in bed, husband still out.

We're wrapped in throw blankets with glasses of wine and candles low, lumped together on the mattress on the screened porch. It's fragile ground because they've both had to recently overhaul their lives, their children's lives, their job situations. This road trip is a nod to their futures.

I'm trying not to think about the future. I just dearly need witnesses to my present. These women seem like the right witnesses, since they've never been afraid of "nakedness."

So I report it all to them. What he said to me upon my return from Italy. How he's been behaving. But I tell them that I'm on his side still. Not getting in his way. I'm creating our family life with or without him. Not that it's right for everybody. I'm careful to acknowledge that everybody's story is different. This is just one woman's way through this sort of crisis. Still, I'm expecting bitterness from them on some level.

And they surprise me with their response.

One of them says, "I wish I'd reacted the way you are when my husband announced that he didn't love me anymore. I was the opposite. I went ballistic. Raised a kitchen knife like a friggin' psycho. But in my case . . . there was a third party," she says.

She gets teary and we console her, hand to ankle, hand to wrist.

She sniffs and goes on like she really has to get this out. "But once I realized what I had to lose, I told him I was willing to forgive and move on. But he didn't want to. Even though he said he'd broken it off. He said he didn't love me anymore. Done. I swear . . . it came out of nowhere. I swear . . . we were happy."

"Fuck happiness," my other friend says, and pulls out a cigarette. "Do you mind if I smoke? Forty-two and I just took up smoking."

I pass her an empty wine bottle to use as an ashtray, thinking about my new definition of happiness. I want to share it, but I don't want to come off obtuse or insensitive. Yet I've never been one to hold back with old friends. "I have to believe that even if there's another woman—and my husband says there isn't—that I can still be happy," I say carefully. "Even if it's just one step outside of suffering, I've decided to call that good. That's how I've been living this summer. Just reeling it back in when my mind wants to freak out. Returning within. Breathing. Grounding myself. Letting go of outcome. Regardless of how it all shakes down. I just want to have some level of inner chill, you know? I guess you could call that happiness. Happiness doesn't need to be this gooey sweet smiley-faced thing."

"Amen," she says—the one who isn't smoking. "A good road trip helps."

"That's what I've felt like all summer. Like I'm on a mental road trip," I say.

The other one has a different story. She was the one who left. "I can tell you that if I hadn't lost my job, if I wasn't the breadwinner, if I hadn't spent my whole adult life building my career only for it to go down the crapper in an afternoon . . . I wouldn't have left my husband." She drops her cigarette in the wine bottle and leans back into the blankets. "But I was in this fog. Couldn't see past my nose. I couldn't deal. I just wanted out. And I got out, that's for damn sure. And my kids hate me for it."

They'll forgive you, we both say to her in our own way.

But she's clear. "I still love him. That's the problem. But . . . I fucked up. And now he's moved on. The judge ruled on his behalf, since he was the primary caretaker for the kids while I worked all those years. And since I was the one to leave. And for the most part, I'm alone. It fucking sucks." She laughs bitterly. "But hey—at least I got my job back! Like that makes things instantly better." She shakes her head.

I don't remember her being the sarcastic type. Or the smoking type, for that matter. I want to hug her, but she seems closed off. She looks stiff; mechanical. Beyond tears. I do not want to become like this.

When they leave the next day, I'm sad to be alone after all that sisterhood and sharing, deep into the night.

Angels.

The days start to smudge by. Me in this place of creating and receiving. Trying to strike some chord of harmony inside myself. Writing this book like a diary when I need to. Working on a few magazine article deadlines.

My husband comes and goes, a phantom of sorts. He's going to work less and less. Making eye contact less and less. He's in the haze my friend talked about as she sat and smoked on our porch.

The kids seem to accept it. They see that he's acting strangely. They know it's something to do with work, as I've let on. They want him, but they also understand that fishing is something that daddies do. Golfing. Boating. Especially depressed daddies. They're following their instincts, too. They have faith in him, too. It's not like he's moved out. The family is still intact; still a wellspring of love for them. Stable, for all they know, in their pre-adolescent, aptly self-absorbed minds.

That's what I'm telling myself. Anything is better than having him here by demand, like a prisoner on the couch watching sports—my kids watching their father resent their mother, the jailor. Or worse, in a house in town somewhere, limping along in some other version of home that they're supposed to somehow claim and even love. There are miles to go before anything like that is even conscionable to me. Miles.

I heard him come in last night. I didn't bother to look at the clock. It was late. The kids decided to "camp" in sleeping bags in the living room, so he had my son's room all to himself; which he chose. He slept until noon. I got our son off to soccer camp, did some grocery shopping, set up our daughter with a playdate, and tried to carry myself calmly. Tried to remember not to take any of this personally. Tried not to feel sorry for myself. Tried not to imagine the script, the play, the scene.

But it's so hard not to.

Fantasy

He: Walks into the kitchen looking guilty and distant.

I: Look at him distantly and say something cunning and cool. *Are you finished celebrating your birthday yet?*

He: Smiles guiltily and goes for the fridge.

I: Smile loquaciously, because I've just gone grocery shopping and the fridge is full of beautiful summer things. Plus, I've just cleaned out the freezer, picked roses and put them in little vases on the windowsill in the sun, placed three delphinium in a vase on the island, cleaned the pantry cupboard, and managed to fit an overhaul of the house into my writing day, so we're in good shape—me and the house. Every pillow is in its place. And I've got on a nice summer dress. I really am Donna Reed.

I: *Want to come with me to our son's soccer championship today?*

He: *Of course. I'd love to!* he says, looking lovingly into my eyes. *And after that let's all take a family swim at the lake!*

No! I'm not playing that game. I'm taking care of what I can control. I'm creating my life, me and my angels.

Here's why you don't do plays, scripts, scenes. They're playing in your head. And not in real life. And yet they bring you real pain. And here's the thing of it—you're not suffering anymore. Remember? You're through with suffering.

Real Life

He: Cuts up an orange at the kitchen counter.

I: Hold court at the kitchen sink a few feet away from him. Not letting myself be desperate for a hug from behind. I love a hug from behind at the kitchen sink, and he knows that. Not, then, being resentful that he's depriving me of that hug.

He: Makes himself some tea, sliding behind me at the sink, not hugging me.

I: Remind myself that I've recently replaced the toaster with a brand-new one from Target, so he can't be pissed off about our broken toaster and somehow blame me for the fact that we've left it broken on the counter for half a year, using the broken handle just so, to maybe half-toast a piece of bread in the one of four elements that works. Even the toaster works this morning.

I: "I'm going to our son's soccer championship at one forty-five. He's on the Spain team. We looked up the flag in the atlas last night. He painted his shirt like the flag."

He: Trumped. He's the sports aficionado in the family. It's one of his talking points to himself, in the case for why he should leave me. I'm not into team sports. He sits down with his coffee and the newspaper. He is exceptionally quiet.

I: "Wanna come?"

He: "Nope. I think I'll go fishing." This from a man who adores his son—takes every opportunity to play ball with him in the yard. Coach his teams.

I: Try not to take this personally. Yet I find it intensely odd that this man would choose fishing over an opportunity to support his son in a ball game. Is this some form of punishment?

I can't help seeing how, in the interest of punishing me, he is punishing our son. Actually, more so, in the interest of punishing himself, he is punishing me, and our son. Plus . . . if he's not going to go to work anymore . . . he and I need to talk about money. But I know if I bring it up right now, he'll blow. He'll take it as punishment.

I decide that I've got to get away from all forms of punishment.

So I leave him there in our beautifully clean and summery kitchen with the nectarines and apricots in the fruit bowl and the corn all laid out on the counter for the great dinner we're going to have with or without him. Maybe he'll even notice the chicken thawing in the sink. He loves a good roasted chicken.

So I go to my office and Google "golden beet and fennel salad," and I'm happy to find out that *Gourmet* magazine has a few pointers on the concoction I've thought up all on my own. I've been vindicated by *Gourmet* magazine, so who cares about any scene that might or might not play out in our kitchen. Oh, but it calls for mint. I hadn't thought of that. Mint would be perfect.

So I walk over to the neighbors' herb garden in my summer dress because I like my summer dress. I don't care if it's not flattering. The whole way over, Sheila tries to get me to think about how he used to call me the prettiest girl at the party. How he used to always say to me that I'd get even more beautiful as I got older. Like Audrey Hepburn. Have I failed his fantasies? Have the twenty pounds I've put on and can't seem to shed actually somehow ruined my marriage? Was it all based on fantasy?

SHUT UP, SHEILA! Still, a woman can tell when her lover objects to changes in her body. I'll leave it at that.

(Weight issues: You fill in the blank ____________________.

Is there a blank long enough?

Be kind to yourself, friend. When you're finished, tell your own personal Sheila that if she cares so much, maybe she could pay for the two of you to go to a spa for a month.)

On the way back, I've talked myself into feeling light and summery again. And I have a bit of an epiphany, as I often do on walks. As much as I'm tempted to feel the heaviness of the last month, I'm going to stay my course, abide by my strategy. I'm not going to get in his way, no matter how miserable he is. I'm not going to be angry, either. I'm not a sucker if I don't use anger. In fact, I'm only a sucker if I let his behavior determine my mood.

So I'm feeling sunny and happy. I've got mint in my hand. He'll find a job that he loves. I'll get a book published. Our marriage will be okay sooner than later. I'll drop those twenty pounds. And darn it—I'm going home to make a *Gourmet*-endorsed golden beet salad.

As I come back up the driveway, I'm looking at our land—our beautiful twenty acres, with two ponds, that he found and called me about, ecstatic, years ago. I try not to feel sad that I haven't heard him ecstatic in so long. Yet looking at the mountain bluebirds on the fence, the hawks riding the thermals above, the wind in the grass—taking in my Montana, and even our Montana . . . I'm happy. Not just a step out of suffering. Leaps.

The dogs stop and look up the driveway. He's rounding the top switchback in his truck—the boat attached to the hitch.

Uh-oh. The boat's going fishing, too. That's committed fishing.

That's not angle-on-the-side-of-a-river-for-a-few-hours fishing. That's all day and maybe all night "fishing." With buddies.

I just stand there with that sinking feeling. That moment of calm is gone, and in its place is an image of my husband and a few guys chain-smoking, stoned, in a boat, on a swampy lake, with a case of PBR, listening to Zeppelin.

But there are options. This could mean one of three things:

1. Yes, he is, in fact, going fishing with his specific fishing friends, and we won't see him again today. Maybe tonight, either. Again.
2. He's taking the boat to the shop.

Or

3. He feels so guilty about his behavior this summer that he's going to do some meditative fishing on his own and then take us all out on a boat ride in a few hours. He'll pick us up at the boat launch like old times. It's Friday, after all. He'd be a real shithead to blow off his family on a weekend.

He has no choice but to stop. Unless, of course, he wants to run me over, which might actually be choice number four.

"Hi," he says. He looks guilty and distant and hungover.

I'm holding the mint a little hard. I bring it up to his window, so it's between us. He loves flowers because his mother loves flowers; he used to help her in her garden. The in-your-face mint is my little reminder of how nice it is to have your parents around you so you can attempt to have a happy childhood.

"Hi," I say.

"What's that?" he says, feigning interest, which means he's been bad. He really looks like shit. And he can't be feeling much better.

"Mint." I smile and hold it up to his nose. I'm not treating him like he's been bad. I've been this sort of bad, and I know that self-punishment is more than enough. I'm staying away from pedestals altogether. I don't even ask what he's doing with the boat.

I remember my son's comment this morning—"Look! Dad's truck is in the driveway!"—off to soccer in sunblock and three blister Band-Aids, a really lovely lunch swinging in a lunchbox from his washed hands. Four hours before his father woke up, in his bed.

But I stay smiling and summery.

He offers this: "I'm taking the boat into the shop. If they fix it, maybe we can go out on the lake tonight." Going out on our boat is one of our favorite family excursions and one he loves to inspire. This is a good offering.

Maybe he's "fishing" for a little redemption. Or he's just plain sick of being an asshole. He knows he's really not an asshole. Though it's a good story he's currently telling himself so he can live up to it and make himself, ultimately, right.

The mind really is our enemy most of the time.

Either way, it's a wonderful opportunity to behave like I actually hadn't noticed the boat was attached to his truck in the first place, or that he stayed out to all hours, again. I can create happiness. I can create beauty. Maybe it'll rub off on him.

I: "Great. Let me know." And then I lean in and kiss him. His lips are soft enough to mine. Then I withdraw the mint, and walk up with the dogs to the house. Where there are apricots and corn and flowers on the windowsill. Where there are things I can make beautiful. Maybe it's just as simple as that.

He: Shouts from his truck, "I'll call. I promise."

I: Didn't ask him to. Interesting.

And when he actually does call a few hours later, he says he's going to camp in the boat and won't be home for a few days. That he needs to be in nature and empty his mind.

He pauses and then speaks, strained. "I'm going to have to shut down the business. We're not making any money. It's time. I've gotta find something else to do for work. We can live off our investments for a while longer. But not much."

And oddly, a clean white relief washes over me. Our investments? Is that it? Is he back? Was my Italian father right? This has all been about his job? A man needs his work. Were my instincts right?

"You go have a good, healing time. Don't think too much. Just be," I say.

Later, I lie in bed leap-frogging all the thoughts that threaten, leveling them with my healing, happy walk through the meadow with the mint. But more, with the idea that he is ending something that needs to end. And it's not our marriage.

Maybe now he'll take a solo road trip somewhere. Think about his old dreams. Merge them with his reality.

Here's the last thought that I let in the door: (emotional pain comes in on thought and thought alone.)

How can a man who vilifies his wife to save his pride ever be an equal partner again? If he ever was to begin with. Pedestals and all.

Free Fall

August.

At this moment in my life, I'm losing steam. This is a ride I want to be done with. I want the county fair that has become my life to pack up and move to the next town—roller coasters, shooting galleries, fried dough, bucking broncos, rodeo clowns, carnies. I'm sick of it all!

And I bet I know what you're thinking. *That's because you're being a pushover. I would never tolerate the shit you have this summer. Never. I'd have told him to go fuck off the first night he didn't call.*

Here's my question, then, to you: *Go fuck off where, exactly?*

It's easy to be a hothead. You just better be sure you can live with your ultimatums.

Instead, my therapist and I agree that this is a time for me to walk my line of power even more. To be indestructible. Unrumple-able. It's his ship to sink, not mine.

But my God, it's terrifying.

With all my summer practice, it's still hard work not to smell his shirts for women's perfume. To dig through his pockets. To peek into his truck looking for clues. I especially resist asking people if they've seen him around town.

And when they ask how I am in passing, I say, "I'm fine." (It's an interesting practice when people ask you how you are to really not tell them. I've always taken that question to heart and answered it truthfully. Now I wouldn't dare. It makes me decide not to ask that question anymore to people in passing. Only behind closed doors.)

All I can seem to eat in the morning this week are plums. I've got acid in my stomach and up my esophagus at night, so I have to sleep sitting up. And I've got two very distinct places that hurt in my gut. I resist more than anything else the notion that my husband has been trying to kill me this summer so that he won't have to be brave and wake up to his life. And that I am somehow letting him.

But still, I love this man.

My therapist asks me why I love him. Actually, I ask her to ask me why I love him. The scene from the movie version goes like this:

Woman sits on mauve leather couch with a balled-up tissue and laughs harshly. She pauses and that's rare—she's a talker. Part of what she's pretty sure her husband doesn't love about her anymore—her talking. She pauses. Silenced by this question. Of course she knows why she loves him. She loves him for obvious reasons.

She just can't think of any right now. In fact, all she can think about is the Thai restaurant down the street and that maybe she'll have some *tom kha gai* soup after this therapy session.

"Surely you can come up with some answer to that question," the therapist says.

"I just love him," she says. "I love his smile. I love the way his skin smells and feels. I love his vibe. He's never asked me to be anything other than who I am. Except for now, but like I've said . . . I don't buy it."

The therapist does not raise her eyebrow. That's a good thing.

She feels sort of shy saying out loud what she thinks so often, but she continues. "When he walks in the room, I feel like everything's okay. My boyfriend has arrived. The fun is here. The safety. The adventure. The cool. I love what a good father he is. Normally."

Her therapist gives her homework. She loves this, when her therapist gives her homework. "All marriages have contracts, whether they're spoken or unspoken. Problems in marriage occur when either one or both of the spouses are not holding up to their contract. Write down your marital contract. Yours and what you imagine was his."

You know, she thinks, *he never even asked me to marry him. We decided together.*

In all truth, the idea of a man on his knee asking a woman

to marry him felt dated and sexist and squirmy. So she'd said something really cool and modern like, "You're not going to ask me to marry you on a chairlift or something, are you? Let's ask each other."

Maybe that was a mistake, she thinks now. *Maybe it took his power away.* She wonders about the times when she took his power away. But can you really actually take someone's power away? If he's being responsible for his power to begin with?

They asked each other by a river in Washington state a few weeks later. They agreed there would be words, fire, and water. She'd like to read his words now. Where did she put them? She must have kept them. In a file in her office. She'll find them and show them to him if she really needs to later on; if he's really going to leave.

Marriage contract. The unwritten subtext behind the wedding vows.

She resists this as much as she resists looking in his pockets or smelling his shirts. But she thinks back in time; climbs into her twenty-something mind. What was lying underneath those vows she took up there at that altar?

Maybe hers went something like: That he'll always take care of me. *Oh, brother. Yuck. Is it true? I'm a liberated woman!* That he'll always adore me. That he'll always be committed to family. That he'll always be an adventurer. Never a sellout.

And for him? This one couldn't possibly be true, but she thinks it is:

That she'll always be thin and beautiful. That she'll be a famous and wildly successful novelist. And I won't have to work. I'll fish my life away on a river somewhere. With buddies.

God.

That rules out ninety-nine percent of reality.

So was their marriage based on illusion? Fantasy? Improbable fate?

What was the "worse" part in his mind when they took their vows? That she'd make less than six figures on her first book advance? That she'd get a few stretch marks after the babies were born?

This homework is no fun. No fun at all. Even the movie version.

I go out for lunch with a recently divorced friend who is in a new relationship and has never been happier in her whole life. Even the kids love this guy. And her ex is getting remarried and he's never been happier and her kids get double the parents and everyone's so happy. Divorce is so great.

I have told precious few locals, but I decide to tell her about my husband because this woman has scope. She, like my friends on their road trip, knows about divorce.

She tells me that it's commendable and all—me using this philosophy—not getting in his way, not freaking out on him, not threatening him. But basically she tells me to tell him to "fuck off." She's the voice of womankind. She's the woman, and I can hear her roar and I feel stupid and weak.

I feel my strategy crumbling around me. "Yeah. You're right. I need to slap him across the face and tell him to wake up. He's an adult. Start acting like one. Or else."

"And if he won't . . . well, I'm here to tell you," she says, "there's a world of happiness out there if your marriage is meant to end. You deserve to be happy."

Happiness. Unlikely happiness. She's dosing me with my own medicine.

"Yeah. It's just that I want to be happy in a marriage with *him*."

I tell my therapist about my lunch with my friend.

"That's great. Like we've talked about before, you can certainly take that tack. The thing about it is, you have to be willing to stand behind your 'or else.' Are you?"

"I just really believe that he still loves me. There are worlds we haven't explored in our relationship yet. This is just a phase. That's what my gut says. And I've got to trust it."

"Then I recommend you stay the course. You can still express yourself. Your emotions. Without placing blame or losing your temper or crying. You can state your feelings calmly. He may throw a tantrum. But you don't have to engage it."

He stays out late two nights in a row, doesn't call, and on the third morning, my son looks out my bedroom window and says for the second time this week, "Oh look, Daddy's truck is in the driveway!" Like it's some kind of guest star making a cameo appearance in his life. I want to cry for my son. This isn't right. How long can I put up with this? This is not the message I want to be sending to my children. And I know he doesn't, either. We've always been so careful with our messages to them.

I look closer and see that the garden gate is bashed in! He's backed into it!!! The one he built so proudly.

I just want to cry or scream or kick him out for good.

But I breathe deeply. The fact that he's doing things that are so unlike him has me know even more that this is a crisis of self. And damn it. Just because he's having a crisis doesn't mean I don't love him. And he's home. He chose to come home.

I hear him snoring somewhere. I browse around the house and find him on the screened porch again under a thin throw blanket. It's cold in Montana at night, even in August.

That morning, he's humble. He drinks lots of water. He does all the dishes. He spends the morning watching golf with our kids.

I send another novel to my agent, who has an interested editor; decide to celebrate and go horseback riding. I feel tough walking through the house in my leather chaps. I make it a point to stop and stand in front of the TV, and when I've caught his eye, I dare to do something I haven't done since the fifth of July. I say, "What do you want to do later today?"

He's mildly amenable. We decide we'll go up to a remote town near Glacier National Park for dinner. Drive the back way over Red Meadow Pass. Something we've done for years.

I push it. Just a little. Hoping that my leather riding chaps and the fact that I'm about to haul ass through the mountains will keep him from thinking I'm a nagging housewife. But I'm not so sure. "What time do you want to leave?"

We make a time. Four o'clock.

I get what I need from the ride—my Morgan going slower than usual. Like he senses that I need calm. When I am on my horse, the rest of the world falls away except for the exact place where his feet touch the ground. It's the most religious practice I've known; it's where the prayers don't beg. They surrender and receive. It's that place of true nature I've been seeking all my life. Freedom. I find myself chanting "Thank you" with each of his steps, hoof to forest floor.

As agreed, we assemble at four and drive over the pass on the sketchy dirt road. We all have some laughs. My husband pretends to drive like a madman—the opposite of my horse today. And that's okay. It's a big act of macho daring and we love it. Not much can happen on this remote, wide-open road in broad daylight. But it reads like a renegade ride he's taking us on and it's a blast. (Reminds me of college.) We're all high on his derelict spirit. He's sharing it with us. After this summer, we'll take what we can get.

As we drive back the paved way and the kids fall asleep, I remember my son's comment about his father's truck being in the driveway, and I begin to fume. I free-fall out of the moment, out of the breath, out of the trusting and going slowly and returning to sleep; out of the getting out of his way. I recall my friend's roar, and I just plain feel like a voiceless sucker.

"Tell him to figure it out or you'll divorce his ass and take all his money and his house and his children," another friend had said. One I shouldn't have confided in.

Yeah. What do I need with a guy like that???

But I want him. I want to live on the beach with him somewhere one day. I want to go on safari with him and brag about our children's killer jobs changing the world. Worlds we have not yet seen. Worlds.

I reel myself back in. Think of my therapist and her mauve couch.

I get to express my emotions. Calmly. State a fact. State my feeling. Leave it alone.

I practice for the rest of the drive home. It's so hard not to say, *Listen, you can try to talk yourself out of this marriage all you want, but there is so much you haven't even tapped in me, in us, and how dare you turn me into the fall guy for your deliberate neglect and bad business choices. I'm not taking the fall. Figure it out. You have everything to lose.*

I said that once to him. That last part. The summer after my father died. I think about it now, and an old hurt throbs in my ribs. He abandoned me that summer, a lot like this one. Adding insult to injury like I've never known. I never dreamed that grief could be so off-putting. Maybe it is when you're dealing in idolatry.

Back then, I played it tough. "You've got a lot to lose! Figure it out!" I said, also in riding chaps. And it worked. But did it? Sure, his behavior might have changed, but that doesn't mean that resentment wasn't building up, like cancer cells. And now, four years later, here we are. Four years of convincing himself he's with the wrong woman in the wrong job under his belt now. He's got a barricade of conviction built around him. I should have played it then like I am now. Straight. State emotion. No threats. Leave it at that.

We pull into the driveway, our kids still asleep in the backseat, and I think I've got just the right words.

I take a deep breath. "Our son looked out the window this morning and said, 'Oh look. Dad's truck is in the driveway.' And I didn't like that to be a surprise—for him or for me."

He digests the words and suddenly he slams on the brakes. "Nice fucking comment at the end of the day!" he says and slams the truck door behind him. Slams the front door of the house and another one somewhere inside.

He sleeps on the screened porch again.

I have a hard time sleeping at all.

Here's what inspires me to fall to sleep finally: he heard those words. He reacted like a child. He knows it. I didn't say or do anything wrong. He got triggered by the truth. He doesn't want to be who he's being. His anger is real and it's scary, but it's anger toward himself. It's not my fault.

And here's what I am convinced of. In fact, I think it's the key to a relationship. Any relationship:

If you get out of someone's way, they will fight and they will kick, but eventually, there's nothing they can do but look at themselves and get real. Very, very real. Or totally self-combust in a life of lies. Or that dear opiate, denial.

But they can all get ugly in the process. Am I strong enough to handle it? What if it gets abusive? Although, he's never really hit me. Threw some groceries at me once. That summer after my father died.

Maybe he thought he was getting out of my way that summer. Maybe he thinks people want to grieve alone in dark rooms. Maybe some people do. But not me. And you'd know that about me if you spent any amount of time with me. Never mind almost twenty years. It felt like abuse. This feels like abuse.

I tell my therapist this the next week.

She says all abuse is just bait. To get you to be the one who freaks out. So the other person doesn't have to deal. Doesn't have to take responsibility. *Oh look—she's the one with the black eye. She's the one crying in the corner. She's the one leaving. What a bitch.*

There's a fist-sized hole in our front hallway downstairs that he made one time when he was pissed off at me. Half a year after my father died. "Why are you still so sad!?" he screamed. He thought I should be over it like a self-cleaning oven. I leave that fist-sized hole there as a reminder of why we should never believe there is such a thing as being "golden."

I think I'm strong enough to see his tantrum after our drive as bait.

Bait?

Yeah, bait.

Here's an example. Maybe you have one or two yourself:

We're out on the lake, on our boat. Our daughter wants to learn how to water-ski. She's in the water, he's at the wheel, I'm in the passenger seat. He's the jock in the family. He doesn't like it when I interrupt him, or give my two cents when it comes to sports. That's where he gets to feel powerful. So I stay out of it, even though I know plenty about water-skiing.

She misses the rope.

He leans over and pulls it in, recoils it and hands it to me because we're too close to the shore and he's driving. "Throw it to her."

I throw it to her and it misses her. It's not far enough.

He throws a fit. And then he cites the adept abilities of one of his fishing friend's wives. "You don't throw a rope like that! You throw it like this." He winds it up in the air and flings it with speed and prowess, perfectly to her.

It's such bait. Because I want to say so much here. I want to say, *Hey—I'd like to see what you do with a horse bridle.* Or, *Listen, dude—you have no right to assume I know how to do something just because you do.*

But I stay silent and practice not taking the bait—not being resentful. Letting it wash over me. Because when I stay here, I am powerful. Very, very powerful. Take note of this. Let him have the middle-aged tantrum. Just be sure to duck!

He thinks she should try a kick-start off the lake bottom. I think that's a poor idea, but remain quiet. She can't manage the ski. She starts to cry. "I can't!"

"God—why don't you help her!" he shouts at me.

Me? Help someone do *sports* in our family? I thought that was a no-no. A bite off his power sandwich.

I jump in and go to her and try to position her ski, but she's crying and mad and she lets go of the rope and I can't reach it in time.

"Forget it," he yells. "Let's just do a regular start."

I want to say, *That's what we should have done before,* but I don't. So much biting my tongue this summer. A new thing for me.

When I get back in the boat, I sit down in the passenger seat.

And he shoots a stare at me and says . . . (BAIT): "God! You're so incompetent sometimes."

I let a beat or two go by.

State fact. State emotion. Leave it alone. This is bait I can live with. For now. This is bait that, if I play it right, might allow me to come up graceful. More graceful than before he said it. He has not hit me. If he hit me, I would have dived off the boat and swum to shore.

But in my mind, I'm not graceful. In my mind it's tit-for-tat. Tantrum for tantrum.

I want to say, *Were you talking to yourself?* I want to list every competent bone in my body. I wish he'd seen what I pulled off in Italy, keeping our daughter safe, and educated, and inspired for three weeks. Has he forgotten about the Pitocin-induced natural childbirth I went through?!

But instead, I try my strategy of choice.

"Incompetent?" I say, calmly. "Ouch."

I can tell that he's waiting for more. He wants tears with my "Ouch." Drama.

No way. Not doing it.

He looks away. I know he's in a fight with himself. That he knows he owes me an apology but can't quite get it out of his mouth.

How much longer can I deal with this? I can't wait for my next therapy session. I'm going to set a date in my mind with her help.

Strangely, he's home a lot after that. For a solid week, it's like old times. Maybe he's had a good talking with himself after his *incompetence* comment. Maybe he's taken a good long look at the garden gate.

And I start to think that this strategy is working in favor of my marriage. It is, at least, for me. I get to pop out of suffering—to shut Sheila up and do the work I know to do. I get to strive for freedom. Even when it feels impossible. And even when I fail. I'm getting better and better at this though. Because I'm not relying on outside forces for my happiness. Even when it's so bloody hard. In the face of such nasty bait. Nasty tantrums. Mine, at least, are internal. For now. Loud to me. But to me only.

The next week I tell my therapist that I'm afraid I'm setting a new protocol that we'll get stuck in. That he'll perceive this as getting away with something. That I'll put up with this shit and he'll get used to the flung verbal blows, poisonous words, tantrums.

She gives me more homework. "Write down your criterion. You get to decide how much you will take. A few months. A day. Six months. A few years. You have choices here. That's where your power is."

I go to the Thai restaurant, order obnoxiously spicy food on purpose—because I can take it, right? I can take that non-bait.

I take out my usually prolific-to-a-fault pen . . . and all I can write down that feels totally true is this: "I will not put up with violence. Or verbal or physical abuse of our children." I can play at this strategy for quite some time. It took us twenty years to get here. But I figure six months would be, for now, dignifiedly pragmatic.

And it's like my imagining an end has somehow infiltrated the psychic membrane to the collective we of our marriage. Because **things . . . start . . . changing.**

He starts coming home.

For dinner. At six.

He calls and tells us where he is.

He sleeps in our bed.

He makes eye contact in the kitchen.

He wants to sit at our well-loved teak table on the stone patio he laid with his own hands. I look out the window, and he's opened the umbrella—tilted it to block out the sun. He's created shade.

The vegetable garden has been giving us so much this summer. I've engaged the kids in it to pick peas, beans, chard, lettuce, arugula, purple potatoes . . . but he hasn't seemed to care. Now he sits down in his shade at the table, and he eats my homemade vegetable soup, and when my son says, "I like this soup," my husband says, "These are our potatoes." Our potatoes.

The Olympics are on and between that and the Cubs doing so well, we're watching a lot of TV. It's okay this way for now. We're together. Stable. A family united in something, albeit a bit bleak.

As if the TV has magical powers and has decided to reward my patience with hope . . . something inanely miraculous happens:

It's Saturday afternoon and I'm upstairs reading a book so different from this one that it balances me out. It's about Michelangelo's life, and it brings me back to Florence, granted five hundred years ago, but anything current feels too hard.

So I'm up in our bedroom, and I hear him talking on the phone below. He's got his polite I'm-talking-to–a-woman voice on. I admit it—I push speakerphone, because this time I want to know who gets to be on the other end of his kindness.

It's the lady from DISH.

My God. He's upgrading our satellite!

He's staying!!!

Granted, every time he waters the lawn, I feel like he might stay with us, but the TV is a whole different ball of wax. Lawns need to look good in order to sell houses. TVs have only to do with the people sitting around them, watching them. A lot of our family life is spent in front of that TV. Whether I like it or not. So a satellite upgrade? That's different from lawn care. That's as good as saying, *I don't know what I was thinking saying I didn't love you, when all I really needed were some more sports channels!*

Is it possible that a thing as banal as television could be delivering me clues to the future of my marriage? If that's the case, I'll remember to look for signs in grocery cart real estate ads from now on! I'm not picky where wisdom comes from, remember? (Calm down, I'm just kidding. Or maybe I'm not . . .)

Monday morning, the satellite guy comes and spends the whole day setting up our house so that we've got TV options in other rooms. My daughter and I go riding in the woods around our house, and my husband stays at home, making life more livable in the foreseeable future. I'll really know he's in for the long haul if a guy comes to put in a bar in the basement. But for now, this is great news.

I try to stay out of it, but when I get back from our ride, I see the satellite guy and my husband going up the stairs to the studio over the garage. And I follow them.

I go over to the area where we've talked about putting in a home entertainment system. Sectional couches. A home office for him. A pool table. A room of his own—a Man Cave—that the family could enjoy, too. We don't have the money now. But just the mention of it in our future, if and when things turn around financially—just his reaction to it will help me to know if he sees himself in this house. With us.

And I risk it all and I say it—right there in front of the satellite guy. "While we're up here, I'm wondering if this area is satellite-ready." I look over to them. Anything could happen. I could be ignored. Called "incompetent." My husband could roll his eyes and leave.

But his eyes widen. "Yeah," he says. "What's the deal there?"

The guy clicks into action and comes over to me and says, "Well, you'd be smart to run the cable now before you put drywall in."

"Yeah," I say. "That would be smart. If we ever wanted to turn this into a living space."

"Yeah, we'd better run cable in here, too," my husband says.

It's like my whole being sighs. I picture us all right here. I picture Christmas morning here. I'll never complain about how much TV we watch ever again—football, baseball—golf, even. I want us to be together. I believe in us. My instincts are my guide.

Later, the phone rings. It's our neighbor returning my husband's phone call. He's a builder. And he'd love to come over and check out the space over the garage. I risk it again, because my husband's stepped out, and I say, "How about Tuesday night?"

We've got a date.

I know I'm meddling. But isn't it more that I'm just guiding a bit? Not getting in the way, but not being blind, deaf, and dumb, either. Regardless, I'm feeling good about us. For the first time all summer, since the day after I returned from Italy, I'm feeling a sense of us. Those are our potatoes. That's our satellite. Damn it. Maybe you think I should require jewelry. Frankly, I'd rather put my faith in potatoes and sports channels any day. More and more, it seems inherently important to be a realist.

And it's like my last weeks of free fall have suddenly yanked me heavenward, and I look up . . . and a giant parachute has opened. Realism seems like the best form of flotation device right now—much more secure than romanticism ever felt.

Heart-Shaped Rock

August still.

But now things are different. Everything, actually. And nothing, too, because we're having coffee and watching the Olympics and planning back-to-school things.

But everything . . . because his sister, who, against all odds, has been winning a fight with cancer for nine years . . . has been given three to eighteen months to live.

His beloved sister, who was like his second mother when they were growing up. Mother of five. Salt of the earth, like no one I know.

I want him to go to her. Help with the kids. Help with the house because, you see, her husband of almost thirty years has taken off with a twenty-something and is going around town saying they're engaged.

It rocked her to the core. And then her cancer came back.

I want my husband to fly to her home and be there for her and her children who are facing every bit of shell shock all at once . . . in what was just moments ago, their happy childhoods. I want him to feel what it is to be a force of strength in the face of real loss. When it's not money that can make you or break you, it's love and death. Forget taxes. I know, because I learned it at my father's deathbed. Whatever crisis he's in has a new reference point: he has his health. He has a family. He has a loving wife who believes in him.

So I'm waiting now.

He's got lifelines: they've presented themselves one by one. Helicopter lessons. Man Cave. Therapy. And now the opportunity to help his dying sister—this may be more powerful than any therapy could ever be.

I want him to go to his sister and hold her in his arms and be still with her and listen to her and climb out of his world of hurt that has had him suffering so fiercely in his mind. I send this message to him by osmosis, because I know it has to be his idea: *Go to her. Go be the strong one for someone else. Forget about your failed business and our mortgage and our debt. Go do more important work. Maybe it'll even inspire you to find a job you love. In fact, practice gratitude for our little jobless uncomplicated mountain-town life where a person can live five miles from work, two from the school, ten from the ski mountain, half a mile from the golf course . . . making it possible to do things like coach your son's baseball team, cheer on your daughter at her soccer game, go skiing, and play golf all in a day's work, depending on the season. No commuter train, no parking issues, no traffic, no four-dollar cups of coffee.*

I'm waiting for him to find himself in the middle of one word, and that word is: gratitude.

Gratitude.

Not the kind of gratitude you might find on a T-shirt in an organic cotton catalog, or spoken through your car stereo by a motivational speaker. Not borrowed gratitude. But your own gratitude. The kind of gratitude you have earned—and feel so truly in your heart. Gratitude that you are alive. That you have people who love you. Not my gratitude. Yours. Can you feel it?

Even if he leaves you, can you feel it?

He buys an airplane ticket to see his sister in a few weeks. I'm proud of him. If he can be responsible to her, maybe he can be responsible to himself. Maybe he'll even start dreaming again. She'll want that for him. Her little brother, once so full of dreams.

It makes me think of something that happened last week. I was driving home after dropping the kids at a birthday party, and I saw his car in front of the bar. And I stopped. Suddenly I wanted to show his "liquid buddies" what he is considering leaving so they can say, *Dude—what the fuck? Do you know how lucky you are?*

It was mildly terrifying. His hallowed ground. What would I find there? But I held my head high, ordered a beer, and saw him over at a table full of people. Married people. Not the guys who spill in every day at five o'clock after work, and pat one another on the back over caught fish and hangovers and football stats.

But a table full of people with great sunglasses and great teeth. People with babies. PLU's, my friend calls them. "People Like Us." Polite people. Men who stand up and shake your hand. Women who take their albeit great sunglasses off so you can see their eyes.

"Hey," I said and introduced myself as the wife. Then I sat down and they resumed their conversation.

He stared into his beer. I'd crashed his party, after all. He doesn't like to have his parties crashed.

One of the husbands said to my husband, "So, tell me more about moving your family to the Caribbean," with awe and envy in his eyes.

My husband hedged.

I stayed cool . . . as . . . a . . . cucumber.

"It's just something I was thinking about," he said.

"Dude, you sounded pretty serious," the other husband said—the one with the newborn.

I was stunned. Pleasantly stunned. Maybe who he's been all these summer nights at the bar is someone who's bouncing his dreams around in public. To strangers. Who don't necessarily hold him accountable. But maybe he just needs new ears to listen to his big ideas. I can understand that. But I want to be in on it.

So I put myself on his dream team. After all, I've been in on his dreams for over half our lives. I helped create some of them. I've even helped make some of them come true. "It's something we've always dreamed of," I said. "Living in the Caribbean."

This is the time for dreams to come true. Maybe dreams start coming true when we speak them. At a bar. In front of babies.

Do I dare allow myself to dream again? Isn't it the dreaming that got me into trouble to begin with? Can you live in the now and still be a dreamer?

I'm thinking about our little Allston apartment with the cockroaches and the Bum Brother and all those wild-colored rooms. I feel the energy of those young people with all those dreams.

This morning I lay in bed next to my sleeping husband. His eyes were rolling back and forth under his lids, and I wondered where he was. Was he scuba diving? Flying helicopters? Climbing Mount Rainier, which he did with his brother so long ago now? I wanted to be with him wherever he was.

I kept eyeing his shoulder, so open and available. And like the worst sort of opportunist, I curled into it. After all, that's been my shoulder to curl into for twenty years. Sometimes you have to steal what you want and run.

He didn't budge. It felt so good to be there. I tried not to think about the idea of him not wanting me there to begin with. Of waking up and shaking me off. Are we really at that point? I just don't believe it.

As much as I want to be with him in his dreams again, I lay there next to his warm skin knowing that before that can happen, he has to see himself in his dreams again. I have to think of his dreams as separate from mine. Guardians of each other's solitude.

I lay there and thought about something that happened last week at the county fair, when it really was in town and not just in my mind wreaking havoc.

Our friends were there publicizing their helicopter school and I plopped down and said, "Dive-bomb our house. I'm not kidding. He's got that three-hundred-dollar gift certificate I gave him for his birthday, and it's gathering dust. He needs inspiration."

"The study books cost three hundred dollars, you know," my friend said, smiling. "It all begins with the books . . ."

"Aha! Interesting. We'll be on our patio on Saturday, at exactly ten o'clock, having brunch."

I suddenly realized it was Saturday morning. I jumped out of bed and went downstairs and started the bacon. Then I made homemade huckleberry muffins from the huckleberries the kids and I picked on a recent hike. (Around here, we're proud of our huckleberries.)

I set the table outside. It was a beautiful morning. The garden was showing itself off in delphinium and pale pink climbing roses. One by one, the family gathered.

I was sunny. Taking secret affirmations from my garden. My sister-in-law has been using affirmations in her battle with cancer, and she has inspired me.

I am peaceful. I am calm. I am alive. I am receiving the abundance of all of Creation. I am creating the life I want. I am creating the way people treat me. I am living in light and love. This, in fact, is my Summer of Love!

And I heard it. *Tap tap tap* . . . my fork rattled . . . then *chop*

chop chop . . . I felt it in my heart . . . then *bap bap bap* . . . the wind came and the umbrellas tipped over . . . and it was there, overhead! The blue and yellow Schweizer helicopter was over our house, hovering low while we were all having breakfast outside at our teak table and under our sun umbrellas like that's what we always do, every morning, bacon and homemade huckleberry muffins . . .

How cool am I? (Maybe not so cool. But can I fantasize a bit here?)

We all stood up and beheld this wonder in our front yard, whipping wind through the patio, tilting the delphinium . . . and I thought this is what they're talking about—what my therapist calls deliberate living, and what the Buddhists call Right Action, and maybe what the Christians call Divine Intervention. When you send out love, and surrender the rest.

I looked at my husband, and he was smiling from ear to ear—something I haven't seen in quite some time. It was beautiful. Like a miracle.

Then his mouth dropped open because he realized that the helicopter wasn't just hovering there to show off its big blue belly.

Out of the helicopter window, attached to a long line, what looked like a black doctor's bag appeared . . . and slowly, it began to lower down into our yard. And I knew what that bag was full of: the books.

"Get your ass out there!" I yelled at my husband like the good old days when I wasn't freaking walking on eggshells all the time in fear of total abandonment.

He ran out into the yard and received that bag like a sacrament. Both arms raised. It was an absolutely religious moment, watching him standing there, receiving this bag in his open palms.

I smiled proudly at my kids, who were standing there astounded.

This is the shit that happens when you're married to me!

I was back. And it felt fabulous.

Today we're going out on the lake in our ski boat with our little family of four. Today we will eat turkey and cheese sandwiches and pull water-skiers and get a little sunburned under the sapphire skies in Montana. With mountains all around.

I pray that gratitude is not lost on him.

I wonder if he knows that I lay this morning in the curve of his shoulder. And dreamed his dreams.

And then we have a date.

Our kids are at day camp, and we have a good old-fashioned date.

His idea. It's like yet another miracle.

It's the first day alone together (alone together—guardians of each other's solitude) in so long I can't remember the last time. Oh, last winter. We had a weekend at a fancy resort. Hotel sex and all that. But here, in Montana. Just hanging out together. Seriously, it might be years. Many of them. I keep catching myself being surprised that he's not on his cell phone talking with a buddy, planning a tee time or a fishing trip.

He's choosing me.

So the first thing we do is have sex.

How is it possible that the sex is great right now? I'm baffled by it. Really. A friend of mine says it's common in couples that are about to get a divorce because it's familiar and both parties are scared shitless of never getting laid again. I don't know if I buy that. But there's a newness to it that I'll admit feels desperate. It's like little red convertible sex. And I try not to think that if he's had an affair, I could now have an STD. But again—no evidence. Should we screen our partners every time we have sex, on the off chance that they've screwed somebody else? What kind of world do we live in? I want to live in one of trust. So I try to rid my mind of that noise.

Afterward, we grab some beer and go to the river. I'm in Supercool Wife mode—still smiling over the helicopter visit, taking full but private credit for it.

So I dive headfirst into the glacial-runoff brain-freeze of the North Fork of the Flathead River, and I don't trip scrambling back up the thirty-foot drop-off and the slimy river rocks. I think I might sort of look like a twenty-year-old river-rafting guide, if it wasn't for my mommy bathing suit, complete with skirt to cover any unsightly cellulite.

I flash on a negative thought: I wish our room had curtains so he didn't need to be reminded of my forty-one-year-old body this morning in bed.

But we're not doing that anymore, remember? We want to be free, even of that—even of our cellulite and that weird paunch we have across our bellies that we NEVER had until just this last year.

We're loving ourselves just as we are because there's no other option but pain. And we're done with pain. So, yeah, we'll go to the gym in September when the kids are back in school, and we'll lose that paunch. And we'll do it for ourselves because we love ourselves, darn it.

But for right now, we get to feel sexy in this body and certainly not try to buff it out just to keep the man around, no matter what your dear mother says to you. We don't do things like that for him because we're scared of being alone. We don't. We do it for ourselves. We are very, very evolved.

So on the river, I feel cool. I throw my shoulders back. I'm a chick, and yet I'm not talking about my feelings, or asking him to talk about his. He's just spent the last hour on the phone with every one of his family members on the subject of his sick sister. They're all on alarm because of the obvious, and I'm watching him be genuinely scared and sad, but showing signs of deep strength. It's like therapy is coming to him.

But I'm not saying a damn thing about it except stuff like, "You are a good brother." "You are a good son."

In fact, when I forget supercool river chick and turn into Elastigirl for a second and say, "How are you doing?" and when he pauses, I just flip it and say, "You know what—it's too heavy. Let's just hang out by the river and not have to talk." This is not my custom—staying on the shallow side of things. And he knows it. And I can tell he's thankful for it.

I stack river stones in a cairn. Then I balance three or four on their ends. Then I soak some willow branches and make a sculpture with them that sort of looks like a dream catcher and I stake it into the rocks and it's really beautiful. That's something I like about myself, and I'm hoping he's remembering that he likes it about me, too. I like to go around making things beautiful.

He rolls a few cigarettes and smokes. This is new. New to me. I'm getting let into something sacred: guy time. This is what he does with his buddies. He goes to a river with some beer and some tobacco and casts out his fly line, and catches a cutthroat, first try. I'm thrilled for him. And I'll admit it—I'm strategically elated that I am his witness.

"Did you see that!" he says. He's just a boy wanting someone to see that he caught a fish. First cast. A pretty decent-sized fish. There's something about watching a man take a hook out of the mouth of a fish he's going to release. It's sort of the way a woman wants to be touched—with gratitude and respect.

He casts his line again and smokes.

I skip a few stones.

Then he sits next to me and does something he's been doing since our Boston days. Something borrowed straight from our engagement ceremony by the river in Washington. He puts a heart-shaped rock in my hand. It's rose-colored and smooth and wet, from the river, like a human heart.

I pull him in and kiss him and whisper something to him that we've been whispering to each other for twenty years. "Everything's going to be okay." It's yet another risk, but it feels right.

He's my buddy and we're escaping the wrath of that shitty wife of his and the pressures of family life, and we're hanging out, playing hooky together on the river.

"It's not going to be okay," he says. "It's going to be really not okay. And then . . . it's going to be okay."

I skip a few more stones and feel my stomach skipping and sinking with them into the river. What does he mean, "not okay"? Which "not okay"? His sister? Our finances? Our marriage? Please, not that. Is "okay" the definition of him living alone, divorced? And me, yeah fine, alone, too? Somehow both of us better for it? No! No no no! Who else would sit there by the river and balance stones and witness his fish? Can't we just do a one-eighty? And be friends again? Be good to each other and our wedding vows. But without any myths or pedestals?

It doesn't have to be hard. As long as we're dealing in honesty. We'll be honest with each other now. There's no such thing as golden. There's no such thing as special. We don't believe in myths. We're just here in Montana in our true nature. In our spiritual birthday suits. The first day of the first morning. We are fallen. But we don't have to run in shame. We can stay in the garden. Can't we? If the garden is a river like this one?

I tighten my grip on the heart-shaped rock.

Our hearts are heavy there by the river. The rock is heavy. The heaviest thing of all, his sister's ordeal. That she's dealing with what will probably be her last year alive, while her beloved husband is divorcing her. So she's having to go through a court case and cancer . . . alone. Isn't it unbelievable? And the five kids have to figure out how to not hate their father. He's who they'll have left. And they'll need him.

I bring it up—another risk. But it feels important to say how important he will be to the kids—a male force in their lives who's on their mother's side, and their side, and coming to Colorado to prove it.

I'm also, of course, subliminally reminding him about the destruction of divorce on wives and children, and that he'll be this same kind of human being if he does what he started the summer out saying he was going to do.

But now it's mid-August and he's been around. So I don't know what to think. One minute he's watering the plum tree and the next he's disappearing with fishing buddies. Though that's been happening much less.

"It's so great that you're going down to Colorado to help. Those kids' hearts are breaking."

It backfires. I'm not the cool buddy anymore.

He says, "Yeah, well, divorce happens. And kids have to deal with it. It's not just death and taxes you can count on. It's death, divorce, and taxes." Didn't I just use this line of reasoning? To no avail.

I'm really quiet after that. He fishes and I stack rocks, palming the heart-shaped rock. I have a whole pathway of these in my garden that we've collected over the years. Including the ones from our engagement ceremony. This one seems like one I want to carry with me to bed tonight. To place under my pillow like a lost tooth.

Then I realize I need to make a phone call and my cell phone is dead, so I reach for his, which he's left on his shirt.

He gets pissed and says, "What are you doing?"

And I admit, I'm looking through his contact list for the number I need. But he's my husband. We don't have secrets. Do we? It's not like I'm sneaking around behind his back. I'm sitting next to him in plain view.

He grabs the phone and pushes some buttons and says, "There's no one in there that you need to be worried about. It's just private. That's all. I don't like people messing with my phone."

Again, how quickly the heart lifts and falls.

Secrets. He has secrets. What kind of secrets? How unconscionable?

Why does someone want their contacts to be private? My options seem bleak.

I try them on for size:

A woman: But I watched him tell me it's not a woman. I have a third eye for lying when it comes to him. I've chosen to believe him, even if I'm a fool. Again—no hard evidence.

Drugs: It's a resort town, yes. But he's not a total derelict, is he?

Denial: Maybe he's throwing me a surprise party for my upcoming birthday? Maybe he's been in touch with my agent and they're plotting to make a big announcement in person with a big New York editor! One of my books is finally selling! Yeah, right.

I choose none of them. I choose silence and breathing.

He moves down the river to fish a different hole.

Then I take the heart-shaped rock and cast it into the river. My heart is rock. The river will keep it for me. It will hold my hope. Maybe one day, it will spill out into the deep blue sea.

Derailed

August 23, 2008.

So it's my forty-second birthday and my family is visiting. It's our annual family summer get-together. And this year, Montana is the chosen venue. There are many generations involved. Rented cabins in the woods. Plans for lavish family meals and sunny outdoor excursions.

I've been looking forward to it. To have my family around. To forget about the challenges of this summer and imagine it could be any summer in a host of summers in the span of my life.

Even so, given our marital ordeal, I'm not sure why I signed up for this. It's challenging enough to achieve a certain level of mental and spiritual health when one is in crisis. But to expect to do it with witnesses, in broad daylight, and not hunkered down in blankets deep into the night . . . is another thing entirely.

And quite frankly, family visits without my father are hard

for me. Seeing that cast of characters assembled in a room still makes me look around for him—followed by the punch to the gut that he's not there. I can't grab him for a walk and bounce around ideas, or rant about something, or brag about some accomplishment that I'd never dare brag about to anyone else. Nobody would give me his response. That kind of blind foolish adoration and praise. Lack of judgment. And advice. Especially now—I want to ask him for advice.

But more than anything, I want him to tell me that I'm lovable. Of course I am. Men go through hard times in middle age. Especially when there's job stress. Right, Dad?

Bottom line: When you're working with living in the moment and trusting that your happiness is solely your responsibility . . . and you're pretty new at its practical application, then maybe don't have the better part of your family of origin come to visit. For two weeks. Especially when your crisis isn't over yet.

It wasn't their fault. They didn't know what they were getting into. We hadn't shared our marital adventure with any of them. Like I said, we didn't want to worry them. And besides, things seemed like they were turning around. My husband was looking me in the eye again. Showing up for dinner. Watching sports, thanks to his new satellite dish.

It seemed like we could pull it off.

But no.

I got derailed. Couldn't find my center. Spun out in a million pieces. Most of it privately. But there was one bad night, when I decided to attach myself to a bottle of vodka.

I think it had to do with having witnesses to my life. That's what triggered it. I'd been such a solo act all summer—walking my line—hunkered down with my kids.

And suddenly there were witnesses.

It was like having an audience to a play you wrote and are now starring in, without somehow meaning to. And it's opening night. And it's a packed house. And you recognize every single person in the audience. Including some pretty highbrow critics. And you can't remember your lines. Or your costume changes. And your leading man is being played by his understudy.

The good news is this: You don't really remember the play. But apparently you went onstage. And the critics panned the whole production, especially your performance, which was sloppy and inappropriate—the worst of all family-of-origin sins.

Fill in the blank with your own best performances. At least I didn't get naked. At least I didn't throw up on anybody. At least I didn't break any bones when I fell face-first in the living room, thanks to my pal Smirnoff—Sheila's favorite Russian uncle.

But it's not over until it's over. And the encore happens the next day in a river raft, in a Class III rapid, on the Middle Fork of the Flathead River.

My mother announces that we're going river-rafting. It's my birthday present from her. Her way of relating to my life in the wilderness.

I try to practice gratitude. That's so sweet. I'm so lucky. My mother is giving me a river-rafting trip for my birthday! I'm pretending that I want this gift more than anything I've ever wanted in all my life—this thing tourists do. Through regimented guide companies. In Barbasol-soaked booties. And not with buddies and beer.

I wipe away the fantasy of galloping away from them all on my horse, into the woods. Alone. I wipe away dreams of sushi. Of a spa. In Ojai. That I can somehow afford again. No. I'm psyched to be going river-rafting with almost-octogenarians and small children. C'mon. I'm a sport. I'm a Montana chick!

Plus, it's an opportunity to show everyone that despite my vodka-induced performance, I'm actually a very grounded, centered, underailable woman who has been a friggin' rock all summer long. A heart-shaped rock. If I must say so myself.

My husband looks like he's about to have a root canal. I can read his mind: he's wondering how we're going to get through a day on the river without cold beer. He hasn't yet looked me in the eye this morning. He hasn't yet wished me happy birthday. He has, however, hugged both our kids and made jokes with them and made them laugh and think he's their hero.

I can tell that he's mad about my performance. Which I can take responsibility for. And I have. But Sheila begs the question: What do his "performances" look like at the bar at two a.m.? I talk her down: We're human. We screw up. We're going through a brutal time in our lives. It ain't always gonna be pretty.

I'm trying my best to tell Sheila where to put it—to pack up her bullwhip and go pick on someone else. It's my friggin' birthday! I love my birthday. Usually.

For some reason it's sixty-five degrees on the twenty-third of

August this year. I'm underdressed. I'm wearing soccer shorts and a sleeveless shirt that's a little on the short side, so that I keep having to pull down the sides to hide my new little paunch. I'm freezing my ass off already, but I'm not saying it, because I'm cool. Everyone else is complaining. I'm a Montana chick now. Not some freaking debutante anymore. I can handle a little chill in the air. It will redeem me.

But God—I want to be home in bed in flannel pj's. I want to be snuggled up with my husband, watching an old movie. Opening a present or two. Nothing big. Just a card would do. Usually he writes "Two Balloons" on my birthday card. Not this year. There's no card. And from the looks of it, there's not going to be. I have "sinned." Just like he wanted me to. I gave him just what he wanted. Fuck me. I'm such an idiot. And I don't need Sheila to tell me so.

At least we share this: he and I are both naturally reacting to this scene the same way.

We Montanans can be a bit cavalier because of the tourist invasion, and what we live through three hundred and sixty-five days a year and call life—forest fires, avalanches, bitter cold, black ice, life with grizzly bears and mountain lions. So we're being cavalier and distant as the river guides tell the tourists local cutesy chuckly jokes and factoids we've heard a thousand times. The tourists nervously raise their hands and say things like, "Can grizzly bears swim?"

Mostly, we just can't believe we have to wear helmets. For "insurance" sake. As if we're the suing type. Suing somebody seems to us like an urban malady. Plus, we've never worn helmets on a river. That's like wearing a Hawaiian shirt to a black-tie party. We're pissed.

In the bus on the way to the river, my mother keeps turning around and saying, "You look so miserable. Why do you both look so miserable?" then turning back around before either of us can give her an answer.

Truth be told, I haven't actually rafted this stretch of river before. The trips I've taken have been more like floats, a little fly-fishing off the sides, picnics on the shore, a cooler of beer with friends. I've heard there are some Class III rapids on this stretch, but I've also heard it's not like Colorado or anything.

So when they tell me to cinch down my life jacket, I sort of smirk and pretend to. Same with my helmet. And I haven't taken their advice and put a back band around my sunglasses. I'm not a spaz or anything. I'm not incompetent.

There are three rafts total on this expedition. We get put with a couple from LA and their two kids. So it's the guide, my husband and me, our kids, my mother and her new husband, and this LA family, who look a bit like they've seen *Deliverance* too many times. They hesitate before stepping into the raft, eyeing us, calmed, then, by my mother's pink lipstick.

Finally, we're all in the raft after much complaining from everybody who is not a Montanan about how cold the water is. It's just above freezing. Ten seconds ago it was snow—surely they all understand this.

There is much discussion about how the others keep their swimming pools at eighty-five degrees.

"The water is straight off the glaciers," I remind them.

Chirp . . . chirp.

When the mother of the family asks what temperature the water is, the guide says, "Cold enough."

We all get in, and my husband and I take the rear. Our kids want to be in front so they can get wet.

My eighty-year-old stepfather announces in his Jack Benny–esque voice, "Why . . . you know . . . I'm not much of a swimmer."

Excellent.

The woman from LA then says, "Paddles? We're paddling? I'm a Jew from LA. I don't paddle."

Even more excellent.

My husband and I make small talk with the guide, who's young and preppy-looking, and we're both clearly trying to relive our twenties by pumping him for local summer stories of women and heavy drinking and dumb tourists. We want him to give us the nod of approval—*You guys are still cool,* that sort of thing.

In short, he gives no one on the boat any information about river safety. Probably because we're too busy chatting him up, trying to feel local and cool.

Actually, that's not correct. He does tell us that we are the motor. Some motor.

And he says, "When I say, 'All forward,' paddle forward, in sync, the ones at the front setting the pace." (That would be my kids. Other than my husband and me, the most capable of the bunch . . . and they're eight and twelve.) "And when I say, 'All back,' paddle backwards." He doesn't say how to paddle.

"All forward!" he shouts.

And suddenly we're in white water. Rocks all around and huge swirling pools of water sucking at us, drawing us through like babies being born, or more—like afterbirths being pulled by the umbilical cord . . . and the family from LA is shrieking. Not with joy.

I'll admit, it's a whole lot more white water than I'd imagined. Our kids are laughing and getting soaked. The senior citizens look sedated. Maybe they think they're watching this on TV. Then our guide says, "All relax," and I want to kiss him. I've been longing all summer for somebody to steer my ship through these familiar waters. A bold but gentle guide who will kindly take over, telling me that I can relax. Let go. Someone's at the steerage.

So I relax, like I'm told. For now, the river is calm and smooth. My mom and her husband are having a good time taking pictures of themselves. The folks from LA are asking us what life is like here, like we are aliens. But my mother makes sure they know the town I'm originally from in Chicago and the lifestyle I left behind, and I can tell they think we're cool whether or not my mother or the guide do. We play it up and point things out—

bald eagles, mergansers (not just ducks—I know my birds), deer drinking at the river's edge.

They take about five thousand photographs of the deer. They've never seen a deer in nature. They start to tell us all about the things they have seen at the Los Angeles Zoo.

I zone out and try to think about breathing. Containing myself again after these two weeks of family visitors.

The river is calm here, and I feel the water swirling around my oar. I paddle in time with my husband. It feels good to be in sync. We've spent so many years being in sync. We're good together. Especially as parents. It would be nice to have a witness to that lately, since we haven't exactly been our best selves.

Then I start to derail because I realize that it's me who notices where we're in sync, and he who looks for where we're not. When did that happen? When did he start needing to make me wrong? We were always such champions of each other. But I focus on something positive. Something I can control. Something I'm proud of. Something I'm good at and that my husband loves about me. I focus on my motherhood. The conversations I have with my children in their beds every morning and night—about friendship and God and playground politics—stroking their hair, rubbing their backs. The bald eagles we've watched, the horses we've ridden, swam with in the river, mushrooms we've picked, bulbs we've planted, meals we've cooked straight from our garden. How my kids are rarely late to anything. How I try with all my might to make every one of their wildest dreams come true. How they eat healthful, well-balanced meals every day; the love notes I put in their lunch boxes.

I'm trying to stay in a place of love. The high road. I'm trying to create a healthy flow of love from me out to the world and everything in it. I breathe deeply. I don't want to fight. Or be angry. Or even vanish. I want to feel smooth like this bit of river. And slowly, the river takes my mind to glass. I've got Montana running in my veins, healing me again in its waters and creature world. I am calm and I breathe.

Then my mother turns around with her camera and shouts, "Get together, you two, so I can take a picture of you."

My husband doesn't move.

I lean across the raft toward him, and she starts to take a picture but then pulls back the camera. "Why do you both look so miserable?" Then quickly she says, "Can you take a picture of us?"

I remember one of my mantras from long ago: sometimes we just have to let ourselves be misunderstood. This summer has been one of those times. This season of family visitors is the crux of it.

Breathe. This is the pain brought by thinking. The *shenpa*, Pema Chödrön calls it. The hook. She's a Tibetan Buddhist nun, and her message is so powerful no matter what your faith base is or isn't. I'm listening to her a lot these days in my car—her CD *Getting Unstuck*. I decide to return to my breath and be with the moment. Stay with the moment. Why do family reunions have to be so lethal?

So now I'm looking at the riverbanks and loving my Montana. Proud of myself in it. For two seconds without thought.

Glide . . .

Sheila dive-bombs like a hungry hawk:

Fuck 'em all! It's your birthday. You should celebrate yourself today . . . with people who want to be photographed with you, with people who, if they think you're "miserable" would give you a good hard hug, not require you to feel any way other than how you feel, and love you through it. You usually start off your birthday by jumping up and down in excitement.

Sheila is so confusing when she takes my side. Most of all, I hate it when she's right.

I decide that regardless of my fragile state, as soon as I'm done receiving this birthday gift, I'm going to go home and cut roses for myself from my garden, peach and pale pink, and put them in a sterling-silver mint julep cup that was my grandmother's and take a bath with them right by my head. I'm going to warm this chill out of my bones which is getting increasingly worse. I'm going to be very, very selfish!

My mother looks back at me again and asks me to take yet another photo of her and her husband, whom she is smiling at adoringly, and he at her. How is it possible that she, a near octogenarian in a thick yellow "slicker," as she calls it (circa 1959), its hood extending under her helmet, a woman wearing khaki "slacks," as she calls them—how is it that this woman can gain the affection of her man, when a forty-two-year-old woman in cool sunglasses and Patagonia cannot?

I take the photo and she looks at me again. "You must be cold in that outfit."

I'm rarely cold. I pride myself on this. But today, it is cold. Unseasonably. I'm underdressed, and I'm pissed that she was right when she said this morning, a know-it-all: "It's going to be about sixty-four today. Shouldn't you be wearing a slicker and slacks?"

I stare at a bald eagle who stares back at me, and I want to keep it just between us, but I realize I should probably point it out.

"I've never seen a bald eagle before," the father from LA says.

"It's there," I say. "In the tree snag."

"Where?"

For all my pointing, he can't see it.

"Don't worry," his wife tells him. "They have one at the zoo."

"It's right there. Twelve o'clock," I say.

They don't know what that means, turns out. I let it go like everything else. I have returned to the breath. For more than a few seconds. More like minutes. I think of the heart-shaped rock my husband gave me at the bottom of another fork of this river. It helps me.

And I decide that this is a good birthday even if my husband isn't observing it this year. Even though I gave him a gift certificate toward his helicopter dream for his birthday a month ago. And arranged for them to drop his pilot study books from the hovering aircraft in our front yard. But, hey. That kind of thinking and four dollars buys you a cup of joe at Starbucks if you're lucky, so I'm just breathing and seeing the bald eagle that

I know at least my kids and my husband can see. And I spotted it to begin with so that makes me the cool eagle chick for right now. People who spot eagles are cool. It's an unwritten law in Montana. So I'm "all good" as the twenty-year-old river guides/snowboarders/bartenders like to say in our fair valley. All good. Return to the breath.

Here's the funny part:

"Okay, folks," our guide says. "This next rapid is a Class Three. It's the one that rafts sometimes flip over on. Not to scare you. And not like anybody's goin' off. I'm not saying that. But just in case, if you do . . . just ride it out with your feet in front of you like you're in a lounge chair, and try to stay as close as you can to the raft and we'll pull you out by the strap on the top of your jacket, so cinch it tight. And when I say, 'Lean in,' lean in to your right. Okay, folks?"

"Okay," we all say in different degrees of fear. But I'm still in cool-girl mode—loose helmet, loose vest. These are tourist waters. I'm so not a tourist.

The woman from LA looks terrified, and even her ginormous Prada sunglasses look dwarfed by the imposing rapid ahead. I am reminded of the seventies movie *The Poseidon Adventure*. She'd be the one to bite it.

I look ahead at the rocks and swirling water. Personally, I'm not afraid for myself. I'm afraid for everybody else on the raft, except my husband. He's not the fall-out kinda guy. But this is like *Gilligan's Island*. There's not a capable one in the bunch, with the exception of me and my husband. I'm hoping that he's thinking the same thing. But maybe he's thinking it's just him. And the guide. Because, remember, I am so incompetent.

We come up to a slick, sloped, rock outcropping that makes up the right bank, and a series of huge boulders in the middle of the river that make up the left bank of the rapid. The guide takes us toward the rock, the current driving hard.

"Now lean in to the right!" he yells as he slopes us onto it, high-lipped so that we're swooping into the air on the right side, like a pancake about to be flipped.

We all lean right.

My mother leans left. The other right.

I lunge forward to try to push her to the right, and with my center of gravity up higher, I swear . . . with every horse-riding, witnessed or not, kick-ass Montana moment I've known these last fifteen years . . . we're goin' over. And I'm not going to ride this Class III rapid with a bunch of inept people and a raft over my head. People die on this river every few years. This is very, very real.

So I do what I do when a horse rears or falls or freaks out. I bail.

It's partly that I've lost my footing, but it's mostly that I need to bail so I can be free from the raft when it goes over, and free to help rescue all these people. Because at least I know: I am competent.

It's as fast and as powerful as anything I've known. The rapid sucks me into it and under. Way under. I'm going down and my loosely cinched life jacket and loosely cinched helmet are pulling up, choking me, and it's all white; a fury. I keep waiting to come to the top, but I'm still going down, and I know what I'm up against. There could be a tree buried down here that my life jacket could get caught on. And how in the hell could anyone possibly control their hands or fingers enough to unbuckle a life jacket to break free? And in that moment, you want your life jacket, because you are ever aware that it is the thing that is going to allow you to surface in the first place and to live out the rest of your shitty forty-second birthday.

There is no buried tree.

I surface, gasp for air, and then, yep, get sucked back down for a longer stint, this time getting twisted in a three-sixty and bashed against a rock before I'm up and over to the side, careening toward the sharp rocky banks, covered in slimy moss, impossible to get hold of. My nose is full of water, and I snort it out and cough up what's in my lungs and try to see the others, surely in worse shape than I. Surely.

The whole scene flashes before me: My new stepfather who can't swim, clinging to a rock. My mother in her yellow slicker, bobbing unconscious. My children grasping an overturned raft.

I see the rafts, two in front, another behind.

Only none of them has turned over. No one has fallen out.

Except me.

Happy fucking birthday, cool Montana chick!

I remember to put my feet out in front of me. I'm still in white water, so it's not easy, but I realize I've still got the paddle in my hand, and my sunglasses are somehow still at the top of my life jacket. I shove them into my bust, and use my paddle to keep from being smashed against the rocks.

The last raft comes up behind me, and the guide yells, "Are you okay?"

I nod. "Yep." Grossly humbled.

"Swim to the raft," he says.

You've got to be kidding. But I've got my paddle, so I reach it out in front of me and he maneuvers the raft toward it, grabs the end of it, and pulls me to the side of the raft. I want to be in that raft. It's splinteringly cold. But there's no way I can hoist myself up, with no footing, in white water.

"Now hold on to this side strap for a bit," he says, "because we've got another rapid ahead of us."

Uh . . . I'm thinking, *a body can't handle this kind of cold for too long.* My hands are shaking with adrenaline and chill. I've heard horror stories of local rafting accidents, and they reel through my mind. I question the notion of knowledge being power right now. Something I've questioned a lot this summer. But I manage to keep hold of the strap, ride out the next rapid from the water, my feet under the raft, my ass hitting rock, and then in an eddy, he says, "Now climb on in."

You've got to be kidding. I honestly have never felt weaker in my life. I try to climb in, but it's physically impossible. My body is shaking with adrenaline and chill. My hands are frozen claws.

So he grabs the strap at the top of my life jacket, and hauls my forty-two-year-old body into the raft, headfirst, feet hanging off the end like a giant squid whose thighs touch, for all to see.

"You held on to your paddle!" he says, and it's the nicest thing anyone's said to me all day. Maybe all summer.

"And my sunglasses!" I say, catching my breath, looking to him for approval, snot all over my face. "Don't worry," I add. "I'm a local." Like now I'm definitely cool. God. All I can think is that my husband officially hates me.

When we come up along the raft that contains my original spot, and I climb in, shaking uncontrollably, they sing me "Happy Birthday," all three rafts, even my husband. The LA chick says, with a look of raw horror, "There's no way that's happenin' to me."

This is where I want to tell them all that I was trying to save my mother's life and potentially theirs, too. But I don't. I shiver. My daughter looks at me, sheet white, and says, "That was so scary, Mom. I feel like I'm going to barf. Are you okay?"

"Yeah. I'm okay," I lie.

Still I don't really get any eye contact from my husband, except he looks at me sort of sideways, the way you eye a car that passes you on the right.

"By the way," the guide says, "that's the death seat you were in." He smiles.

I'll add in here that originally, my husband was sitting in it, but I asked to switch because my back was hurting. I wish it had happened to him. The part where he had to try to save my mother's life, and the part where he got to be humbled by the river.

I ride the rest of the river with my life vest cinched as tightly as I can get it, ditto my helmet, and I realize that if the float lasts much longer, I could get hypothermia I'm so cold. But I don't say anything. When is the last time you shivered like a little kid who's been in the pool too long? Purple-lipped.

But I rode it. And I lived. And I felt better for it—another chance to take the high road. Right ear ringing and all. It was a whole lot like the rest of my summer. I'd had weeks of practice but this was the ultimate test because in that moment under the water, I felt it: true surrender. True powerlessness and then, true surrender.

Not state-of-emergency. But . . . really . . . nothingness. Zen's no-mindedness. Detachment. The moment of waking. Before thought. True nature. It all came together in that moment in the river. Even more than in my boarding school walk in the woods. Or my moment in Italy. Or even in natural childbirth with my first child, where I felt like I was in the perfect cusp of all that was life and all that was death. Like I would die to have the child live. Again, it wasn't scary. Because the mind was quiet. Sometimes, I guess, we have to be very close to death to find this place.

It was afterward that the fear rushed in. I took that fearless, no-minded moment in the rapid as my real birthday gift. It would be my reference point from now on. Marital adventures and otherwise.

Later, at the car, I'm changing into a fleece and yoga pants, and my husband comes up to get something out of the car and I grab him and say, "Give me a goddamn birthday hug."

A girl can ask for a goddamn hug on her birthday.

He hugs me.

"That was scary," I say.

I don't defend myself and try to explain away why I was the one who fell out. I just stand there, shaking, allowing myself to be misunderstood, being hugged on my birthday by my husband. Breathing.

Community

Labor Day weekend.

It's gloomy and cold. I'm making myself not comment on the amount of football and golf and tennis and boxing and baseball and more football . . . that's being watched in our household. I'm being a realist. This is what is. Nor am I commenting on the fact that my sweet adorable sensitive eight-year-old son is now screaming, "Take him down, ya retard!" at the TV screen, lying on the couch, next to his father, scratching his balls.

This is not the time to have a talk with my son about discriminatory language or what we do in private with our bodies. I'm choosing instead not to say a thing. Because I know that now, on top of not having a job . . . my husband's sister is dying.

If he needs to use TV sports as a drug, so be it. This is not a time to ask anyone to be their best selves. Especially since I know that he's about to be called upon to be just that.

His sister has qualified for a clinical trial in Chicago and she wants to try it; to see if it will stop her tumor from growing. The odds are minuscule that it will add up to anything more than just a little hope in this time of preparing for death. But she's willing to try. For hope alone, perhaps. She is remarkable. Her hope inspires me.

It will be a fall and maybe even a winter of helping her along in this process, whichever direction it goes. He is the family member that lives closest, though the others have come with all their hearts.

The truth is that even though he's scouring the Internet for a job, he is the one without job requirements at the moment. Though nothing makes sense about her cancer, it does make sense that he, among so many dear ones, will be called to be of comfort to her. Now is his turn.

It's changed him overnight. He's reliable again. Fixing things that have long been broken. Painting over bald spots on the porch railing. I keep catching him gazing off into the woods, mid-fix, like he's checking for bears or mountain lions on our property. But I know that's not what it is. I know that he's heartbroken about his sister. It just doesn't make sense that she'd have this form of rare and aggressive cancer. Such an amazing woman. The very definition of mother, wife, healthy lifestyle, community volunteer. Not even fifty.

And I know he's thinking about his own life. Feeling unworthy of his health, and all that he has at his table, especially since lately he's treated it carelessly. Even so, I wish he could see that he's given us so much for so long in ways that have nothing to do with financial success. And he's given us that, too. I wonder if in his mind, the last seven years have undone the first eight when he was financially successful. When he did love his job. When he was so linked to the community. When he felt so powerful and "worthy." Like he's been stirring the sauce backward.

I want him to go forward. "All forward." I want him to find his way to the man who doesn't need to be defined by his outward success. Because there I know I can find an equal partner. But even more, there, I know he'll find freedom.

Something tells me being there to help his sister . . . will do just that. And knowing her, she'll be working this angle. She believes in inspiring people. She has quotes all over her house to this effect:

"You miss one hundred percent of the shots you don't take."

"The end of something is always the beginning of something else."

"You gain strength, courage, and confidence by every experience in which you really stop to look fear in the face. You are able to say to yourself, 'I have lived through this horror. I can take the next thing that comes along' (Eleanor Roosevelt)."

I especially like that last one. It reminds me that suffering is a relative term. And pain is pain is pain.

It also reminds me of the opposite of fear—my high school discovery that still rings true: love. Sure, that love has to start within, but how can we beam it out to the world? I bet his sister would say through family. And community. Through inspiring people.

And I think about how people need community as much as it needs its people. My husband and I used to be so much a part of things in our Montana town. Movers and shakers. As much as you can move and shake in a town of five thousand or so. But in all our feelings of failure, we've pulled away from our community. I haven't really seen it until this moment. I used to be on boards. Spearheading fund-raising parties and street dances. Attending writing conferences and volunteering to teach in the schools in their creative writing courses. Singing and playing guitar for the kids in school. Showing up at rallies in support of our local environmental issues. I was a giver. And so was he.

When he ran the brewery, people came to him daily wanting his support. He rarely turned anyone down. He had the respect of local politicians and prominent figures, regardless of their politics—everyone from the chief of police to the rancher/farmer who used to pick up the spent grain from the brewery to feed his livestock. That man is our governor now. My husband has the ability to wear many hats. Well. People love him for that. I love him for that.

His sister and her kids will be a community for him in this next phase of his life.

Knowing this, I decide to help create this moment of comfort for him. Father and son lying on the couch. Even though I loathe football—don't really even understand it. Looks like glorified war to me.

But I think, *What do football wives do?*

I open the pantry door and scan the contents for something football-ish. As if by magic, a bag of Doritos appears. I have never bought Doritos in all my life. It's a leftover from the last batch of visitors. Doritos. Cool Ranch Doritos, even. And another bag. The kind that turns your tongue blue. Perfect. I put them into a bowl. This is the Dorito debut in our healthy home, and I place them on the coffee table as if I've done it a thousand times before.

My husband and son assume it's hummus and they ignore it.

But slowly, the tangy aroma infiltrates their football haze, and they perk up. And start power-loading their mouths with God-knows-what's-in-a-Dorito.

I relax into the rocking chair, making sure that I am within their line of peripheral vision. I feel very football-ish. I want him to feel my support. And I'll admit it: I want some credit for it, after a summer of feeling so unappreciated.

My hands rest in my lap. I start rocking harder, catch myself, and slow down. My God, I'm bored out of my mind. That's when I see my laptop innocently lying on the hearth, just inches from my right hand. And in the spirit of the game, a conversation I had earlier that day with one of my best friends instant-replays in my mind. "I can't believe you're not on Facebook! It's so much fun. Especially you, living out in the boondocks. It's excellent networking and totally addicting."

"Isn't it for, like, high school kids?"

"Hell, no—you're definitely hip enough. You don't want to lose your groove, do you?"

Lose my groove? Certainly not. I'm hip. I'm happening. I'm popular. Aren't I?

I eye the laptop. Then I reach for it. *Click. Click click click*, and I'm creating a password. I choose: *Football*. I'm going to see what all this Facebook ruckus is about.

You know Facebook, right? You're obviously more hip than I am, living in the middle of nowhere Montana. In case you don't, I'll cover it in a whisper—don't tell your kids or colleagues and definitely not your spouse. It's a networking site on the Internet where you join for free, search for people you might know, and if they are a member of Facebook, you can "request" their friendship. If they accept you, you're invited in to their personal page. If not, you can still view their Friends to look for more people you might know, or might want to know, and try to poach them. In short, you get in touch with people you sort of meant to lose contact with and you spend a lot of time checking if that old boyfriend who dumped you in the eighties will at least Accept you as a Friend so you can show him your home page full of the best photos you could find of yourself, and your tragically attractive children, and your insanely cool life in the mountains. Also, you are proud to point out that your Status is still Married.

In one night of doing Facebook, you've posted a photo of every impressive activity you've done in recent memory—dogsledding, river-rafting (in the caption, you don't add the part where you almost drowned), skiing, boating, snorkeling, water-skiing, horseback-riding, hiking. And you've been highly strategic in posting your best exotic travel shots, even though most of them include you in a bathing suit—which isn't necessarily a good thing. So you've found the ones where your children are standing in front of your thighs. And there you are with your Italian family in their living room feeling like a million bucks after a long time of not feeling like a million bucks. You realize how starved you've been for community. And heck, you've got friends all over—after all the places you've lived through the years, from coast to coast.

So you search like a madwoman. Turns out a lot of people you know are on this thing. Just not anyone you know . . . well. Which means you are the most immature of all your best friends. Or that they're too busy for this shit. Or . . . or . . . maybe it's that they don't know about Facebook. They've become old and un-hip and jaded. But not you. You're eternally young!

At first, you're discerning. Why would you want to be in touch with him? Eww. Didn't he try to put his tongue down your throat at a dance in high school? Wasn't she like . . . one of the mean girls?

"Touchdown! Oh yeah!" Husband and son do a little couch dance and spill the Doritos.

My daughter comes in to see what all the racket is about, takes one look at the sports and one look at you, decides you're all losers, and retreats back to her room where she can sit in bed and roll her eyes all afternoon. But not without saying, "Mom, isn't Facebook for like . . . young people?"

This is what puts you over the edge.

You hungrily proceed to request the friendships of every single person whose name you even remotely recognize on every network you can think of. You rip off friends of friends like the worst social climber. You shamelessly flirt with guys you know had a crush on you thirty years ago, enticing them to accept you as a friend with PG-13 innuendo.

And then you wait. And you upload more cool photographs of yourself onto your profile so that when they come, they will find an even better you than even you imagined possible. They'll drool over your life and wish they were you. Or that they'd married you. They'll look at that picture of you and your husband in Belize and say, *God—look how happy they are. Still look like movie stars after all these years. I bet they have rock-star sex.*

You click on Profile and it says, You have no friends, and you actually get depressed for a second.

The first person you hear from is your niece. She's crazy about Facebook.

"Aunt Laura, that's so funny you're on Facebook! College is great. I love my roommate. Luv ya."

She sends you a pudgy bunch of cartoon roses. It's not missed on you that she's just sent all her friends, instead, pudgy rounds of beer.

Then you go back into Search mode. You only have one friend

and she's related to you, and that's pathetic. You can't let anybody see this.

Must . . . have . . . more . . . friends.

"What are you doing?" your husband says, staring at you straight for the first time today.

"Facebook," you say, nonchalant.

He outright laughs.

"What? It's cool. You can't believe the old friends I'm getting in touch with." You are being sucked into the vortex of high school behavior.

Then, lo, you see that a request has been made for your friendship. By the most powerful girl in high school. The girl you were afraid to speak to; who made you shake in the knees. And you get to Agree or Ignore her. The power is tantalizing. So you spend approximately ten seconds ignoring her. You are SO high school.

And then . . . and only then . . . you point your last remaining fingernail to the track pad, and you tap: Agree. And like you just happen to be running into her in the cafeteria line, you tap again on her profile. And you see that she has exactly 1,753 friends.

This . . . my Friend . . . is war. And this from a woman who scoffs at football!

All three days of Labor Day weekend go by, gloomy and football-full. And you sit in that rocking chair with the computer hot and bothered in your lap, and you network. Your kids make fun of you. "It's great for my career," you say. Now they all outright laugh.

The whole thing is like one big orgy.

Then you get a message. Not even a private one. A Wall message for all to see. It's from a local friend. It says, "Get off Facesmack for a change and get over here immediately. There's an idiotic subdivision that we need to fight. We need your support. The meeting's tonight. Come over and I'll give you the lowdown."

Oh, yeah! My real community, you remember, but not before you ashamedly realize that people can monitor how long you've been on friggin' Facebook.

You log off fast. Slide your laptop into your old courier bag where it used to travel to important community meetings back when you were a mover and shaker and not a social networking whore, and you gently say, so as not to sound aloof to the sports viewers in your living room, "I'll be back in a little bit. I'm going to a meeting about some subdivision they're trying to sneak in."

Husband looks up. There is just the glimmer of old respect in his eye.

You'll take what you can get.

And as you drive to the meeting, you realize your Facebook bender is something not to repeat.

But you cut yourself some slack: for three solid days, you didn't feel lonely. Or rejected. You felt like your old self, who, by anyone's estimation (well, maybe not the girl with the one thousand some-odd friends) was popular again. And pretty. Desirable. Twenty. Golden again. Even though, at forty-two, I know all about clay feet.

His Sister's Gift

Back to school.

This is what it would be like. I'd be alone like this. In my bed. With the covers pulled high or low, the way I want them. Not having to dread his snoring. Knowing that unless my mind or my dream mind gets in the way of it, I'm going to have an excellent sleep. I can read late with the light on and not worry. I can watch Letterman, as loud as I want. It's not that bad.

Except that I'm a little scared for some reason, without the idea of his strength and testosterone somehow protecting us. I realized tonight in the pitch black of the Big Sky—coyotes barking and howling—how much I don't fear in life because of his testosterone. (Funny what you admit to yourself in the dark.)

He's used it at her house already. He's done heavy lifting household tasks for his sister in her husband's permanent absence.

Helped with her new garden vision; she, too, loves to make things beautiful. He's proud of helping to create that beauty, as his mother did in their childhood home, and yes, maybe as his wife has done in his adult one.

He calls me to report it: "I mowed the lawn, fixed the sprinklers, dealt with the garbage." He's got that First Day energy high.

But I can hear that he's scared, and I can hear that he feels powerless. This isn't a time to gloss over things as is his usual approach. This is a time for drastic measures. Real and difficult conversations. Granted, it's also time to do household tasks. I just fear that he'll hide behind them. I want him to be deeply affected by this. I want this to change his life. Awaken his soul.

And maybe it's happening, because later, when we call him, he answers right away. Not exactly his practice of late.

"What are you doing?" I ask.

"Watching the U.S. Open with everyone." When he lists who's there I realize that everyone includes: his sick sister, her two daughters, his other sister, his brother, and his brother's ex—all of whom have come to help.

In other words, he's sitting in a living room full of women, some of whom have been devastated, and maybe even fatally sickened, by marital abandonment. This seems like the perfect place for him to be, in my estimation. Of course, I would not wish this sort of pain on anybody. But it is possible to look at this as an opportunity for my husband to grow—as some sort of gift of soul from his sister to him. To our family.

I call his sister one night. She doesn't normally talk on the phone, but we talk for hours. We talk about how it is for her, physically and mentally and spiritually—and she gives me this at the end: "Good karma," she says.

Good karma. You listen differently to things from a dying person. There's no bullshit there. I memorize it for later—her voice in my ears. Good karma. I know to take it and fasten it to my heart as the best kind of blessing. A call to live life believing anything is possible. Especially from my husband's "second mother." A woman as graceful as she.

And it's bizarre. In the absence of him, just the kids and me in the house, the television cool and the hearth warm, classical music swelling in the bookshelves, tea in a pot on a tray . . . I feel a sense of relief.

After all this long summer, I want to sigh and keep on sighing until all the strands of fear and practiced surrender unwind into the foam of the couch, down through the floorboards, down through our foundation, into the ground, through layers of rock and clay and silt, all the way to obsidian. Mostly, I don't want to have to be competent or good or sexy or anything of substance. I want to put the kids to bed early and crawl into my bed and watch TV. Mindless TV. And nothing with balls.

For a while, I click back and forth between *Will & Grace* and *Sex and the City* reruns, *Iron Chef*, and Letterman. I cannot remember life feeling this uncomplicated and this uncharged. I feel myself letting down. And I sleep and sleep and sleep. No dreams—not that I can remember. I wake up in the exact position I fell asleep in eight hours ago. With a no-minded first glance at the trees out my bedroom window. This might be my first good sleep since Italy.

I take the kids to the first day of school, and everything goes so smoothly. Everything is easy. Even going to the county Planning Department and having a crash course in aquifers, riparian zones, floodplains, and storm drainage to arm myself for the upcoming subdivision fight . . . is easy. Even though I know we're going to have to move fast and it's going to be stressful.

By our county law, a developer proposing a subdivision larger than five lots has to notify only those neighbors within 150 feet. Which can mean, with large rural parcels of land divided by rivers and roads, that sometimes only one or two people are privy to their plans.

That's the case with this proposed subdivision. So, unless you're astute enough to read the legal notices in the daily paper or happen to spot the smallish sign on the property, you might just be seeing Eagle Vista Ranch going up in your relative backyard in the middle of rural Montana, which has been, for the most part, left pristine up until now. And there's nothing you can do about it except for wave good-bye to the eagles, because they are so out of there. And soon, your "vista" will be of a person in his/her plaid flannel pajamas, looking for eagles on a paved driveway next door, wondering why the L.L. Bean catalog lied to them.

So, thanks then to the eagle eye of one of the two neighbors of this parcel of land, at least we know what's up. But still, we only have five days to fight what could set a new precedent for growth and development in our rural area, forever. Because once you okay a one-acre parcel, there's no stopping suburbia in our neck of the woods. Montana just doesn't have the forward-thinking laws it needs to ensure responsible growth. Not yet.

Responsible growth. It feels so good to imagine it. In the land. In my marriage. In myself. It is so good to be focused on something other than my marriage and my well-being. To focus on my community again. But I'm not taking it personally like I might have in the past. I can be passionate but not attached to the outcome. I can dream a little.

I can apply my sister-in-law's wisdom that has had her triumphing over cancer for so many years. I can visualize:

The valley will not be chopped up into one-acre plots. On a floodplain. Polluting the river. It will be open and wide . . . a basin to hold its night sky in case it should ever choose to drop.

I don't have that desperate, powerless feeling of impending doom that I usually have when some asshole comes in and tries to do something ridiculous with the land in rural Montana.

It's one of our largest local issues: land use. Too often, outsiders come in and try to rape what has been protected by locals for generations. Locals understand how to live with the natural world—preserve it, respect it, with some level of harmony. Yet the people in positions of power in our community all too often give in to the carrot the developers dangle in front of their faces: Money. A future of wealth in a state that is mostly poor.

It breaks my heart how quickly some local politicos lose their perspective and forget what it is to be rich in open space. What a greater wealth that is when it comes to the future of our state. Our country. Our planet.

Don't worry. I won't go on and on. I can tell you this, however—you can't believe how fast people come together, regardless of their politics, when there's land rape in their backyard. Backyards in Montana can go for miles. And that won't be the case if we don't work together.

For the record: I'm not against change, growth, development. Heck, I bought my land and built my house. But this area is one of the last pristine wilderness areas in the lower forty-eight and I feel a responsibility to try to keep it that way on some level. With the focus off my marital adventure, I'm back to my old self, mouthing off at the café, the school parking lot, the soccer field . . . about stuff I care about. One-acre lots? It's totally reckless and uncharacteristic for this rural area. We have to fight.

But I'm using my new strategy. I'm not letting the fight control my well-being.

"We don't need one-acre lots. What's wrong with ten, or better yet twenty, like ours? The river is already on the Impaired list—one of the major drainages for Flathead Lake, which, according to the county Growth Policy, is supposed to be a barometer for watersheds from the Mississippi to the Pacific Ocean!"

It feels great to put my energy into something besides my

personal life. I can fume and not worry about it having marital repercussions. And I realize how insular I have been since Italy. Not just in a community-minded way. But socially, too. I've been a hermit during this stressful time, even though I promised myself I wouldn't be. I don't like myself this way. It's not who I am. I realize that, with the exception of the visitors, I haven't had anyone over for dinner all summer long. Suddenly I feel energized and alive.

But what I come to find after two hours at the Planning Department is that this fight is similar to the fight for my marriage: there are no promises. Shamefully few protective laws in matters of the heart. I guess all worthwhile fights come with these inherent realities. Over and over I hear, The Growth Policy is fluff—has no teeth. And the developers know it. They always win in the end. The little guy has no power. It's all about greed.

The Planning Department employees look tired and Mafia-run. They deal with this land rape every day, and they really can't do much, because even if the Board denies a proposed subdivision, the County Commissioners can still pass it. They've got *powerless* written all over their faces. I empathize. But it's thrilling what this brings up in me. After the summer I've had, I don't feel powerless in this one bit.

I'm in process. And I have energy and experience "fighting" without taking on other people's garbage. Here, my strategy is a little difficult, but damn is it great to be so active and verbal again, rather than so contained and quiet. Both have their place.

So I make copies and copies of the developer's application,

letters, FEMA studies, maps. And I bring them to everyone I can think of who knows anything about this sort of thing: a biologist, a hydrologist, the guy running for County Commissioner, the Land Trust, a landscape designer who has excellent scruples when it comes to development, an environmental engineer, a lawyer—and I phone everyone I can think of who might possibly show up at that meeting and speak to the total inappropriateness of this sort of high-density subdivision in the rural West, so far out of town. I feed them "talking points":

It is simply out of the character of our rural area and the impact would have devastating effects on the environment, the wildlife that lives here and migrates here, the aquifers, and the people who call it home.

And it's not the only subdivision of its kind in the making. There are a bunch of them, slated to go in all up and down the river. This is a very important migration corridor for the animals that live in these climes.

But I am not fighting mad. I'm not going to go manic like I usually do when I'm on a mission. I'm calm. Maybe I'm the one who's grown this summer. It is possible, then, to think of it as his gift to me. That line of thinking requires ultimate maturity. Of the spiritual sort, perhaps.

So I catch myself talking to myself in the car as I drive all over the valley, making copies and delivering them, and still factoring in my kids' music lessons, soccer practices, pick-up and drop-off times and places. I'm saying, "You're going to the copy store now. That's all. The copy store. For now."

When I get to the copy store, I give them the stacks of files, and then I go outside to wait in the sun. If I smoked, I'd be smoking there in the sun.

A school bus pulls up and a Hutterite farmer (think Amish with trucks) comes up to me in his standard suspenders and blue work shirt. In his odd accent (think: *Trow the ball to turd*) he asks me what kind of produce I am interested in buying. These guys are excellent persuaders, these Hutterites. I admire their style.

I scroll down the list. Roma tomatoes. I've been wanting to make my Italian mama's tomato sauce—the pomarola sauce that the Tuscans make in the height of summer, the open-air markets teeming with bright red, vine-ripened Roma tomatoes. But on our side of the Rockies, there are no promises in the way of tomatoes, given our harsh climate.

My Italian mama had added, "Make sure that you get tomatoes from as close to the sea as possible. For flavor."

I look up at this man, whose beard crops his chin line. "Where do you live?"

"Over there in Du-puyer over there near Browning there. Valier."

"Over on the east side. It's sunnier there."

"Yeah. Much sunnier. Five generations of farming. We also have rhubarb wine."

I think of Freezeout Lake and the snow goose migration I drive over the Rockies to witness every year for "spring cleaning"—spiritual scum removal. And it's always sunny. That whole area was once an inland sea. Dinosaur land. I figure that's as close to the sea as I'm going to get and find tomatoes around here.

"How many cases do you have?"

"Oh, three or four."

"I'll take three."

As I go on his bus with him to pick out the best three cases, I catch myself whispering, "I am picking out tomatoes on the Hutterite school bus." When I first moved to Montana, this sort of thing used to blow me away—so far from the world of the private sector that spawned me. I used to say, nervously, "They don't teach ya this in finishing school," all the time, just to let the pressure off what was cooking in discomfort inside me. That's all gone, especially now. I am officially at home, and present in this Hutterite bus full of vegetables.

I'll wait to buy the rest of the vegetables from my organic farmer friend, but I buy some of the rhubarb wine just to be polite.

Then I go back in the copy store. Now I'm picking up copies. Now I'm paying for them. Now I'm in my car listening to mantras.

A friend gave me a CD of them. I'm not picky when it comes to wisdom, remember? So I memorize a mantra about affliction. *Omarkayanahmaha*. I have no idea what the actual words mean—just that it's about freedom from affliction, and that's what matters. It feels good to be in mystery. In the intention and the commitment. I am committed to that.

I chant it all the way up the highway, noting the ridiculous and the sublime, until I get to Petco. I need to go in there and buy rat food for my daughter's pet rat, Houdini. My daughter's heart belongs to Houdini. We all love that rat. We love that rat so much that we paid a hundred fifty dollars for the surgical removal of her tumor last month. Rolling in the dough as we are.

I'm in Petco buying rat food. I love a rat.

Then I go to Target because I need to get my son a three-ring binder. *I'm in Target. Everything is red and fluorescent.*

I chant all the way to the environmental lawyer's office, where I drop off the documents and notice the hip conference room with the corked bottles of wine and the espresso machine. I get back in the car. Drive to the County Commissioner–hopeful's home and drop off the documents on his front porch, which is covered in kids' dress-up stuff, and I think it's sweet. It feels so good to bear witness to people's private spaces today. Especially in the name of community interest and hermitage busting.

Then I drive to my friend's organic farm to leave a petition. Her well-loved, hard-won quilt of green manna is a triumph in the short season and harsh weather of northwest Montana. My farmer friend knows the land better than anyone around; her fingers steeped in it for thirty years. She'd fight for the land like a mother would fight for her child. And the proposed subdivision, with all its pollutants, abuts the same river that winds through her farm. Hers, then, is not just a community of people, but of soil, water, flora, fauna.

Her concern for this development is deep in her suntanned face. "I'll tell you a story that would make the developers weep.

I have to believe they have consciences." She turns toward the river. "There's a forty-acre piece of state land down there along the river. It's really hard to get to. No roads attach to it. I go there by canoe sometimes because it's so much the way things used to be." She looks at me and tears fill her eyes. "It's where the animals come to die."

I swallow.

"All the animals that have been pushed out by developments in the hills . . . they come here. I found a dead bear along the river last year in late autumn. She should have been up in the hills by then. I looked along her spine because it was a strange shape, and I saw that her back had been opened a long time ago, by an arrow. And her spine had healed around it. She was a tough bear."

I swallow and breathe, and we both nod. I want to lie by that tough bear by the river and spend a day weeping.

In the spirit of her profuse farm and her hard work—what is . . . I say, "I'm canning sauce with my kids. Do you have any celery ready? Or flat-leaf parsley or basil? I need carrots and garlic and onions."

"Sure. How much do you need?"

"Lots."

We go out to her field—five acres of organic produce growing so beautifully along the river. She squats in the ground and cuts out seven heads of celery. And I take the runs of her Italian parsley for free because they're not pretty, but they still taste good. And her interns help dig up a crate of carrots and another of garlic and onions and bunches of basil.

We have a long hug before I go. "Thanks for doing this work with the development," she says.

God, it feels good. Good work. And none of it has anything to do with my marriage.

Then I go out to the horse ranch, most threatened by this subdivision, and owned by one of my dearest friends. We sit in her home and I tell her everything I've learned and we plot. She's never felt more powerful in her life than when she's in the woods on a horse. Now is the time for her to feel powerful, right here in her kitchen.

Forget Facebook. This is community. We don't have to be alone. We create our lives. We create community.

My husband calls. He's still with his sister. He and his brother have spent the day planting bulbs. They hope she'll live to see them in the spring.

In the same form, I spend two days making and canning the tomato sauce with my kids. It is as if that sauce strikes a compromise between the hard times and the good times of this summer. Each jar will hold our tears and our smiles, but mostly the latter.

Sixty pounds of Roma tomatoes, cut in half. Stacks of celery, cleaned and chopped. A fleet of carrots, peeled and chopped by my daughter, who knows her way around a knife. Leaves of fresh Italian parsley and basil, cleaned and cut with kitchen shears by my son. A tower of onions, peeled and diced. Heads of garlic sorted into naked cloves, peeled and minced. All put together with love. With my kids.

I remember my Italian "grandmother's" voice, as I stand stirring the sauce. "Don't stir backward. You'll undo the sauce." I am not going backward. Not anymore.

I set the sauce into hot water baths in sterilized jars and lids. Remove them and place them on the kitchen table to cool—the lids vacuuming and popping to a seal, one by one.

We sit in the kitchen, spent, drinking hot cocoa and listening for it: twenty-one pops. Total success.

By the end of it, we're all up to our ears in tomato sauce. Labeling each jar with careful script and tired fingers. When we're through, we proudly place twenty-one twenty-eight-ounce jars of canned homemade organic Italy-kissed sauce into our pantry closet, looking forward to giving them as Christmas gifts and eating some ourselves on cold, tomato-less winter nights.

We've been through something together that is raw and real.

But nothing like my husband has.

When he returns from his trip, I can see it in his eyes: what really matters. His sister's gift. He has so very much to lose. He is gentle with me. He comes up behind me in the kitchen and gives me a hug. Kisses my neck.

Our children point him to the jars of sauce on the pantry shelves. He is proud of our sauce.

My Italian Family's Pomarola Sauce Recipe

This is a light sauce that is the epitome of the summer harvest and is usually canned to capture summer in the middle of winter. It must be made with the freshest Roma tomatoes to get the right consistency, preferably from somewhere close to the sea.

Sauce for one pound of pasta. Serves six.

2½ pounds unpeeled ripe Roma tomatoes

1 onion

1 clove garlic (Americans generally use more garlic than is the Italian custom.)

1 stalk celery—just the white part, not the leaves

1–2 carrots (depending on how big they are)

3–5 leaves basil

3 sprigs flat-leaf parsley—no stem

A pinch of salt

A pinch of pepper

A pinch of white sugar

2 tablespoons extra-virgin olive oil

Cut tomatoes in half. Cut vegetables into small pieces. Rough-cut basil and parsley with scissors. Put all ingredients into stockpot. Simmer, covered, very slowly until the carrot is soft and can be easily mashed with a fork (about an hour and a half). Then pass everything through a *passatutto*, or food mill—a wide-mouthed hand-cranked strainer. Keep turning the *passatutto* until only the seeds and skins are left. Then put the sauce back on the stove until it reaches a boil. You may need to cook it for a bit longer to ensure desired consistency.

If you'd like to make a big batch of this sauce for canning, then adjust ingredients proportionately, adding an extra hour or so before passing the ingredients through the food mill, and after returning the sauce to the stove. Working with eleven pounds of tomatoes at a time is a good amount.

At this point you can serve or keep it in the refrigerator for a week, or put it in jars. Use the ones that have a self-sealing lid—which pops as the sauce cools and provides a vacuum seal, making it possible to store for months. The wonder of this sauce is in its fresh ingredients and its simplicity.

The Good Fight

First week of September.

We won. At least the first fight. There may be more ahead. In five days we put together an opposition to this irresponsible subdivision that consisted of a rancher, an organic farmer, a dog musher, a horse trainer, a restaurateur, a real estate broker, a farmer, a mule breeder, a millionaire, a handful of people on food stamps, a Harvard graduate, and a whole lot more.

I'll admit—I got a little bit manic after all. I took all that energy I was throwing into Facebook—my fake community—and hammered my real one with one of the things I care most about, and that's land.

Most of the people who showed up did it not expecting to be heard. To be duped. Again. By The Man. In a state where we have only three electoral votes, where only recently our primary votes mattered, even the millionaires have gotten pretty used to falling into the cracks. Some of us like it that way. But when you live in Montana, the land creeps into your soul. I don't care who you are. You want to fight. It's places like ours that they were referring to when they coined the phrase "our neck of the woods."

The Planning Board meeting was the single most inspiring event I've witnessed in recent history. Because regardless of how they've fallen through the cracks, these people got up and spoke. There were tears. There was rage. There was good common sense. And the Planning Board voted down the subdivision unanimously.

In those five days, the fever of this fight swept me off my feet. I made it a full-time job, and I was able, by virtue of some bold phone calls to the Department of the Interior, a few lawyers, a few land-use consultants, and some high-alert e-mails to everyone I could think of who might care to fight this, to put together a binder for each of the nine members of the Planning Board and present them with it at the meeting.

They were impressed. I don't mind bragging. Because maybe it'll rub off on you—how good it feels to really stick your neck out for your neck of the woods. Especially when you've been in and out of feeling powerless for months. I'm telling you this because I want you to consider what it feels like to be powerful. To create something with your passions and skills. Whether or not the people who are supposed to love you the most are doing their best to slice and dice your heart. I believe when we act powerfully, we get treated powerfully. That's what happened to me. Apparently, it reminded my husband of why he loves me. If at least partway. At least for a moment. But not with pedestals.

Because . . .

I got a note, in his handwriting, on the kitchen table that morning of the county meeting. It said, "Go Mama! We're proud of you!" Imagine the note Erin Brockovich got. And she got to go to the Oscars. I just want to preserve our little family and my marriage and my community.

To celebrate, I spent a good part of the morning in our hot tub. I felt like I'd woken up. Like it was the day after I returned from Italy, only bright, and I'm-not-sure-I-love-you-anymore free. I was finally enjoying my grace period. Sending out light and love. To everyone. Even those who have hurt me. It felt positively remarkable.

I was reliving my Italy epiphany. It's all here. It always was.

And check out what happened:

So I'm blissing out in the hot tub with my cup of jasmine green tea and the French doors open and it's him. He's in a towel and then he's in the hot tub. In the past few years he's made a point of never getting in the hot tub with me and now I know why, even though I've known it in my gut all along: HE THINKS I'LL TALK. He thinks I'll bring up hard subjects. Try to drag him into my personal mission to go at life in perpetual full-frontal passionate honesty—even to the derailment of my own health and happiness. No more!

So I don't talk.

I just temporarily helped save a pack of wolves. I don't need to talk. I sip my tea, smile at him, and lean my head back on the hot tub, basking in the sun and the fact that I'm a chick who doesn't need to talk.

So guess what? Yep. You got it. He talks . . .

It comes out calm and vulnerable.

"You know," he says, "being with my sister . . . who's fighting for her life—I just . . ." He stops and starts again. "I just realize what matters. It's not your job. It's your relationships."

He pauses and I am stone still.

"It's been great this summer not torturing myself with a dead-end job. I see how miserable it was making me. And I see now that I'm not going to live the rest of my life hating my job. Waking up at the crack of dawn to do something I hate."

Oh, this is good, I'm thinking. *He's getting it. And he hasn't even had any therapy!*

He continues, "I've just needed to get through this hard time. It's like I'm just waking up to the fact that I'm in the middle of my life. This is it. I'm a forty-two-year-old who wants to be in a twenty-year-old's body, and it's not working. And there are so . . . many . . . messages pummeling me from all sides. You have to be young and fit and successful and rich. And it's gotten to me."

Yeah. It's called a Midlife Crisis, oh dear one. Or a "Midlife Opportunity," as it's now referred to. But I am silent. Sunning myself. My eyes are closed.

He continues, "And all that other stuff I said to you earlier this summer . . . after Italy . . . I've let go of it all. I've let go of everything that was bugging me. I can never repay you for what I put you through. It's just the way I've always done things. I have to hit rock bottom and then, when I'm bloody and bruised, I rise up."

Grace. Finally, his heart in his hand. I think of the heart-shaped rock at the bottom of the river. I wonder if it will ever make its way to the sea.

But here's how the suffering me wants to handle it. She wants to throw a tantrum: *That's it!? That's all you've got to say??!! Well, thanks for the fucking memo, Mr. Rising Phoenix. You've ruined my summer. I've probably got a brain tumor now, thanks to the stress you put me under. Never mind the fallout on the kids. And I'm supposed to have some sort of sympathy for you because you finally got that you've been acting like a twenty-year-old frat boy for the last three months? Bruised and bloody, my ass. That's just a story you've told yourself to excuse yourself for being irresponsible. I want an apology. I deserve an apology. A clean: "I am sorry."*

But I put on the brakes. I DON'T WANT TO SUFFER. I am not in denial if I keep my mouth shut, as long as I sweep those thoughts off the front porch of my mind. If out of that swept surface I find a few true words. Measure them before I speak; if I utter any at all. I'm protecting myself from pain, and that is my first priority. What he's just said has worlds in it that, yes, I might have to decipher. But I'm great at deciphering code when it comes to interpersonal relationships. The must-be-fully-self-expressed-at-all-times police can go home. I really really really don't want to suffer.

Oh, but it's tempting.

So I hold my position in the sun, feeling the jets working my back. I take in a deep breath. Think about my tea and how it's just the right temperature by now.

I open my eyes, reach for the mug, and take a nice sip. Then I put it back on the hot tub, lean my head back in the sun, and say, "One thing you might want to look at is your relationship with resentment."

That's it. It's perfectly rational. It doesn't take sides. And it's true. I resist the urge to go into a forty-minute dissertation on all that I've learned in therapy about resentment and how it screws with you. Makes double damn certain that you suffer. Keeps you in victim mode.

He has a retort. This astounds me. This might just be the first conversation we've had all summer, except for the first one—the kickoff—the bad one. This one is good. He says, "I've given that some thought. And I'm through with resentment. I'm at a true crossroads. A true beginning."

To this I look at him straight on. But I don't say anything. For a while. I sit there and feel what it is to trust myself. To take care of myself. To be the sole proprietor of my happiness. Finally I say, "It feels good to be responsible for your own happiness. It feels good to be forty-two. That's what I've learned." And then I lean back and close my eyes again.

"Yeah," he says. "I just wish my back didn't hurt. And that we weren't so broke. And that my sister wasn't dying. And that I knew what I wanted to do with the rest of my life."

And I think of him at age twenty. And I think of us as equals. And I say, "You can be anything you want to be."

When it really comes down to it, what more of an apology do I need? The police and parole officers and Sheila have gone home. We don't need them anymore. They never did anything but shout in our ears and freak us out anyway. Putting us constantly on red alert.

To borrow from the Johnny Mercer song: We've been happy and unhappy together. It seems important to know how to do both.

Indian Summer

I have a friend who has what she calls her "pickle jar philosophy." She says a whole host of tensions can be solved in her marriage when she hands her husband the pickle jar.

It's simple like a Zen koan is simple:

She's having a hard time opening the pickle jar.

She passes the jar to her husband.

He opens it.

She says, smiling, "Yeah, well, I loosened it for you."

But they both know it was a meeting of intention.

Talk about a marital contract. They both walk away with a result that works for each of them (and let's not forget the plain fact that there will be pickles today). Things are right with the world.

All she had to do was state her need. Acknowledge his

"strength." Ask for his help. Get out of his way. And receive what he had to give. How is she powerless? She's not.

I have my own example.

I've wanted a horse trailer for eight years—since I found what balanced my family life, my writing life, and my soul's life and remembered how much I love horses.

Nothing fancy. Just something to haul my horse in to the vet, and so I can join group rides around the valley. But I've told myself that I am not a candidate for a horse trailer. My reasons have been twofold:

1. It's another expense.
2. I've been chicken.

Nice horse trailers can cost in the tens of thousands of dollars, but it's not like I'm in the English show circuit. I have a good horse with a good mind, and I trust him in the woods. That's what I'm in it for. If I could ride my dog, I would. I just want to play around and feel lighthearted. Canter a bit. Jump stuff when the opportunity arises.

But the thought of loading a twelve-hundred-pound animal into a metal box with me in it feels like suicide. The margin for error, seemingly nonexistent. And then the fact in question that a little steel ball on my truck can haul two or three horses plus the weight of a trailer . . . that seems like we're destined for a ditch. And what about the deer flinging themselves in front of my truck? What would that impact be with thousands of pounds of horse and trailer behind me? And there are the logging trucks and the ice and the Montana-ness of where I live. Moose. Bear. Elk. Redneck hunters on meth.

It's amazing how we talk ourselves out of our dreams. (You should have heard my Italy list—complete with Mafia bosses.)

For years I've seen women, of all sizes, loading horses into trailers, shutting the door, getting into their diesel mega-trucks, and heading down the highway.

That's not me, I think. I'll take the little covered arena where I board my horses in the winter . . . and I'll do it at a nice easy trot. Maybe a walk in the meadow. A dip in the river.

But when I'm driven by fear, sooner or later my bullshit detector usually wins. And yesterday, it did.

Because a friend called me to join her and a few gals for a ride. And once again, I had to decline. No horse transportation.

It was just like the friend in the grocery store who called me out on not returning to Italy. "What's your problem?" this friend said over the phone. "I can't believe you don't have a horse trailer. It's not like you need to get anything fancy. They're practically giving them away in *The Mountain Trader*. I don't get it. What's the point of having a horse in a place like Montana if you can't go out and ride?"

She's right, I thought as I hung up.

I'm sick of saying no to so many excellent opportunities to join the community of horse people out there. It's what's here for me that I love. It's time to start fully stepping into the things that bring me joy. Things outside of being a mother and a wife and a writer. I need a hobby that's healthy and inspiring. Arena riding is one thing. But seeing Montana on a horse's back is soul food. Even if I'm chicken. I just have to ask for help.

So I went to the shoe box in which for years I've been squirreling away writing money for horse "emergencies." And I counted out just under two grand. Just enough for a decent horse trailer.

The possibilities unfolded in a way I hadn't mentally let them. Galloping on the beaches of Lake Koocanusa up on the Canadian border. Meeting my friends at the other end of the valley for a ride in the Swans. Finally accepting the annual invitation to join a group of pack trip veterans in the backcountry of the Bob Marshall Wilderness. A whole Montana opened up to me, as big as the Big Sky. A Montana I'm ready for.

Downstairs, my husband was at the kitchen table on the Internet looking for jobs. I grabbed *The Mountain Trader* and sat across from him.

"Anything good in there?" he said. Finding hilarity in *The Mountain Trader* is old practice for us. It's our "porn," as my designer friend says about his *Architectural Digest*. Used to be that *Architectural Digest* was my porn, too. But now it's horse trailers and cheap fencing.

"Here's one," I read. "'For sale—two mutt puppies and one four-wheeler—needs wheels. Will trade for snow tires. Will throw in puppies.'"

He looked up and laughed.

"Or 'Wanted—your farm rabbits and game birds. Not for eating.'"

We both laughed.

"Looking for anything in particular?" he said.

"A horse trailer, actually. Nothing fancy. I've been saving up for one for a while. I have a few grand." I felt instantly guilty. Like I have no business going shopping for a big item when he's looking for a job. When I've just gotten back from Italy. Even though I paid for it myself. "I don't want to stress you out, though."

"Heck—I've got a dirt bike. I get a ski pass every year. Do what you need to do. It's your money. You earned it." I love this man.

He knows how badly I've wanted a horse trailer—ogling them in traffic for almost a decade. And I think he even sees that it would be an investment in sanity for a woman he knows has not had the best summer of her life. Still, it's generous of him.

"Thank you."

So after eight years of talking about wanting a trailer, sort of in the next breath after wanting to return to Italy, I finally made a call on one in the *Trader*.

The woman gave me directions to her ranch.

"Will you go with me?" I asked him. "I don't really know my way around horse trailers. At all. Truth be told . . . I'm a bit chicken."

It's the pickle-jar philosophy. An equal-opportunity way to be with another.

We drove through the valley, sunny and dry. We commented on the threat of forest fires.

"You do the talking," I said. I've seen him negotiate a deal. He's good. It's been his job, after all, for many years.

But Montanans are tricky. They're so honest, you wonder if it's some sort of a scheme.

"What year is this trailer?" he asked the disheveled seller, failing at trying to keep her dogs from jumping all over us. "How many miles does it have on it?"

I made a sisterly comment. "It's okay. We're dog people."

She smiled. But then it faded. "I don't know what year it is. My husband used to do all this. But he took off to Alaska." The seller managed to crack a smile, but I could see the pain.

And it was hard not to think that I had so nearly dodged this reality. Still, who knew what would happen. I could be her in a year. Selling my trailer to a woman and her husband. Thoughts like this humble me in a way I don't need humbling. At this point.

Walking around, looking at the tires, he asked, "Any idea when's the last time the bearings and the axle were greased?"

She cracked up. "Heck if I know!"

I opened the door to the tack room, and my heart lifted like a little girl's. I imagined my saddle in it. My reins hanging from that hook. The smell of manure and leather. Maybe a few horse postcards taped to the walls. Hawk feathers from the trail. If times got tough, we could sleep in it if we had to. If I had to. My horses outside on makeshift hitches. We could roam around the country in this Circle J Apache 2000 three-slant load trailer covered in rust, indelible horse-shit Jackson Pollock on the walls.

I caught her watching me. "We used to take the horses camping in this trailer. We'd use the tack room to hold the hay and the wood and the tents and all." She looked sad again. But not exactly sorry for herself, hard times such as they are.

My husband got under the trailer and banged around. "Floor looks like it's in good shape."

Then he emerged from the noxious weeds and dry grass and said, "How much do you want for it?"

"Two thousand five hundred," she said.

"We've got two thousand cash," he said.

I felt bad taking an asset from her that held such fond memories of her husband. "Literally, in fives and ones from a shoe box under my bed," I said, stupidly—as if admitting that we weren't millionaires would make it any easier on her.

But she nodded and smiled. This woman appeared to have a similar shoe box under her bed. "Two thousand's fine with me."

"We'll be in touch by the end of the day," my husband said. "What size is the hitch?"

She told us and we shook hands.

I felt tough driving out of that ranch with my husband, talking two-and-five-sixteenth balls. "Oh my God! Are we really going to do this? I can't believe it. I'm sort of terrified. I have no clue how to haul a trailer around or how to hook it up and back it up. That sounds terrifying. Is it hard?"

"You'll get the hang of it pretty quickly. You're a good driver." BIG COMPLIMENT.

"Will you show me how? I want to get the hang of it before I load my horse."

"Of course." He actually slid his hand into mine. And I thought of the pickle jar philosophy. When was the last time he had the opportunity to help me with something in one of his fields of expertise? Something he offered me? Yet I was taking responsibility for my part. Paying for it. Having the dream to begin with. Loosening the jar, as it were. So what if I had to ask? Sometimes we have to ask.

Later, we were in our kitchen, calling around, doing our homework. I was on the phone with used trailer salesmen all over Montana, Texas, Wyoming, who were all telling me that two thousand dollars for a 2000 Circle J three slant is a steal. They weren't even bothering to try to sell me what they had in their lots. One even said, the Montanan of course, "Heck, I've got the same one in my lot for five thousand, five hundred. You better get that trailer or you'll regret it. Ain't never gonna find that price again."

My husband had the phone book open, making calls on his cell. He had that important-guy business tone. But he wasn't making tee times. Or fishing dates. He was talking to the car dealer. About my truck. Seeing how much weight it can haul. And then he was talking to a guy he knows at the Napa auto body shop—a guy who knows his way around horses. It was endearing the stuff he was asking. Innocent and revealing in a way that he doesn't usually let himself be perceived. In short, he didn't know shit about horses.

I already knew way more than he'd know after he'd exhausted his three resources, but I didn't let on to any of it. That's not his part in this. His part is the driving.

It felt so good to have calls being made on my behalf, by my husband. I basked in this feeling of love and care. I hadn't felt it in a long time. Who cared if I got a horse trailer out of it? We were unified.

I went upstairs and got my shoe box. Took out all the bills and sure enough there was nineteen hundred dollars in there. I'm proud of this. I earned it from my writing. Even though it's not much. Lately my writing has been paying for my dreams to come true. I wonder how much that fact has to do with intention.

Then I took the wad downstairs and while he was on the phone making his important-guy calls, I started counting it out on the kitchen table, like I hadn't just done the same thing upstairs—twice.

It got his attention. Cash. He got off the phone quickly and watched as I put the bills in stacks of hundreds, perpendicular to one another, the way you do in bridge, as if to prove to him that we are responsible for our own dreams coming true. Even if we need some help sometimes.

"Are you a drug dealer or something?" he laughed.

I smiled and counted out loud, "Seven hundred, eight hundred, nine hundred. I do make some money as a writer, you know." I finished arranging the bills and looked up. "Listen. I don't want to do this if it's not okay with you. I'm perfectly happy to put this in our joint checking account to help pay for bills. I want to be fair. I really mean that." And I did.

He perked up, I imagine, in the same way that my friend's

husband perks up when she passes him the pickle jar. "Oh no," he said. "Two grand isn't going to make us or break us. You've wanted a trailer for a long time. It's silly that you don't have one. Go for it. I'll throw in that extra hundred dollars since I didn't get you a birthday present."

The power of stating your need. Asking for help. Being responsible for your part. Being more concerned with your intention than the outcome. It's like Italy. He gets it now.

"Let's pick it up and surprise the kids with it at school," he said.

We bought the right-sized hitch, drove back to the ranch, and paid for the trailer in cash, and gently, carefully, he showed me how to hook it up. Gentle and careful have not been personality traits in him this summer.

I think it has to do with pride. But it's not just his pride. It's our pride. There's room for me in it because it grows from pride in me. I'm buying myself something important to my passion. I'm taking charge of something that is within my realm of happiness—only something that I can control. Like Italy. He gets it now.

His cell phone rang and it was a friend and he referred to the trailer as *our* trailer.

I haven't felt so aligned with him all summer. And it feels like healing salve. A horse trailer? Who knew?

We laughed and nervous-giggled all the way to school pick-up and all the way home because now we are the proud owners of yet another addition to our limping fleet of slightly decrepit motorized vehicles—vestiges of a shinier time in our lives.

When we pulled into the driveway, we made comments on what our parents would say, in their tennis whites, off to their respective country clubs in the suburbs of New York and Chicago. Seems that in Montana, the more broke you are, the more vehicles decorate your driveway, front yard, and sometimes even your backyard. It has nothing to do with keeping up with the Joneses. It's all about resourcefulness.

We, then, look like real Montanans.

We are real Montanans. We like that about each other. And dreams need vehicles every so often. Even if they're rusty ones.

That night he gave me driving lessons. No arguments. I did just fine.

It felt like our college days. We even cranked music on the stereo. "Why don't you go for a trail ride tomorrow," he said, looking into the side mirror as I backed the trailer in a perfect circle. "I can pick up the kids. It's supposed to be a beautiful day. Go for a ride. You can handle this thing fine."

So the next day, I hooked up that trailer by myself, drove only semi-white-knuckled up the highway to pick up my horse where I'm currently boarding him, loaded him without incident, brought him to a trail system I've been wanting to check out for years, met a friend and her horse there, and off we went. It was the Italy in Montana. It was both of them in me. Receiving the joy the mountains were singing all around me and my horse. I decided I'd sing that song to my husband when I got home as thanks.

In the last mile, I heard a clanking and stopped my horse. "Loose shoe," I said, sliding off his back.

I'd never taken off a loose shoe before, but these are the moments where riding in the woods teaches you who you are. Gives you practice. Just like the trailer.

So I pulled a hoof pick out of my saddlebag and, with more strength and less acumen, pried off the shoe. My horse seemed relieved. This horse speaks the same language as the people who pay attention to birds.

I walked him in a circle and saw that his hoof was tender, so instead of getting back on, I led him out of the forest, not wanting him to be lame. I need my horse to be trail-ready—until the snow flies and this long summer will hopefully be over.

And suddenly, I thought of asking my farrier to pull all his shoes off like so many horse people are doing these days. Going barefoot. Letting him build up his own calluses. It's how I've felt this summer: shoeless. It's been a good thing.

"The wild horses didn't need shoes," I said to my friend. "I bet it sucks to walk around all the time on those things."

I held the shoe, smiling at its symbolism of luck, yes. But also of how it binds—how without it, there is the chance for being open and naked and free. True nature.

When I got home, I took that shoe and hung it, pointing upward, on an old nail on the front porch.

Inside, I took off my boots and told my kids about the ride. About how great it was to be able to haul a horse somewhere new. How my horse seemed to like it also, breathing in and blowing out with gusto. About the sweet streambed where we stopped for a drink. Groves and groves of aspen and river birch.

Moose prints. Fairly uneventful, save for a loose shoe.

My husband made buffalo burgers for dinner, and handed me a plate, proud of his perfectly cooked medium-rare burger and of his competent horsewoman wife. "You pried that shoe off yourself?" he said, smiling.

I saw its root, and said back, "You always cook the perfect burger. What's the secret?" Equals in praise. A good place to begin.

He went into a long speech about the perfect burger. (Here's his trick, by the way: you don't turn the burger until the juices are bubbling. Then you turn it, and it goes fast on that side.)

We all begged for popcorn for dessert, because he does that perfectly, too. We want him to feel good.

In bed that night I said, "Thank you for helping me with the trailer. It really meant a lot to me."

"Of course," he said.

"You do realize you may never see me again, however." I poked him literally in the ribs. A month ago, I was afraid to touch him at all.

He protested and poked me back, and we kissed good night.

He fell swiftly to sleep, and I lay there and basked in the idea of us being on equal ground again.

It's happening. I can feel it. Tomorrow is our anniversary. I'm going to get out of it what I want. I'm not waiting around for anything anymore. If I'm a garden and I need to be tended, then I'm going to do the tending. And I have to believe he'll follow my lead. Either way, it's a great way to live.

Two Balloons

September 25, 2008.

So. It's our anniversary. Fifteen years. Really twenty, with our years of courtship.

I take the kids to school and leave a card for him on the kitchen table with the Rilke and Rumi quotations. And a picture of two hot-air balloons.

When I get home, he's drinking tea and he thanks me for the card. I'll tell you the highlight of our anniversary, and really, with the exception of Italy and the horse trailer, it's the highlight of my entire summer. It happened at the end of the day. And I'll skip to it for a moment. I'm feeling like I can skip to the end of at least this day, at least here.

I was pulling out of the driveway to pick up the kids. Car windows were up.

He turned the corner on the lawn mower.

I've grown accustomed to how he doesn't say hello or good-bye, and I've built up tough enough skin to learn how to come and go without lingering in want of it. Sometimes, I just go to him and kiss him and say good-bye or hello or I love you whether he likes it or not. More and more, I'm doing that.

But there he was, looking up at me. Smiling. From the lawn mower.

I pushed the button to lower the window, and amid lawn mower noise, in the fading evening light, amber shoots filtering through the fruit trees, heavy with fruit . . . from his seat on the lawn mower, he mouthed in exaggeration, I LOVE YOU! So there would be no mistaking it.

This from a man who started July off with the words "I can commit to a future with you. But not with any confidence . . . whatsoever."

I resist thinking of those words, and replace them with this very recent and very real string of mouthed vowels and consonants: Eye luuuuuuuuuv yooooooooooo.

My Evil Twin Sister Sheila attacks from behind. She's crawled back from exile. She wants blood . . .

He doesn't love you. He doesn't know his ass from a hole in the ground. He's faking. He doesn't want to lose his house and kids so he's faking that he loves you. He's so terrified right now that he'll say or do anything. Be careful. I wouldn't trust that shit for one moment. You need to open up your own bank account. This guy's going nowhere. Just because some guy tells you he loves you from a lawn mower and looks at you—you're on the verge of tears?! What the hell is he doing at home on a Thursday afternoon, anyway? That should be the gardener mowing the lawn. Your husband should be at work, making some goddamn money!

Get thee out, Sheila. You are trouble. You are *All-My-Children-in-the-eighties* trouble.

And I take my husband's "I love you" all the way into town, through school pick-up, through kids' music lessons, through picking up dinner—sushi and Veuve Clicquot because it's our anniversary, and I just got another paycheck from a magazine article, and shit, we've been through it this summer. I take his "I love you" through family hot-tubbing, and then a quiet night of non-snoring and sleeping, undisturbed until sunrise, in the same bed.

Even though Sheila's not happy about it, I have that "I love you" now, as I write. She keeps pointing out how I'm clinging to it. How I'm setting myself up for pain once he's in a place of power again, and he doesn't need all this nesting and safety. There will be another night when he doesn't call and doesn't come home and soon, she tells me. (She has a thick New York accent suddenly, which is a little daunting. You should hear how daunting she used to be at the gym when I was standing in front of the mirror, lifting weights next to a blond bodybuilder who doubled as my husband's personal trainer.)

But I'm ignoring Sheila. Returning to the breath, chanting my mantra. (I still haven't found out its exact definition—so I'm chanting in Sanskrit probably *Praise to Sheila!*) It works. I feel calmed and energized by that mantra. I can write this today and still feel his wide-mouthed "I love you" and report that our anniversary was one of the best I can remember.

It had to do with cars. Just like when we met.

It was nothing fancy. We had no plans. We just took off in his truck and went for a ride. We didn't know where we were going, and we didn't go prepared. Still, we both knew to have hiking shoes and a few warm layers because there was a frost the night before and it was autumn in Montana—snow in the hills. We banded together, like broken children running away from their parents; who don't want to talk about it, sitting huddled close around the train yard hobo bonfire.

Not that different from twenty years ago. He drove fast. We cranked music. I stared out the window thinking about a novel I want to write next.

It's funny where we went. We drove the length of the valley down to the state park on Flathead Lake where we first went when we were deciding to move here from Seattle. Without really talking about it, we'd both pictured us there, sitting on the rocks staring at the osprey and mountains all around.

In the car, we didn't talk about our kids or money or his sister. We didn't really talk about much of anything, but it wasn't because we were boycotting each other. The lines were open. I felt them—wide open. I felt like gushing a little: "You know, of all the primary people in my life, there are only two who haven't tried to control me. My father. And you. Thank you."

"You're welcome," he said.

I realized the disservice I'd done (with a lot of help from Sheila) to my marriage by taking this non-controlling behavior as neglect. What if I flipped it, like Byron Katie talks about in her book *Loving What Is*? What if I took it as freedom? I decided, from then on, to look at it as freedom.

I recognized what pressure can do to a person. I thought about how he's been to me in the last years, and I wondered how much of it has been in response to pressure he's felt from *me*. How much I've played victim to him without knowing it. So I can blame him for my woes? So I don't have to be responsible? *God, that is twisted if it's true.* I decided to be willing to look at it all.

To live pressure-free. To live in the drive. At least for the moment.

And we did. We lived the drive—commenting on things we saw—*Montana moments,* we call them: three old people walking alongside the road holding a heavy bucket. A nun sitting on a lawn chair on the highway shoulder, holding religious literature out to passersby clocking ninety mph. Our builder friend who was in front of us at a traffic light and whose truck was missing its left brake light. We got his number off his truck and gave him a call. Migrating geese. Newly golden aspen trees. A golden eagle on a stop sign.

We stopped at a Hutterite farmstand and got gigantic apples and hand-churned butter. We stopped at a ranch for sale and picked up one of the papers giving its stats, commenting on what it would be like to have a horse ranch. We commented on the price of hay and how it's driving people to leave the horse business, and we thought about what it would take to plant our bottom five-acre meadow with hay as a side job.

"I'd love to do that," he said. "I've always wanted to work land."

We spent a lot of our day making comments and surprising each other with them. We met a couple from Toronto who were driving their motorcycles on only back roads from Calgary to Silver City, New Mexico, and we called a friend who had just moved to Silver City and hooked them up the next week for a drink. We were the way we used to be when we were unmarried—playing with life and people and our environment. Flirting. Not needing it to add up to anything in particular.

Then we went to a restaurant that was, surprisingly, open in this non-tourist time, and we sat out on the deck and listened to jazz and ate appetizers and drank Flathead cherry-infused Cosmos and wine and leafed through magazines, commenting. On houses. Maverick artists. Trips we'd like to take to remote places. Sipping wine in the middle of the day like we were people of leisure without a care in the world.

Then we drove back, had a little sex, pretty good sex, actually. And then he went out to mow the lawn, and I went out to pick up the kids, the sushi, the champagne. With the "I love you" that I still have, nesting softly in the palm of my hand.

We were equals. Not a pedestal among us.

Thanksgiving

9:00 a.m.

A Tuesday in November.

I wake up and it's light. Too light for seven a.m. I smell him in the sheets next to me, still warm. I hear the truck pulling out of the driveway. I go past the kids' rooms and they're empty. I've overslept. I'm a light sleeper as a rule. How is this possible? But I figure, I must be catching up from so many restless nights.

There's a note on the kitchen table, in his handwriting:

"Got up early. Took the kids out for breakfast before school. Thought you might need the rest. I love you. Good luck writing today!"

I pick up the note. It accompanies me while I make tea, the teapot heavy and still hot. He's filled it for many cups of tea. And not just his.

It's been almost a month of this now. I've been finishing a rewrite on a novel for a big editor in New York City—the one my agent sent in earlier this summer—possibly my first book deal after so many years, so many books, so much rejection. But now I'm looking at it like so much practice.

There's a job opportunity that has come his way in the green building field—something he can hold in his hand—and it doesn't start for a while. We have enough money to get by for another half a year, tops. If I can get this book deal with my novel it will turn everything around financially. I'm hopeful. My agent is hopeful. Yet another editor is hopeful. I work on the revision, but with a new surrender, dedicating myself to loving the process. But I just don't have the time I need.

Then one day he announces, "You're the one with the career heat right now. You work. I'll hold down the fort." Time. Space. A writer's food.

His hard work is different for now. He's planning on helping his sister travel to and from her clinical trial in Chicago and in her continuing fight with cancer. That will be his focus in this upcoming cold season. If he needs to, he'll take a job working the lifts up on the ski mountain. Or bartending. I've been thinking about restaurant work. Just like we did twenty years ago when we were slumming it in Boston. Only now it's all too real.

But we're not going to lose the house. We'll figure it out. We'll get by. For now, most important of all, we have a family.

For now, it looks like this:

He wakes the kids. Makes their breakfast and packs their lunch boxes. Gets them to school on time—earlier than I do, actually. He reminds them of their music lessons and soccer games and book reports. He runs back home when they forget their binders or library books.

I see them off with hugs and kisses and good wishes for their day at school. Then I get my tea and go to my office and write.

I'm working twelve-hour days on my novel—balancing the 350-odd pages so that I know them by heart; hold their pulse in my waking and sleeping.

And on the side, I'm still writing this, like a trusted journal I've grown used to. Usually in the early mornings. As a warm-up to the novel I hope to publish.

I have never felt more in tune with my craft—the intersection of heart and soul and mind that is writing. I've never been more proud of turning in a book rewrite. I have him to thank for it. The gift is vast and he knows it. He's giving me the time to work hard at what I love so much. And to potentially support our family financially for a while. I am proud that he thinks so highly of me as a writer, after what he said in June. I'm glad I didn't buy it. It was a bum deal he was trying to sell, after all. Instincts are everything, especially when it comes to crisis.

Pride.

I see it in him again. A pride that I trust maybe for the first time ever. Because there are no myths in it. No rebellion in it. No pedestals.

I report this to my therapist.

She smiles and says, "This is wonderful news. I couldn't be happier for you two. Let's see . . . how long did that take?"

I count on my fingers. "Four and a half months."

"Not bad," she says.

"Not bad at all. And while I was waiting to hear back from editors on my last novel this summer . . . I wrote a book about it. A memoir," I say. "I'm almost done with it, I think."

"A book?"

"Yeah. I've been writing it to process this time in my life. Moment by moment. I'm a writer. That's what I do. It's not like fiction. It's not made up. It's real life. I'm scared to put it out there. But I think it will help people. It's why I write in the first place."

"I think it will help people, too," she says.

"I just have to clear it with him . . ."

I'm afraid, actually, to clear it with him. It's not like everything's perfect all of a sudden. It's not all tied up in a perfect pink bow, not that it ever should be or that I'd ever want it to be.

But I remember my Author's Statement:

"I write to shine a light on an otherwise dim or even pitch-black corner, to provide relief for myself and others."

I've lived through something truly difficult with some level of grace and some level of success. I wrote it down. Which brought me relief. I want to bring that relief to others.

Still, it's new territory. And it's scary. There is so much to lose. Yet I suppose, nothing is as scary as having to live through it.

Later, he's back home doing projects. Much more than watering and mowing the lawn. He's systematically dealing with everything that drives him crazy around the house. Stuff he's let build up for years. Stuff he'd let run his life with resentment. He keeps saying, "Man—I can't believe how I've neglected things around here."

Amazing the power of fixing the toilet seat. The screened-porch door. Cleaning the gutters. Fixing the garage door opener. Telling your wife you love her. Saying hello and good-bye.

Now, he's standing at the door next to my office, determinedly holding Windex in one hand and an Allen wrench in the other. I think of the horseshoe hanging on the other side of the wall, on the outside of our house.

"How's the writing going?" he says, like that twenty-year-old college boy who used to brag about his girlfriend's early career aspirations.

I pause, eyeing the three-hundred-page memoir sitting on my desk. "You know—aside from the novel I'm revising . . . I have another book I'd like to send to my agent. It's a . . . memoir. About this summer."

His eyes do not glaze over.

I say, "Not that it would ever really get published. It's just a little story. About you and me."

He holds the doorknob. "Whatever you wrote, I probably deserve it," he says, shrugging.

"No, it's not about punishing anybody. It's not some angry exposé. It's about the process of self-responsibility. It's about dashed dreams and climbing out of breakdowns. Yours and mine."

"Okay." But he looks a little downtrodden, and I obviously understand why.

"I promise, it's written in love. It's written for people who are going through a rough time—in a marriage. Or anywhere in their lives. It's written to help. But it's really, really honest. It has to be, if it's going to be something people can relate to."

"Well, do whatever you've gotta do. Especially if it'll help people. I trust you." He understands so much about help these days, given the help he's passed to his sister.

"Uh—you might want to read it first," I say.

"Does it make me look like a total asshole?"

"If it does, then I look like one, too, I guess. But I didn't write down all the gory details. It's more about the journey of the mind of a person going through a tough time and wanting not to suffer, even though she's not always, or even remotely, successful. I tried to stay on high ground. And to encourage the reader to do the same. To fill in the blanks with their own lives when it got too personal." I look deep into his eyes to see if he's still with me. He is.

I continue. "It's really not about our family. It's more about my process. It's about not taking things personally. Even when you feel the world is crumbling around you. It's about choosing happiness over suffering. It's about retraining the way we think. But I'm not sending it out unless I have your approval."

He smiles, his eyes pooling with humility.

It means everything to me in that moment in my life.

"I trust you," he says. "I'll look it over tonight."

"Thank you. I love you, by the way."

"I love you, too," he says with an honesty that is unquestionable.

And for now . . . that's the end.

And for now, let's call that good.

Epilogue

Midnight.
Thanksgiving.

The meal is done, the family asleep, my grandmother's china washed and drying on tea towels on the kitchen counter. My great-aunt's silver, dried, counted, and put back in the silver chest. The Steuben crystal goblets that my grandfather gave my grandmother for their wedding gift, drying upside down next to my other grandmother's china. It's like they're all saying, *We were here. Now it's your turn.*

I feel stitched in. Safe. So many sleeping, beating hearts under this roof—children, husband, dogs, cat, fish, rat. So many mothers' eyes watching over me today, as I polished the silver and dressed the table, the turkey, ourselves, in all our finest for the feast.

It was just us. The four of us. They would have been happy sitting in pj's around the dining room feast, eating on our everyday china plates. But of all the Thanksgivings I can remember, it seemed essential to celebrate this holiday well.

We sat by candlelight sparkling off sterling candelabra—the first candelabra from our rebel days. We each spoke our thanks. My husband went first. Eager this year.

"I am thankful for my family," he said, his eyes filling with candlelight. "It's all that matters to me. I love you all."

When it came around to me, I said a gentle, "I am thankful . . . for this moment in our lives."

And we held hands, blessed the food, and ate.

The Perversely Vertical Half-Cracked and Sometimes Devoured Stack of Books on My Bedside Table

The Message: The New Testament Psalms and Proverbs—Eugene Peterson

The Bhagavad Gita

The Book of Love—Rumi

Letters to a Young Poet—Rilke

The Cloud of Unknowing—Anonymous

The Upanishads (classic of Indian spirituality)—Eknath Easwaran

The Way of a Pilgrim—Anonymous

The Roaring Stream: A New Zen Reader—edited by Nelson Foster

The Essential Sermons—Meister Eckhart

Thoughts in Solitude—Thomas Merton

Selected Poems—Czeslaw Milosz

Living Buddha, Living Christ—Thich Nhat Hanh

Pilgrim at Tinker Creek—Annie Dillard

The Brothers K; *The River Why*; and *God Laughs & Plays*—David James Duncan

Illusions—Richard Bach

Discourses—Meher Baba

Collected Poems—Wendell Berry (especially the poem "The Country of Marriage")

The Theory and Practice of Rivers—Jim Harrison

Challenge of the Heart: Love, Sex, and Intimacy in Changing Times—edited by John Welwood (essays—especially Rilke's "Learning to Love")

Refuge: An Unnatural History of Family and Place and *Finding Beauty in a Broken World*—Terry Tempest Williams

Christian & Oriental Philosophy of Art—Ananda K. Coomaraswamy

Siddhartha—Hermann Hesse

Franny and Zooey—J. D. Salinger

The Power of Intention and *Change Your Thoughts—Change Your Life: Living the Wisdom of the Tao*—Wayne Dyer

Living in Process—Anne Wilson Schaef

When Things Fall Apart: Heart Advice for Difficult Times—Pema Chödrön

The Power of Now and *A New Earth*—Eckhart Tolle

The Four Agreements—Miguel Ruiz

Loving What Is—Byron Katie

Codependent No More: How to Stop Controlling Others and Start Caring for Yourself—Melody Beattie

Your Sacred Quest: Finding Your Way to the Divine Within—Joan Borysenko

A Wrinkle in Time—Madeleine L'Engle

The Little Prince—Antoine de Saint-Exupéry

Lafcadio: The Lion Who Shot Back—Shel Silverstein

Amos & Boris—William Steig

Horton Hears a Who—Dr. Seuss

Older Love

His wife has asthma
so he only smokes outdoors
or late at night with head
and shoulders well into
the fireplace, the mesquite and oak
heat bright against his face.
Does it replace the heat
that has wandered from love
back into the natural world?
But then the shadow passion casts
is much longer than passion,
stretching with effort from year to year.
Outside tonight hard wind and sleet
from three bald mountains,
and on the hearth before his face
the ashes we'll all become,
soft as the back of a woman's knee.

—JIM HARRISON

Acknowledgments

Foremost, I offer my deep gratitude to my husband for being willing to share our story in the spirit of my Author's Statement, and for all his above-and-beyond help and support in the last months of my writing this book. You are a rare and good man. I love you.

To my children: I am more proud of you than you could ever imagine. Thank you for knowing how much I love to write, supporting and/or tolerating it, and for trusting that there will always be room for you in the Grandmother Chair. Let's always make "the sauce" together. . . .

To my family of origin and extended family: Thank you for your grace in trusting me to be careful with your personal lives. It's never easy having a writer in the family. Especially, I would like to thank my mother, Virginia Munson McTier, and my sister, Cathy Rogerson, for listening to my dreams from the beginning.

To the voices of wisdom and reason; there are many. Limitless thanks to these in particular: Vim Tesar (MS, LCPC, LAC, CRC), upon whom the therapist in this book is based; Rossell Weinstein, certified personal coach and founder of Intendit Coaching, LLC; and Bobbi Hall (Stillwater Horse Whispers Ranch), who have all been, and continue to be, my living examples of personal responsibility.

To my friend and agent, Tricia Davey (Davey Literary & Media), who believed in me against the odds, and whose brilliant ideas and hard work on my behalf are a massive part of why I have acknowledgments to offer. A river of heart-shaped rocks to you, Tricia. Also to Beth Davey for her exceptional professional advice, and sisterly encouragement, too—thank you, both!

To my editor, Amy Einhorn: Your instincts are those of a grizzly bear in a Montana forest; your vision, like that of a hawk riding thermals in the meadow where much of this book was born. Consider this page wept over, every tear circled with an AE beside it. Thank you.

To Marilyn Ducksworth, Stephanie Sorensen, Halli Melnitsky, Leigh Butler, Lance Fitzgerald from Montana, Bonnie Soodek, Ivan Held, Kate Stark, Catharine Lynch, Katie Grinch, Victoria Comella, Emily A. C. Osborne (and the late Faith Sale, who saw the sculpture in the stone years ago and encouraged me to keep going), and all the other wonderful people at Penguin Group who did so much to back this book and this author. I've been practicing these words in countless versions for what feels like an eternity. And here I am with only a few. That's all I needed, it turns out: *Thank you.*

To Dan Jones, editor of *The New York Times*'s "Modern Love" column: Thank you for giving me my big break! And for your good work editing my essay "Those Aren't Fighting Words, Dear." I know you know how much I appreciate you.

To my many early-draft readers over the years, and especially to Amelie Dawson and Kim Ludlow for their invaluable third eyes in the eleventh hour. Thank you.

Alla famiglia Renzoni: Vi voglio tanto bene! Grazie di cuore.

To the Seattle Writer Ladies: Jayme Lynes, Christine Johnson-Duell, Kim Ludlow, Mary Casey, Jocelyn Scott, Reba Bliss, and Felicity Oram. Your quilt has many squares now. Thank you, sisters in words.

To my many, many dear friends who have listened to me fantasize and rant about the writing life and publishing world for twenty years . . . and either tried to stay interested or at least faked it well, thank you. You know who you are. I love you all. Special thanks to the ever loyal ears, hearts, and minds of Kirsten Gottschalk, Jay Clarke, Cindy Kuchman, Chris Hanson, Peter Naylor, Elisabeth Massey, Alison Scherer, Melissa Demopoulos, Jennifer Schelter, Toby Malina, Hannah Plumb, Helen Pilling, Swithin McGrath, Sandy Anderson, Ky Sandelin, Kate O'Brien, Laura and Bill Donavan, and Amy and Leif Peterson. And to Melinda Sullivan, who inspired creative wings in me a long time ago, reentered my life this year, and charmed it. Thank you.

Immeasurable thanks to the writers David James Duncan, Jim Harrison, and Terry Tempest Williams, who all, in their own way, have been daily at my writing table for years, influencing my words, breathing life into my muse when I don't seem to know how.

In loving memory of Sandra Nora (1960–2009) and in honor of her great legacy. You will forever be the God of the Fourth of July to us. Rainbow and all.

About the Author

Laura Munson lives with her family in Montana, where she writes novels, memoirs, short stories, and essays. This is her first published book.